Political and Philosophical

University of Liverpool

Political and Philosophical Debates in Welfare

Allyn Fives

Consultant Editor: Jo Campling

First published 2008 by
PALGRAVE MACMILLAN
Houndmills, Basingstoke, Hampshire RG21 6XS and
175 Fifth Avenue, New York, N.Y. 10010
Companies and representatives throughout the world

PALGRAVE MACMILLAN is the global academic imprint of the Palgrave Macmillan division of St. Martin's Press, LLC and of Palgrave Macmillan Ltd. Macmillan® is a registered trademark in the United States, United Kingdom and other countries. Palgrave is a registered trademark in the European Union and other countries.

ISBN-13: 978–1–4039–8738–9   paperback
ISBN-10: 1–4039–8738–6   paperback
ISBN-13: 978–1–4039–8737–2   hardback
ISBN-10: 1–4039–8737–8   hardback

This book is printed on paper suitable for recycling and made from fully managed and sustained forest sources. Logging, pulping and manufacturing processes are expected to conform to the environmental regulations of the country of origin.

A catalogue record for this book is available from the British Library.

A catalog record for this book is available from the Library of Congress.

8   7   6   5   4   3   2   1
15 14 13 12 11 10 09 08

Printed in China

For Anne Marie

Contents

List of Figures and Tables

Figures

Tables

Preface

The idea of writing this book was first raised by Joe Mahon. He suggested that I write something based on a course that I teach called Theories of the Welfare State. He also put me in touch with a commissioning editor, the late Jo Campling, and she guided me through the process of securing a book contract. In teaching political philosophy I try to remember that my students may be approaching many of the ideas and thinkers for the first time. Nonetheless, I do assume that, by and large, these students, and the readers of this book, have already begun to explore this area and are willing to take their studies further. For that reason I hope this book will be of some help to those who want to become political philosophers. And a political philosopher is, at the very least, someone with the capacity to engage in a critical analysis of moral issues that arise in politics. Jo Campling was clear that she wanted a textbook, not a monograph. I have therefore tried to write a book that provides an overview of contemporary political theory. At the same time, it is a critical overview. After all, the analytical and critical skills that students are encouraged to develop are just those that research requires. For that reason, I do not just recount the arguments of others here. This book looks at the way in which arguments are constructed so as to analyse their cogency, and in doing so I develop and defend my own line of argument concerning a number of key themes.

What are the main themes of this book? This book is concerned with theoretical accounts of the moral basis for welfare provision. First, I give special consideration to the question of whether moral goodness is part of a person's welfare. Secondly, in doing this, one must also look at the requirements of a good argument: what makes some consideration a good or compelling reason to accept a conclusion? Finally, I address the issue of modernity, and analyse its problems and potential, and address the arguments of its detractors. In short, this book has been written so as to address the following question. What counts as a good reason to justify welfare entitlements? More precisely, can a moral argument be made, one that is rationally compelling, which shows that justice requires us to acknowledge and guarantee the welfare entitlements of others, and which also shows us just what those welfare entitlements are?

Welfare is often approached from an 'empirical' perspective. That is, theorists of welfare often set out to show how welfare *is* distributed. They may show us what reasons are, in fact, given as the rationale for such policies, but they do not (and of course they do not want to) address whether such a distribution is just and whether such a rationale is sound. I am interested in welfare as a moral issue in politics, but there are different 'normative' approaches to welfare. Some theorists assume that a rational argument about what justice requires of us must *not* rely on, or draw from, a perfectionist conception of the human good. That is, such theorists of welfare try to remain neutral or impartial about what is and is not a 'good' life. They believe that we cannot make rational arguments about such an issue, but nonetheless that we can have rational grounds to accept or reject a theory of justice.

In this book, I question the assumption that, if it is to be rational, normative theory must be non-perfectionist as well. A long line of thinkers, from Aristotle to J.S. Mill to Alasdair MacIntyre and Joseph Raz, accept that we can and must make value judgements about what is or is not a good life. And this is the case precisely when we address the issue of welfare. The term 'welfare' refers to the way in which a life is going. If it is going well, one is approaching, or one has attained, well-being. It seems strange to these thinkers to say that a life is going well, and yet refrain from saying whether or not it is good. Not only that, Aristotelians try to show that we have the resources to make a rational argument about the goodness of a life. To live a good life, we need material goods, good fortune, and fully developed capacities, but these things have no value without moral virtue. The virtues are character traits, habitual dispositions, such as wisdom, moderation, courage, and justice. It seems hard to imagine a life that is lived well without such virtues. To put the same point another way, we pity the person who is incapable of exercising virtue because it is reasonable to assume that we benefit from having such character traits.

This book also addresses the question of what counts as a good reason to justify welfare entitlements. We will be looking at whether a perfectionist account of welfare can be defended. Another important issue is relativism. Many theorists accept something like the following position: 'a claim can be rational relative to the standards of some particular context, but not rational as such'. This is a position of relativism. On this account, a consideration is reasonable (or not), it is compelling in an argument (or not), depending on the community or aspirations or interests of the persons involved. There are no rational standards that are independent from each context, standards with which we can assess what is claimed in such contexts. We cannot take 'the view from nowhere' when we address moral issues; we are always already speaking from within a given context.

Universalists, however, believe that relativism can be refuted. The refutation of relativism is twofold. I return to it in detail in Chapter 8, and I offer only a sketch of the argument here. First, relativism involves a logical contradiction: relativists state there are no context-independent reasons to accept a proposition as true or right, but they make this very statement about every context, not just their own. If relativists can make such a statement about the nature of rationality in other contexts, this seems to undermine the claim that all rationality is relative. Secondly, relativism misconstrues morality: moral ideas rely on standards that we often find exacting, and they relate to demands that often are onerous. If we could equate what is 'good' with what is in our interests or what we tend to think and feel, then the term would be emptied of its distinctively normative content.

I do not think it is going too far to say that relativism is alarming. This is the case as a rational refutation of relativism simply does not have any importance for relativists. The argument I have sketched above, the relativist might contend, represents just one view on an issue. To insist on the primacy of reason is simply to adopt one tradition and to speak from one perspective that is, they would probably go on to say, a narrow, uninspired, and self-deluded perspective. However, in this book I want to proceed as if relativists are willing to enter into a rational debate about the reasonableness of their own approach. I also want to address a variety of positions that not only reject relativism but also feel unable to accept universalism.

Now there is one final issue that this book raises. Is modernity an ongoing project, one that has many positive features (as well as contradictions and shortcomings), or is modernity something to be challenged and even rejected? Often, support for a comprehensive and ambitious welfare state has been closely tied with arguments for modernism. The welfare state derived some justification from humanist ideas about the moral equality of each person, and humanist optimism about the possibilities for social reform aimed at recognizing that equality. The welfare state also often relied on, and contributed to, the idea of a national community, which could justify and motivate the sacrifices required in a welfare state. And the welfare state expressed the modernist view that the material well-being of each person (along with such things as dignity and respect) has great moral significance.

In this book I address a number of challenges to modernism. I hope to show that even though society (perhaps increasingly) is pluralistic, a moral basis for welfare provision can still be found in ideas about the human good. Even though economic actors may refuse to accept moral obligations for those less fortunate than themselves, it does not follow that the state has lost the power to intervene in the economy so as to promote well-being. However, does the state (under any conditions) still have the moral authority to do so? This book will explore ways in which to connect perfectionist arguments about well-being to a politics of state welfare.

Acknowledgements

A number of colleagues and friends were kind enough to read and comment on some parts of this book. They were generous with their time, and their help was indispensable. I only wish that I had resolved all the problems they discovered and attained the standards they pointed to. In particular, I would like to thank Keith Breen, Richard Hull, Russell Keat, Joe Mahon, and Pete Morriss.

Professor Chris Curtin and Professor Markus Wörner have given me the opportunity to work in two departments at NUI, Galway: the Department of Political Science and Sociology and the Department of Philosophy. I would also like to thank the Social Science Research Centre for providing me with office space between 2002 and 2006.

I would like to thank my PhD supervisors, Russell Keat and John Holmwood. And I would like to mention and thank other friends and colleagues from my time at Edinburgh: Emilios Christodoulidis, Bregham Dalgleish, Richard Freeman, Tim Hayward, John Holmwood, Kimberly Hutchings, Raymond Plant, and Andrew Schaap.

My family has given me support, understanding, and encouragement all the way along, and many pleasant distractions as well. And their numbers keep expanding!

I dedicate this book to my wife, Anne Marie Power, without whom I would have written something else, far inferior.

CHAPTER 1

Introduction: Political Philosophy and Welfare

Political philosophy

This book looks at different approaches in political philosophy to the issue of welfare entitlements. However, it is also very much a book about political philosophy, or political theory, itself. Every political philosopher discussed here attempts to engage in a rational analysis of moral issues that arise in politics. They leave to one side those moral issues that arise only outside politics. 'Political' moral issues concern the right and wrong ways to exercise political power and also the claims of justice that can be made on citizens and on the state (Plant, 1991, p. 2). Moreover, the theorists discussed here assume 'that questions about political morality ... can be answered in rational and objective ways' (ibid.). They do not accept that moral issues are a matter of sentiment or inclination alone and that the realm of rationality extends only so far as facts and logic.

Political philosophers deal with the basic issue of political obligation. They ask, *why and when ought we to obey the state*? We may have good reasons to obey the leaders of a local community, but it does not follow that those considerations will count as good reasons for obedience as citizens. There is another basic question political philosophers address, the question of justice: *what is due to others and how should we be disposed to treat others*? While we may have good reasons to be charitable to the needy, it does not follow that the needy have rights of justice that we ought to accept and respect. Welfare is an issue that arises at the boundary of these questions about political obligation and justice. Most political philosophers deal with the issue of welfare at some length, and differences between positions become clear when the question of welfare is addressed. Welfare is not the only significant moral issue in politics. However, it draws attention to the contentious question of the precise limits to both the power of the state and the just claims of its citizens.

A political philosophy of welfare is concerned with the boundary between individual and collective responsibility. It is not immediately clear when and in what ways the state should perform a collective duty to support individuals, families, and other social groups. And the state can perform such collective duties in many different ways. A political philosophy of welfare also is concerned with the 'well-being' (or welfare) of each individual. The political philosophers we discuss offer various definitions of well-being, but they agree that the well-being of each individual has moral significance. That is, they do not assume that we can, or ought to, neglect the well-being of some individuals or groups; for instance, religious minorities, the disabled, manual workers, and so on. Finally, political philosophers of welfare set out to offer an argument that is rationally convincing and compelling. However, they disagree about the nature of a good reason in such an argument. They disagree as to whether such a reason can be derived from what is called 'the human good'. They also disagree about the scope of any such argument: to whom can an argument be addressed? to all rational, mature persons or to the members of more restricted groups?

Political philosophy and welfare

I have begun discussing political philosophies of welfare. They offer different approaches to three important questions, as summarized in Table 1.1.

(1) *What is welfare?*

Some theorists provide a 'perfectionist' view of welfare. They assume that 'welfare' denotes a life that, morally speaking, is 'lived well'. Perfectionists assume both that some forms of human experience or activity have special value and also that morality requires us to respect and/or to promote this value. They contend it is possible to judge that a life is lived in a way that is better or worse, more or less perfect. This is the case with Aristotle's conception of *eudaimonia* (flourishing or happiness). Aristotle [384–322 BC], living and writing in Classical Athens, assumed there are two mutually necessary aspects to flourishing: moral goodness is difficult to attain without health, wealth, honour, and pleasure; but the latter are pointless, or even dangerous, without moral goodness. Flourishing just is a life

Table 1.1 Three basic philosophical considerations

Basic considerations	Opposing positions
What is welfare?	**Perfectionism**: welfare refers to a life that is, morally speaking, 'lived well'. **Non-perfectionism**: welfare refers to all-purpose means to attain one's aims and/or the satisfaction of one's desires and preferences.
What is a good reason?	**Universalism**: a rational argument always appeals to standards that transcend a given context. **Non-universalism**: what counts as a good reason varies, and rightly varies, with each context.
Is modernity an ongoing project?	**Modernism**: the project of modernity is ongoing and incorporates commitments to humanism, the nation state, and material well-being. **Counter-modernism**: modernity dissolves social networks needed to attain well-being, or heightens power and instrumental rationality.

led exercising the virtues. 'Human good turns out to be the activity of the soul exhibiting excellence, and if there are more than one excellence, in accordance with the best and most complete' (Aristotle, NE, I. 7, 1098a15).

We need material goods throughout our lives so as to be in a position to exercise virtue: '... it is impossible, or not easy, to do noble acts without the proper equipment' (I. 8, 1099a30). However, material goods are only of value to the extent they do contribute to virtue, and indeed, their pursuit may on occasion be an obstacle to virtue. For instance, the pursuit of wealth may lead to a 'grasping', unjust, state of character, the vice of *pleonexia*. Perfectionism continues to find adherents. The utilitarian John Stuart Mill [1806–1873] argued that people are truly happy only when they are striving towards flourishing [see pp. 23–31]. 'Now it is an unquestionable fact that those who are equally acquainted with, and equally capable of appreciating and enjoying, both, do give a most marked preference to the manner of existence which employs their higher faculties' (1861, p. 139).

Other political philosophers reject perfectionism. They contend that we cannot make objective value judgements about the moral goodness (or badness) of a life. Rather, welfare refers to the possession of all-purpose means to attain one's aims, and/or the satisfaction of one's desires and preferences. It is important to note that, for the non-perfectionist, although it is possible to argue that a person has not chosen the most appropriate (rational) means to attain his or her ends, it is not possible to argue that the choice of ends itself is irrational or unworthy.

This is the case with John Rawls's [1921–2002] welfare liberalism [see Chapter 3]. What he calls 'justice as fairness' 'distributes certain primary goods, that is, things that every rational man is presumed to want. These goods normally have a use whatever a person's rational plan of life' (1971, p. 62). Rawls does believe that a life is good only if it is rationally planned. For Rawls, 'one long-term plan is better than another... if it allows for the encouragement and satisfaction of all the aims and interests of the other plan and for the encouragement and satisfaction of some further aim or interest in addition' (ibid., p. 413). Nonetheless, his liberalism leaves individuals free to do what they want with primary goods, including, to take Rawls's example, spending one's life counting blades of grass (ibid., p. 432).

Some of those who reject perfectionism at the same time defend a 'substantive' conception of well-being. A substantive position states that well-being is possible only when certain resources can be enjoyed and also when certain capacities are developed. Martha Nussbaum [see pp. 62–5 and 137–43] argues that justice requires distribution of the goods needed to develop capabilities; in particular, practical reason, affiliation, and emotion (2000a, pp. 78–82). Nonetheless, she contends, political authorities are *not* justified in making value judgements about the ways in which people then choose to employ or utilize their capacities. Similarly, Raymond Plant [see pp. 203–8] argues that although it is not possible to agree on what is or is not a good life, it is possible to agree on what he calls 'positive freedom', which 'can only be made intelligible in terms of a conception of human agency' which in turn 'cannot be formulated without reference to human abilities, needs, capacities' (2003, p. 4).

So, Plant and Nussbaum offer a non-perfectionist, substantive view of well-being. Aristotle and Mill offer a perfectionist view of well-being, but this view is also substantive to the extent that '... it is impossible, or not easy, to do noble acts without the proper equipment' (Aristotle, NE, I. 8, 1099a30).

(2) *What is a good reason?*

Some contend that an argument always appeals to standards that transcend the given situation. This is the position of universalists; and they reject relativism. If I say that a certain distribution of benefits and burdens is right or just, or if I say that a certain type of life is lived well, I also imply that, should my interlocutor wish it of me, I can give reasons to accept this statement that should prove to be compelling. What is more, I imply that these are reasons *any* person I address can accept as good reasons, reasons to agree with the conclusion I have reached. Also, they may continue to count as good reasons even if my listener refuses to accept them.

Jurgen Habermas [see pp. 182–6] contends that when we engage in an argument about a moral issue such as welfare we always implicitly invoke the following universal rational principle: 'Only those norms can claim to be valid that meet (or could meet) with the approval of all affected in their capacity as participants in a practical discourse' (1990, p. 66). Habermas assumes that we cannot hope to agree about what is or is not a good life; all we can hope to agree about is the fair distribution of benefits and burdens: a distribution that is in the 'general interest'. We can analyse questions of justice 'from the "moral point of view" of whether something is "equally good for everyone"' (1994b, pp. 122, 123). In contrast, ideas about the 'human good' are 'based on strong evaluations and determined by the self-understanding and perspectival life-projects of particular groups, that is, by what is from their point of view "good for us," all things considered' (ibid.). Note, not all universalists accept this requirement of impartiality. Mill and Aristotle assumed that their perfectionist accounts of well-being were universally valid.

Non-universalists, in contrast, contend that what counts as a good reason varies, and rightly varies, with each context: each community, or tradition, or set of interests, or inclinations. According to Alasdair MacIntyre [see pp. 145–50], we can determine each person's just claims only if we first agree about the nature of the (Aristotelian) human good. However, only membership of a community can ensure the requisite moral consensus.

> There must be some *common enterprise* to the achievement of whose goals those who are taken to be more deserving have contributed more than those who are taken to be less deserving; and there must be a *shared view* of how such contributions are to be measured and of how rewards are to be ranked.
>
> (1988, pp. 106–7; emphasis added)

Tradition can provide a conception of 'the good and the best for humans', which is the first premise in any rational argument about

what is right and just. However, MacIntyre also assumes that 'tradition' and 'rationality' are mutually reliant:

> standards of rational justification emerge from and are part of a history
> in which they are vindicated by the way they *transcend the limitations of* and
> *provide remedies for the defects of* their predecessors within the history of
> that same tradition.
>
> (ibid., p. 7; emphasis added)

Where is there such a tradition now that can also provide the moral
consensus needed for rational debate about welfare? MacIntyre
assumes that Aristotelian perfectionism is possible now among
those who share an 'Aristotelian tradition'. This is the case in the
United States among Irish Catholics, Orthodox Greeks and Jews,
and Protestants from the Southern states.

(3) *Is modernity an ongoing project?*

Some assume that modernity is a series of ideals to which we
should aspire, although modern society is replete with examples of
conflicting interests, institutional inefficiency, and injustice. This is
perhaps most evident in utilitarian thought. It claims that an act is
right in proportion as it tends to promote happiness (or utility). Its
primary concern is the justification and implementation of social
reforms, the betterment of the human condition (and the condition
of all sentient creatures) through collective action. According to Mill,

> The ultimate end, with reference to and for the sake of which all other
> things are desirable . . ., is an existence exempt as far as possible from pain,
> and as rich as possible in enjoyments, both in point of quantity and quality.
>
> (1861, pp. 142–3)

Moreover, utilitarian morality requires us to ensure such an existence is 'secured to all mankind; and not to them only, but, so far as
the nature of things admits, to the whole sentient creation' (ibid.).
Modernists are committed to some, if not all, of the following.

(a) *Humanism* – For humanists, the end of moral action is the
welfare of humanity. The claims of fellow humans are given priority
over the claims of not only transcendent beings (such as the Judeo-
Christian God), but also non-human animals, such as the animals
used for food and experimentation.[1] They also believe in the moral
equality of each person. We should be treated with respect; we

should be treated as moral equals. Moreover, social reforms can remove obstacles to the attainment of mutual respect. Collective action can be taken that is to the benefit of each. Therefore, humanists are optimistic about the possibilities for truth, freedom, and justice: humans have the capacity to identify injustice and restrictions on freedom, and also solve social problems and implement those solutions.

(b) *Nation State* – Modernists may also assume that the 'state, society, and economy are . . . co-extensive within the same national boundaries' (Habermas, 1999, p. 48). The nation-state is the political agent through which much social reform can be carried out. The nation-state may have the power and authority to intervene in, and regulate, the national economy so as to implement these reforms. Also, a national society consists in shared expectations and understandings as well as reciprocal relations of contribution and benefit. A national society may provide the moral basis to justify the welfare state. I include this as one element of modernity with the following qualification: belief in the moral authority of the state to act in the provision of welfare does not entail either insularity concerning the worth of other cultures and peoples, or an aggressive chauvinism in the promotion of a nation's interests.

(c) *Material Well-Being* – The modern spirit gives great importance to material well-being and material goods. Some argue that in modern welfare policies far too little significance is given to spiritual well-being (Giddens, 1994). However, physiological health and the possession of material goods are necessary, if not sufficient, for well-being. Moreover, the distribution of material goods is often necessary, if not sufficient, to show respect for other persons. There are limits to the value of material well-being in modernity, however. It is possible to be healthy and contented and yet fail to be respected. This is the case with slaves who, although skilled and well-fed, passively accept their bondage. The modernist position, as I have outlined it, cannot condone such a situation.

Modernity itself is the subject of controversy. Its critics contend that the project of modernity must be challenged. They may argue that modernity has displaced and dissolved many important social institutions and shared beliefs, which are important networks in which to live and attain well-being. Some conservatives [see Chapter 4] and communitarians [see Chapter 7] criticize modern markets and modern bureaucracies because of their effects on small-scale communal groups. These groups are 'structures of authority . . . which all require a substantial degree of autonomy – that is, a corporate freedom – in order to perform their necessary functions' (Nisbet, 1986, p. 35). At the same time, others argue that a communitarian political movement can harness the state so as to protect or foster communal groups and cultures. Charles Taylor's example is the attempt to ensure the cultural survival of Quebec's Francophone culture (1992, p. 58).

Post-modernists [see pp. 170–6] claim that modernism rests on a number of politically sinister fictions. Michel Foucault [1926–1984] argues that although the drive to reform society is thought to arise from noble aspirations (justice, truth, and freedom), reform itself intensifies power and instrumental rationality. It creates practices in which bodies are disciplined and persons are subjugated. For instance, the provision of education imposes not only a single curriculum but also a strict surveillance of each student's movements.

> The body is molded by a great many distinct regimes; it is broken down by the rhythms of work, rest, and holidays; it is poisoned by food or values, through eating habits and moral laws; it constructs resistances.
>
> (Foucault, 1971, p. 87)

The post-modernist response is to 'construct resistances', and modernity itself is the chief object of this struggle.

Three theories of welfare

I want to look briefly at three of the main thinkers discussed in this book: MacInytre, Mill, and Rawls. This is shown in Figure 1.1.

1. Aristotle's work has influenced many political philosophers, not least Alasdair MacIntyre. Aristotle assumed that flourishing refers to

	Universalism	Non-universalism	
Perfectionism	Mill	*Taylor*	**Modernity**
	Aristotle	MacIntyre	**Counter-modernity**
Non-perfectionism	Rawls	*Later Rawls*	**Modernity**
	Habermas	*Foucault*	**Counter-modernity**

Figure 1.1 Combinations of opposing approaches to the basic philosophical considerations

a life led exercising virtue. We exercise virtues when we engage in a city-state [*polis*], as they are the characteristics needed to think and act for the good of the community: 'man is by nature a political animal' (Aristotle, Pol. I. 2, 1253a2). However, agreeing with contemporary Athenian practice, Aristotle argued that some people are naturally fit for slavery, and women and manual workers are unfit for full citizenship (Pol, I. 4–7; I. 12–13). Aristotle therefore did not share the humanist belief that collective action can be taken to remove injustice or bad luck. He also did not give great significance to material suffering (or well-being). Aristotle did argue that a multitude of great events, 'if they turn out ill they crush and maim blessedness' (NE, I. 10, 1100b24). Nonetheless, ' . . . even in this nobleness shines through, when a man bears with resignation many great misfortunes, not through insensibility to pain but through nobility and greatness of soul' (ibid.). The city-state should distribute needed goods to its citizens (Pol, VII. 10), and yet flourishing cannot be improved on by the addition of more material goods.

Although he rejects Aristotle's views on women, workers, and slaves, MacIntyre accepts the Aristotelian conception of flourishing. However, MacIntyre contends that we can only make reasonable arguments about welfare (among other things) from within a tradition, and mainstream modern society and theory are inimical to tradition-based thought and life. Therefore, Aristotle's ethics cannot be used now to *justify* arguments for a welfare *state*. An Aristotelian, perfectionist politics may be possible now, but only within small-scale communities on the margins of modern society (MacIntyre, 1985, p. 252). His Aristotelian approach would give priority to the principle of merit along with what he calls 'just-generosity'. Excellence and need are the primary reasons that generate justified claims to valued goods. Moreover, despite MacIntyre's claims to the contrary, I will argue that he is a relativist. That is, his position implies that a claim 'can be rational relative to the standards of some particular tradition, but not rational as such' (1988, p. 352). This is the case, as MacIntyre believes that our ability to reason about a moral issue like welfare is constituted by traditions: we cannot gain access to 'rationality-as-such'. In short, he is a perfectionist, non-universalist, and counter-modernist.

2. Mill is a perfectionist. As we saw, Mill assumes that utility refers to 'the manner of existence which employs their higher faculties'. Once people experience such a life they will clearly see its value.

He also claims that utility refers to the exercise of virtue and that virtue is an end in itself. However, while Aristotle shows little concern for the consequences of exercising virtue, Mill is a 'consequentialist'. For Mill, 'actions are right in proportion as they tend to *promote* happiness, wrong as they tend to *produce* the reverse of happiness' (1861, p. 137; emphasis added). Mill's consequentialism is combined with a humanist (modernist) commitment to social reform. He assumes the virtuous person should be disposed to bring about this kind of good life for as many sentient creatures as is possible, men and women, non-human animals and humans.

Mill is a universalist as well. He defends a single principle of life and a single basic principle of morality. He contends not only that an act is right in proportion as it tends to promote happiness, but also that happiness (a life of virtue) is at all times the final end, that 'for the sake of which all other things are desirable' (ibid., p. 142). Mill also believes that one form of treatment can be extended to all persons. He calls for basic rights protecting each person's liberty (1859, p. 68). These are justified as the most likely means to promote happiness. He defends individual rights that the state then guarantees. Perhaps Mill provides one way to join Aristotle's commitment to flourishing with a humanist view of social reform.

3. Rawls is a non-perfectionist. While we can hope to agree on rules of justice, Rawls argues, we must acknowledge 'a diversity of conflicting, and indeed incommensurable, conceptions of the meaning, value, and purpose of human life (or . . ." conceptions of the good")' (1987, pp. 424–5). Rules of justice are rationally justified if they could be accepted by anyone in what he calls the 'original position'. This is a thought experiment where we put knowledge of our own interests to one side, and then choose principles of justice anyone could accept. However, while we can hope to agree about principles of justice that would benefit anyone, whatever interests they end up having, we cannot hope to agree about the value of different lives.

Rawls assumes that fair principles of justice would ensure the distribution of 'primary social goods'. These are goods that are required no matter what one's plan of life. He believes that we should always respect rights to such goods, even if on an occasion we could (perhaps) promote a greater amount of utility by infringing those rights. He is also an egalitarian, and this is evident in what he calls the 'difference principle': 'Social and economic inequalities are to be arranged so that they are . . . to the greatest benefit of the least advantaged . . . ' (1971, p. 302). Rawls does not allow natural or social advantages to count as reasons to receive primary social goods; unequal distributions of income and wealth are justified if (and only because) they make the position of the least advantaged as good as possible.

Principles of justice

What considerations are relevant to a discussion of justice? What principles of justice can be defended as the bases from which to make decisions about welfare entitlements? There are three principles and two quasi-principles of justice as shown in Table 1.2.

(1) *Need* – According to the first criterion, I have a just welfare entitlement because I am in need, and welfare resources should be designed to meet that need (Spicker, 1988, p. 5). It follows that I have an entitlement to such goods even if I do not have the resources to pay for them. Also, if I have a needs-based entitlement to some goods, I do so irrespective of whether I can be said to deserve such goods (on the basis of some other consideration) and irrespective of whether or not my enjoyment of such goods brings

Table 1.2 Three principles of justice

Principles of justice	Competing interpretations
1. Need	Objective or socially constructed need. Threshold or relative need. e.g. Plant: needs of well-being.
2. Merit	Ideal or conventional. Universal or contextual. e.g. MacIntyre: virtue and moral consensus of community.
3. Equality	Equality of liberty, of opportunity, of basic income, or of outcome. e.g. Rawls: equal liberty, fair equal opportunity, the difference principle.
Quasi-principles	
4. Right	Established rights or inherent human rights. e.g. Plant: social rights (but relies on criterion of need).
5. Utility	Welfare interests or exercise of 'higher faculties'. e.g. Goodin: welfare interests (but relies on criterion of equality).

about a more preferable social environment (e.g. one that is more equal). However, there is no agreement about what the criterion of need refers to. Does it denote human needs or socially defined needs? And should we seek to meet the needs of those below some threshold, or should we seek to reduce the relative measure of the neediness of the worst off or even their subjective sense of neediness?

Raymond Plant has defended welfare entitlements as human rights, alongside the traditional rights that fall into the civil and political categories (e.g. freedom of expression, property rights, the right to vote). He argues that there are certain needs of well-being without which a human cannot be autonomous: they include physical integrity and health, an appropriate level of education, and income and social security (2003, p. 17). He goes on to note that rights are justified as necessary protections for freedom. As the autonomy of humans cannot be guaranteed without meeting their basic needs, all humans have the same rights to certain social and economic resources.

(2) *Merit* – Perhaps when we say that a person needs income (or some other resource), behind that statement there is the idea that the income is needed for some other end that is itself important and significant. If that were the case, we should be more interested in a criterion of merit that would help identify just what is and is not meritorious (deserving, valuable, or excellent). According to a merit-based theory of justice, welfare should be distributed to those most deserving of that benefit, and in proportion to their desert. Perhaps, as well, welfare should be distributed only if the recipient meets some explicit requirement, such as to actively seek work, which acts as evidence of the merit or desert of the recipient.

As we saw, MacIntyre employs the principle of merit. MacIntyre derives the criterion of merit from an 'ideal' standard of excellence: merit is a matter of the 'virtue' of the agent. Others may instead believe that standards of merit are already evident within a given society in its conventional (not ideal) standards of reward and punishment. At the same time, MacIntyre does not make an argument based upon 'universal' standards of value. His is an argument about merit that can only be made to those who share certain ideals within a community. Others may argue that any genuine standards of merit must be based on universal (not contextual) principles.

(3) *Equality* – Finally, perhaps the notion of equality is itself the closest we can come to an expression of our sense of justice. Rawls starts from the assumption that all persons have moral equality, and goes on to argue that, because we are all equal, society may not infringe the rights of any person so as to promote some other goal. He calls for a distribution of 'primary social goods', as we saw. However, this involves three variants of equality. First, 'equal liberty' guarantees an equal measure of civil and political rights; second, the principle of 'fair equal opportunity' guarantees the same opportunities for all those similarly motivated and endowed; and third, the 'difference principle' states that inequalities in income and wealth are justified only if they serve to improve the expectations of the least-advantaged members of society.

Not every egalitarian agrees with Rawls, however. Some argue that moral equality requires no more than a guarantee of equal civil and political liberties along with formal (not 'fair') equal opportunity (Nozick, 1974). This position calls for the removal of any barriers preventing access to opportunities but it does *not* call for the provision of social resources so as to equalize opportunities for all those similarly motivated and endowed. Others think that Rawls's egalitarianism does not go far enough. Some call for a guaranteed basic minimum as a right of all (van Parijs, 1995), while others call for a much greater reduction in inequality than Rawls insists on (Cohen, 1995).

I want to discuss two further contenders for the category of principle of justice. I believe they are only quasi-principles, however, as they must, in the long run, be subsumed under one or other of the above three principles.

(4) *Right* – Perhaps welfare entitlements can be justified by reference to the rights of the recipient. There are, broadly speaking, two different ways that such a position can be developed. First, we could argue that, as I have *inherent human rights* to social and economic goods, it follows that I have entitlements to such things as income maintenance and health services (Plant, 2003). However, the following question still must be answered. Why can an individual claim such a right? And here we are forced to fall back on one of our principles of justice: I have such a human right because of moral equality, or perhaps because of my significant need. Second, it could be argued that as a member of a given community, who has performed certain valued roles and made valuable social contributions, I have rights to the social and economic goods that are *conventionally*

provided to the members of this community who perform such roles and make such contributions. These would be *established rights* (whereas human rights are ideal and inherent). However, the same question of justification arises here. Perhaps such conventional rights appeal to the criterion of merit.

(5) *Utility* – The utilitarian argues that actions are right in proportion as they tend to promote happiness. By extension, rules of distribution are just if adherence to those rules tends to promote happiness. R.E. Goodin [see pp. 39–42] has argued that there are certain fundamental aspects of each person's happiness or utility, what he calls 'welfare interests', and justice requires that we secure each person's welfare interests. However, Goodin also seems to fall back on the principle of equality. He argues that basic goods have 'diminishing marginal utility'. The less I have of some good, the greater the contribution to my utility any addition in such a good will make. Therefore, if we are to promote utility, an egalitarian policy is the best one. It seems as though Goodin derives the principle of equality from the principle of utility. However, we could instead say that Goodin implicitly relies on the assumption of the moral equality of each person when making his argument that the best way to promote utility is to promote the welfare interests *of each*. He assumes that we must give equal consideration to the utility of each person, one by one.

It should be noted that combinations of our three basic philosophical considerations ((non-)perfectionism, (non-)universalism, (non-)modernism) are relevant to the question of which principle of justice to defend. Certain combinations of basic philosophical considerations may rule out a principle of justice, or at least shape the interpretation and application of such a principle.

For instance, Rawls's conceptualization of equality is clearly shaped by his basic philosophical commitments: his defence of the distribution of primary social goods rests heavily on his universalism, non-perfectionism, and modernism. He rejects the criterion of merit because conceptions of merit are derived from substantive conceptions of the good, and, he argues, there is no way to reconcile different and incommensurable conceptions of the good. Rawls's commitments are controversial, and indeed, any critique of Rawls's approach to welfare will involve a reconsideration of the steps in the argument between basic philosophical considerations and principles of justice.

The same can be said for MacIntyre's rejection of egalitarianism and defence of merit and need-based principles. Due to his

perfectionism, MacIntyre conceptualizes merit in terms of contributions to the realization of 'goods', but also, due to his non-
universalism, these are the goods of specific communities. In
more recent work, MacIntyre defends something like a needs-
based entitlement to welfare (1999). Just-generosity requires that
we respond to the needy in direct proportion to their human needs.
This has led some to suggest that MacIntyre is moving away from
contextualism and towards universalism. However, my point still
holds that any critique of MacIntyre's approach to welfare will
involve a reconsideration of the steps in his argument between
basic philosophical considerations and principles of justice.

So far, very little has been said about welfare entitlements as they
may or may not be implemented and enjoyed. I want to suggest that
the position defended with respect to principles of justice also
shapes our argument about policy tools and benefit-types.

Welfare as a benefit type

I want to look at three different categories of welfare entitlements
(Table 1.3). They are different benefit types or policy orientations.
These different benefit types are already in use in different welfare
regimes (Esping-Andersen, 1990; Ginsburg, 1992).

(a) *Selective means-tested entitlements* – Recipients of these entitlements have to show abject need, and the benefit may be offered for a
limited period only. It may be the case as well that recipients are
deemed 'worthy' of aid only if they are incapable of earning an
income in the market, or if the aid will help them attain such
independence. The purpose of this entitlement is to help the

Table 1.3 Principles and policies

Principles of justice	Benefit types – Policy orientations
■ Need	Means-tested income maintenance and services (health, education, and housing); special needs provision; and universal human needs.
■ Merit	Social insurance schemes; conditionality of welfare receipt; equal opportunity (meritocracy); and counselling and training.
■ Equality	Guaranteed unconditional basic income; universal public services; equalization of income; fair equal opportunity; and affirmative action.

needy or most needy, and them alone; and/or to maintain the market and family as the primary sources of welfare. The principle of need is evident here, as welfare entitlements are to respond only to those in greatest need. However, the principle of merit is evident as well, as welfare entitlements are conditional and will be only granted to those deemed 'worthy' of such aid. This is typical of Anglo-Saxon regimes such as the United States or the United Kingdom (the 'liberal market model').

The following can be included in this category: means-tested income assistance; supplementary income for the unemployed or the working poor; free health care or education or housing for the poor; 'welfare to work' retraining and counselling programmes for the unemployed.

(b) *Contribution-based entitlements* – Not only must the recipient of contribution-based entitlements fit the description of those deemed eligible to receive the benefit (unemployment, illness, retirement, etc.), but also the level of benefit is proportional to the recipient's previous contributions to an insurance system (Goodin, 1995, p. 185). These benefits are 'passive' and 'transfer-oriented'. They are enjoyed by members of all social classes, but they do not eliminate inequalities. They transfer resources from earlier to later stages in the life cycle (Van Kersbergen, 1995, p. 4). The state plays a more significant role here than in the selective means-tested model. However, the system encourages a plurality of welfare providers (public, private, and occupational). It is usually organized on a federal, decentralized basis. Also, it incorporates employer and employee organizations.

The idea of receiving rewards in proportion to one's contributions may appeal to the criterion of merit. Also, the criterion of need plays a marginal role here. Flat-rate benefits are paid to the needy, but such benefits usually involve judgements of the worthiness of recipients. This is typical of corporatist or Christian Democratic regimes in continental Europe.

(c) *Universal and unconditional entitlements* – This 'refers to programs embracing the entire citizenry and to those allocating benefits or services without the application of economic needs-testing (or means-testing)' (Rothstein, 1998, p. 20). That is, anyone may receive such benefits, and do so irrespective of their employment and income at present or in the past. These benefits may be designed to reduce inequalities in the distribution of some important social good (e.g. income) or to ensure all people receive the same benefits (e.g. education, health, or housing). This is the case with an unconditional basic income guarantee, and publicly provided universal services in health and education. This type of benefit is associated with Scandinavian countries and their social democratic approach that gives priority to the criterion of equality.

The social democratic regime provides other kinds of benefits as well. They include a right to employment; a right to a 'fair wage' from employment; democratic representation within work; a right to paid leave from work for purposes of health and education ('welfare time'); and social insurance coverage that extends to all adults and provides services of a 'middle-class standard' to workers. These latter benefits are not unconditional as they are linked to employment. However, when compared with the Christian Democratic model, under social democracy fewer distinctions are made between those who are and are not in employment, or those who have and have not contributed to an insurance scheme.

I have tried to show how principles of justice can inform the rationale for welfare policies. However, it was noticeable that it is possible to develop each policy orientation in a variety of ways. Moreover, each of the three policy orientations employed more than one criterion of justice. The important lesson to be learned is that 'movement' from philosophical commitment to principle of justice and from there to benefit type is not a process whose steps are automatic. It is a rational movement in the sense that it involves argumentation. Each step along the way needs to be argued for, and an analysis of welfare theory does not just focus on the reasons for adopting a criterion of justice but also on the way such a criterion is fleshed out argumentatively.

We can note also that a number of quite different welfare policies can be argued for on the basis of the principles discussed. We have already seen Plant's argument that all humans have human rights to the goods 'needed' for well-being. However, others argue that some needs are not universal, and welfare policy should focus on (for instance) the 'special needs' of the intellectually and physically disabled. The criterion of merit can be the basis for meritocratic policies: equal opportunity to all to develop and use their native gifts. Alternatively, it can provide the rationale for the provision of counselling and training designed to improve the recipient's 'human capital' or employability. Finally, with respect to equality, Rawls calls for fair equal opportunity and a distribution of income and wealth determined by the difference principle, as we saw. Others have called for affirmative action, which is to compensate those discriminated against in the past or ensure such discrimination does not recur in the future.

Chapter outline

I want to give a brief outline of the chapters to come. The first part of the book (Chapters 2–5) looks at four key political philosophies.

Utilitarianism (Chapter 2) obliges us to act so as to promote utility (or welfare). We should reform major social institutions if in doing so we will better promote utility. This approach combines consequentialism, welfarism, and sum-ranking: actions (and rules) are judged with respect to their likely *consequences*; consequences are analysed in terms of people's experience of *welfare*, and those experiences of welfare can be *summed* so as to determine the right course of action.

Rawls's liberalism (Chapter 3) gives primacy to individual rights rather than the promotion of utility. Welfare entitlements can be justified only if they do not infringe individual rights. Entitlements must ensure each person's autonomy is respected, they must be part of a fair distribution of benefits and burdens, and they must not involve judgements about the relative worth of different lives. I give particular attention to Rawls's 'difference principle'.

In Chapter 4, I make a distinction between two strands of conservative thought. Conservatives often claim that welfare entitlements must be closely tied to social duties and also that intermediary groups like the family and church should control welfare provision. However, other conservatives try to justify the state's role in the redistribution of property, and even go so far as to justify welfare payments whose purpose is to improve the position of the worst off.

Socialists (Chapter 5) reject the conservative defence of existing social groups and the social hierarchy based on the existing division of labour. Socialists share a conservative commitment to community, but socialists call for a new community based on historically unique principles. Socialists are egalitarians, like liberals. However, unlike liberals, socialists believe that the principle of equality should be applied to work relations as well as to the distribution of income and wealth.

The second part (Chapters 6–9) of this book deals with theories that arise from challenges posed to modernity. It is argued by some that the state, economy, and society are no longer co-extensive within the same national borders; there is a heightened awareness of the plurality of moral doctrines and conceptions of the good; and a standpoint of suspicion is required given the pervasiveness of power within social institutions and even within political theory.

'Political Liberalism' (Chapter 6) is the name Rawls gives to his later work. He has taken on board the communitarian argument that his first formulation of the theory implicitly relied on a liberal substantive moral philosophy that cannot be accepted by all. I will focus on Martha Nussbaum's feminist interpretation of political liberalism. She argues that a position concerned with human capabilities (not resources) can adequately account for women's experiences of injustice and it can also be the fair terms of social cooperation in a pluralist society.

Communitarians (Chapter 7) assume that welfare benefits should help foster human flourishing and also that entitlements are justified when they are derived from such an Aristotelian conception of the good, that is, a life of virtue. MacIntyre provides a thoroughgoing defence of Aristotelian perfectionism. However, he concludes that such insights cannot motivate systematic politics now as they are only available to the members of traditional communities with clearly understood shared ethical commitments. I explore the possibility of a non-relative (universal) communitarianism, which is based on the idea of our flourishing as humans.

Radicals (Chapter 8) contend that mainstream theories have remained unaware of the pervasiveness of power. Post-modernists like Foucault insist that even well-intentioned welfare programmes simply implement various new 'disciplinary regimes' that 'subjugate' individuals. However, Habermas's critical theory promises a way out of unjust, illegitimate power relations. According to Habermas, in an 'ideal speech situation', where each person can participate and where each is treated as an equal, we can generate legitimate welfare entitlements that will guarantee each person's autonomy. However, Habermas's response to post-modernism is made at some cost, as he relegates ethics and virtues to a secondary role.

Chapter 9 looks at the New Right (neo-liberal) critique of extensive state provision of unconditional welfare benefits, and recent attempts to respond to that critique. Neo-liberals argue that state welfare is inefficient, an unjust infringement of liberty, and the source of a culture of dependency. The Third Way does not challenge the basic terms of the New Right critique. In contrast, liberal socialists have defended welfare as a human right; perfectionists have argued that the market must be limited so as to enhance well-being or flourishing; and recent Marxists have argued that even a Rawlsian liberal should (logically) be committed to virtually unqualified equality itself.

CHAPTER 2

Utilitarianism

In this chapter, I explore utilitarian political philosophy, and John Stuart Mill's ideas will provide our starting point. Mill argued that 'actions are right in proportion as they tend to promote happiness...' (1861, p. 137). It follows that entitlements are justified *if* they tend to promote happiness. He also defended an Aristotelian or perfectionist theory of happiness, arguing that people, with experience of both, 'do give a most marked preference to the manner of existence which employs their higher faculties' (ibid., p. 139). Therefore, well-being refers to a life that (morally speaking) is lived well. Utilitarian thinkers still play a major role in political theory (Goodin, 1995). Utilitarianism first arose, however, at the end of the eighteenth and the beginning of the nineteenth centuries. Its main figures were Jeremy Bentham [1748–1832] and Mill. It was a progressive position, known as 'philosophical radicalism' (Plamenatz, 1963, vol. 2, p. 24). This is the case for at least three reasons.

First, it was argued, the focus of morality should be the well-being of ordinary people. To be more precise, utilitarians argued that the happiness of all sentient creatures (human and non-human) was the end of morality. Morality may require sacrifices from us, but the reason for a sacrifice must always be the happiness of our fellow sentient creatures. We cannot be morally obliged to make sacrifices so as to please a Deity or to conform to the opinions of the majority; but we are obliged to act so as to promote the welfare or happiness of all, ourselves included (Mill, 1861, p. 148).

Secondly, utilitarians believed in the equal moral worth of each sentient creature. We are morally obliged to act so as to promote the general happiness, but each sentient creature's welfare counts equally in the calculation of the general happiness. Bentham's dictum is 'everybody to count for one, nobody for more than one' (Mill, 1861, p. 199). According to Mill, this 'involves an equal claim to all the means to happiness' (ibid.). However, utilitarians *need not* believe that persons ought to be equal in their welfare or utility, that is, equal in their opportunity to attain welfare or equal in their resulting experiences of welfare. Utilitarianism is an egalitarian position because it insists on the equal moral worth of all, and this is compatible with accepting unequal outcomes.

Finally, utilitarians were active campaigners for the reform of social institutions (Plamenatz, 1963, vol. 2, p. 24). Institutions are justified not by longevity, as conservatives argued (see Chapter 4), nor by human rights or a social contract, as liberals argued (see Chapter 3). They are justified only if they are the most likely means to promote the general happiness, and institutions that fail to do so are legitimate objects of criticism and targets of radical reform. Utilitarians attacked restrictions on free trade and restrictions of the franchise (Mill supported women's suffrage) not because they believed humans had natural rights to economic and political freedoms, but only in so far as these freedoms best promoted the general happiness (Ryan, 1984, p. 104ff).

A number of questions need to be raised about utilitarianism: (1) Can utility be clearly defined and identified? In utilitarian theory, utility variously refers to pleasure, preferences, and human perfection; (2) Can utilitarianism provide a grounding or foundation for individual rights? Mill and Goodin believe that it can, but liberals argue that utilitarians will be forced to accept infringements of individual rights *if* this best promotes happiness; and (3) Does utilitarianism provide good reasons to support any one criterion for the distribution of benefits and burdens in society? In particular, can it justify egalitarianism?

I focus on two utilitarian theories in this chapter. Mill defends an Aristotelian or perfectionist theory of happiness. He also argues that happiness is best promoted by respecting rules that defend each person's liberty. However, while the protection of each person's liberty is a matter of justice, for Mill, the receipt of goods by the needy is (by and large) a matter of self-help and charity. In contrast, Goodin argues that the vulnerable have unconditional rights to the goods needed to promote their utility. He does not accept Aristotelianism. Instead, he defines utility in terms of each person's basic preferences ('welfare interests'). He argues that a guaranteed unconditional basic income best promotes happiness, and the state, as a moral agent, can perform each individual's duties in respect of the welfare rights of others.

J.S. Mill's Perfectionism and the 'Harm Principle'

Mill is perhaps the most important of utilitarian thinkers. Although profoundly influenced by Bentham's utilitarianism, Mill brought many changes to the philosophical position of his predecessor. In particular, Mill insisted that pleasures differ in respect of quality, as there are higher pleasures, while Bentham argued that pleasures differed only in quantity. Moreover, Mill believed that utility is best promoted by certain rules, in particular, those that guarantee liberty, while Bentham concerned himself with each action and its likely consequences.

Higher pleasures and liberty

I want to start where Mill begins *Utilitarianism*. He first asks, 'What is utilitarianism?' In prioritizing 'utility', it may be thought to neglect pleasure. However, Mill insists that utilitarianism is not concerned solely with what is useful or instrumental. In *Hard Times*, Charles Dickens created a distopian vision of a society that valued only what was useful, what his characters referred to as 'fact':

> "You are to be in all things regulated and governed," said the gentleman, "by fact. We hope to have, before long, a board of fact, composed of commissioners of fact, who will force the people to be a people of fact, and of nothing but fact. You must discard the word Fancy altogether".
>
> (1854, Chapter 2)

Mill's utilitarian 'theory of life' could not be more different:

> pleasure, and freedom from pain, are the only things desirable as ends; and . . . all desirable things (which are as numerous in the utilitarian as in any other scheme) are desirable either for the pleasure inherent in themselves, or as means to the promotion of pleasure and the prevention of pain.
>
> (1861, p. 137)

Therefore, utilitarianism does not neglect pleasure for the sake of what is useful. According to Bentham, pleasures differ as to intensity, duration, certainty, propinquity (nearness), fecundity (being followed by pleasures of the same kind), purity (not being followed by sensations of the opposite kind), and extent (the number of persons to whom it extends) (1789, IV. § 2–4). However, Mill argues that pleasures differ in quality. Utilitarianism can show that some pleasures are more valuable than others; it is *not* 'a doctrine worthy only of swine' (1861, p. 137).

> Of two pleasures, if there be one to which all or almost all who have experience of both give a decided preference, irrespective of any feeling of moral obligation to prefer it, that is the more desirable pleasure.
>
> (ibid., p. 139)

Further, it can be said that people of experience prefer the higher pleasure, 'even though knowing it to be attended with a greater amount of discontent' (ibid.).

This is perhaps a paradoxical conclusion for a utilitarian. Utilitarianism states that something is desirable because it is pleasurable, but Mill defines 'happiness' in such a way that the highest form of happiness may bring discontent. Discontent is surely a type of pain. If Mill is really giving priority to individual happiness, then why conclude that we should act in such a way as to promote discontent? However, perhaps Mill must adopt this approach if he is to avoid moral relativism and moral subjectivism. Mill has *not* argued that happiness could refer to whatever is thought to be pleasurable in a given situation (relativism) or to each individual's expressed desires whatever they may be (subjectivism). Mill can also make his argument by appealing to the heritage of political thought, in particular to Aristotle's account of flourishing (*eudaimonia*). Aristotle assumed that, in the soul of the good person, desire obeys reason in aiming for good ends (NE, I.7, 1098a2). That is, the good person only does what gives him or her pleasure to the extent that he or she takes pleasure from doing what is good.

Mill develops what Bentham called 'the greatest happiness principle'. That is, we ought to do that which best promotes pleasures and diminishes pain, and we ought to give equal consideration to the pleasures and pains of each. For Mill, according to this principle, 'the ultimate end ... is an existence exempt as far as possible from pain, and as rich as possible in enjoyments, both in point of quantity *and quality*' (1861, p. 142; emphasis added). As this is the 'end of human action', it is 'necessarily also the standard of morality' (ibid., p. 143). Moral rules and precepts are those which, by their observance, 'an existence such as has been described might be, to the greatest extent possible, secured to all mankind; and not to them only, but, so far as the nature of things admits, to the whole sentient creation' (ibid.). The end of life is happiness, and pleasures differ in quality as well as quantity. Morality requires us to promote the happiness of all, that is, all sentient creatures.

I want to turn now to Mill's second major innovation in utilitarian thought. Mill makes use of 'rule-utilitarianism'. Act-utilitarians assess the likely consequences of each act, taken one by one. It may be the case that the best way to promote happiness is to infringe a conventionally accepted entitlement. For rule-utilitarianism, in contrast, the utilitarian criterion is 'applied in the first instance to the basic general rules governing individual acts' (Harsanyi, 1977, p. 41). A moral rule is correct if it is 'what maximizes social utility if followed by all' (ibid.). Mill's version of rule-utilitarianism is a defence of the 'harm principle' (also called the 'principle of liberty') as is shown in Figure 2.1.

> That principle is that the sole end for which mankind are warranted, individually or collectively, in interfering with the liberty of action of any of their number is self-protection. That the only purpose for which power can be rightfully exercised over any member of a civilized community, against his will, is to prevent harm to others. His own good, either physical or moral is not a sufficient warrant.
>
> (1859, p. 68)

The harm principle itself is justified because it best promotes happiness, that is, 'utility in the largest sense, grounded on the permanent interests of man as a progressive being' (p. 70).

Mill is often thought of as a liberal; indeed, one of the leading liberals. This is accurate to the extent that Mill defends liberty of thought, liberty of tastes and pursuits, and the 'freedom to unite for any purposes not involving harm to others' (ibid., p. 71). Mill rejects the paternalism that infringes personal liberty *for the sake of* the good

Mill	Bentham
Rule-Utilitarianism – the harm principle.	Act-Utilitarianism.
Perfectionism – the manner of existence which employs higher faculties.	Non-Perfectionism.

Figure 2.1 Two versions of utilitarianism

of the individual. However, Mill never leaves utilitarianism behind, for, in the final analysis, rights guaranteeing liberty are required only because they contribute to utility.

Mill combines the Aristotelian conception of happiness with the harm principle. He does so in the following way. First, he equates the highest end with 'individuality'. Referring to William von Humboldt, Mill argues that the end of each human is 'the highest and most harmonious development of his powers to a complete and consistent whole', but we should, therefore, aim towards 'the individuality of power and development' (ibid., p. 121). Flourishing (development and excellence) can be equated with individuality. To be 'happy' as individuals, 'our understanding should be our own' and 'our desires and impulses should be our own' (ibid., p. 124). Secondly, society is justified in coercing the individual on one condition alone, namely so as to prevent harm to some other individual or individuals. However, Mill argues, I am 'harmed' if I suffer some injury to my 'permanent interests as a progressive being'. I am not harmed when denied a trivial, fleeting pleasure, but when I am hindered or prevented from attaining and enjoying 'happiness', that is, flourishing.

Happiness is the only thing desirable as an end

Mill argues that an act is right in so far as it promotes happiness. This is the criterion of moral judgement. Mill derives it from a utilitarian 'theory of life', namely 'Happiness is desirable, and the only thing desirable, as an end; other things being only desirable as means to that end' (1861, p. 168). This is the case for each individual. Further, 'each person's happiness is a good to that person, and the general happiness, therefore, [is] a good to the aggregate of all persons' (ibid., p. 169). This moral reasoning is consequentialist and welfarist. When we judge actions we are concerned only with the consequences of the act. We assess motives only when we want to judge a person's character (as virtuous or vicious). Further, a consequence is good if it promotes welfare, that is, if it is 'productive of happiness'.

Can Mill defend the claim that happiness is the ultimate good? According to G.E. Moore, Mill commits the 'naturalistic fallacy' and his approach falls prey to the 'open-question technique' (1903, pp. 12–13). Mill's argument is an attempt to define 'good' as 'productive of pleasure'. Moore's contention is that 'good' (like 'red') cannot be defined although we know what it means. One may agree with Mill that 'employing higher faculties' causes happiness, but one may still doubt whether this property (happiness) is good. Good cannot be defined as productive of happiness. To do so is to commit the naturalistic fallacy: to define good as being some other natural object. In one sense 'good' is like 'red', as neither can be verbally defined as some other natural object. However, it is possible to agree on the meaning of red, as it can be defined 'ostensively' (we can point to red things). When it comes to 'good', different people may point to different things as having this property. Some point to the humble person, others to the proud; some to the skeptic, others to the person of faith. For Moore, 'good' describes a non-natural property, something we intuit, as we can use 'the good' to denote many and varied things. 'The good' can denote not only 'all the things that produce happiness', but also friendship, aesthetic enjoyment, and wisdom (Hudson, 1983, p. 70ff).

One response to this criticism is to state that there is an internal relation between the word 'good' and the 'objects' to which it refers. Philippa Foot, an Aristotelian moral philosopher, denies it is possible for 'just anything' to be called 'good'. Rather, good connects to certain 'human wants' which are satisfied when we exercise the virtues. We want the ability to resist temptation and to face what is fearful, and the virtues of moderation and courage are 'good' because they are connected to these human wants (Foot, 1958, p. 125). Mill, like Foot, defends an Aristotelian conception of happiness.[1] One could say that Mill does not equate good with what people *do* desire. Instead, good denotes what people, given their needs and potentials, *ought* to desire. That is, Mill's argument makes sense if we take him to be employing a 'moralized' conception of happiness or flourishing. It may not be the case that we all do desire 'happiness' as the ultimate end. However, we can judge that people ought to desire happiness as the ultimate end.

As we saw, Mill also argues, 'each person's happiness is a good to that person, and the general happiness, therefore, [is] a good to the aggregate of all persons' (1861, p. 169). Does the statement in the first clause of this sentence entail the conclusion? Some argue that Mill is guilty of an 'error of composition' here. For instance, even if John's happiness [JH] is a good to John, and Peter's happiness [PH] is a good to Peter, it does not follow the entity 'JH plus PH' is a good to each of John and Peter (Hudson, 1983, p. 75). This is a peculiar criticism given that utilitarians espouse the individualist view that society is nothing more than the aggregate of its individual members. We are to promote the *general* happiness, but the 'interest' of the community is 'the sum of the interests of the several members who compose it' (Bentham, 1789, I. § 4–5). Further, Alan Ryan has argued that it may be possible to deduce the greatest happiness principle from both the principle of universalizability and every man's natural desire for his own happiness. As a sentient being, every person has a desire for his or her own happiness; as a rational being, every person recognizes that all others have as much right to their happiness as he or she has to his or her own; and as both a sentient and a rational being, therefore, every person must (logically) recognize that the ultimate moral end is the greatest happiness equitably distributed (Ryan, 1966, pp. 424–5).

Mill contends that a life of virtue is good, and desirable. Is that the case? Those 'who are equally acquainted with, and equally capable of appreciating and enjoying, both, do give a most marked preference to the manner of existence which employs their higher faculties' (Mill, 1861, p. 139). No intelligent person 'would consent to be a fool', even if the fool 'is better satisfied' (ibid.). Mill has argued that happiness is the only thing desired as an end 'in itself'. At the same time, he claims a person is virtuous only if he or she considers virtue to have *intrinsic* worth (ibid., p. 171). That is, for the virtuous person, virtue is desirable 'in itself'. Mill has not contradicted himself *if* it is the case that the exercise of virtue is not just a means to happiness but a part of happiness itself (as Aristotle contended: NE, I. 7, 1098a2). Mill also argues, however, that the virtuous person willingly exercises the virtues 'without any thought of either pleasure or pain' (1861, p. 174). Nonetheless, he assumes 'nobleness of character' increases the happiness of the virtuous individual (ibid., p. 142). This is 'the Greek ideal of self-development'. In developing 'individuality', a person 'becomes more valuable to himself', and 'capable of being more valuable to others' (1859, p. 127). The summary of the above-mentioned points is given in Table 2.1.

Table 2.1 Critiques of Mill

Critiques of Mill	Possible responses
■ Naturalistic fallacy.	His conception of happiness is not merely factual; it is moralized.
■ Error of composition.	Utilitarianism is individualistic.
■ Virtue valued in itself (but only happiness is desired only as an end).	Virtue is valuable in itself because it is a constitutive element of happiness.

Justice and charity

Can Mill's utilitarianism justify positive action taken by the state to promote welfare? Duties of justice are 'perfect', he argues. My performance of my perfect duty is something another definite individual can claim as his or her right. In contrast, duties of charity are 'imperfect', as I am not obliged to give any particular thing, at any particular time, to any particular person. Mill does argue that we 'ought to shape our conduct by a rule which all rational beings might adopt *with benefit to their collective interests*' (1861, p. 188; my emphasis). Mill would justify rules of justice with reference to their consequences for the general happiness. Rules of justice 'make safe for us the very groundwork of our existence' (ibid., p. 190). Nonetheless, Mill does not defend the state's proactive role in providing welfare entitlements. The perfect duties of justice are 'negative': we are duty-bound to refrain from wrongful aggression, and wrongfully withholding what is due to another (ibid., p. 196). These rules do not oblige us to give help to the deprived and vulnerable. It also follows that many of our moral obligations to others are not those of justice, but of charity.

How is welfare to be distributed, and on what principle is welfare distribution justified? Mill calls on political society to distribute certain goods, and equality may be an important consideration here. It would seem that he believes the goods concerned have what is known as 'diminishing marginal utility'. According to Peter Singer, 'for a given individual, a set amount of something is more useful when people have little of it than when they have a lot' (1993, p. 24). For Mill, it is 'one of the most sacred duties of parents . . . after summoning a human being into the world, to give to that being an education fitting him to perform his part well towards others and himself', and 'if the parent does not fulfil this obligation, the State ought to see it fulfilled at the charge, as far as possible, of the parent' (Mill, 1859, p. 176). However, society should provide education to the children of families who do not have the income and wealth to provide it themselves (ibid.). Nonetheless, Mill does not believe that children can (or should) be made equal in their educational resources or educational attainments.

The purpose of education is to fit the child to 'perform his part well'. Mill does not support the state's proactive role as a provider of welfare entitlements that would significantly diminish social inequality. In the work of Bentham as well, the strong case for equality is overwhelmed by arguments for 'security'. The constant redistributive efforts required to establish (and then maintain) equality would so frustrate individual expectations that even those who would do well from equality would suffer from insecurity (Ryan, 1984, p. 105). Mill's rights of justice extend only as far as protections against theft and violence. At best, the state's welfare role is residual: the state should provide a basic welfare good (like education) only when the family can no longer do so. The principle of need may motivate charitable acts. However, in the market place, people will receive benefits because they are thought to merit or deserve those benefits (at least in so far as we can equate the preferences of others in the market with judgements of merit). For these reasons, Mill's thought can be compared with the 'liberal market model' of welfare (Figure 2.2). This model is perhaps best represented by welfare policy in the United States.

The US welfare policies include social insurance (contribution-based) entitlements along with means-tested, selective benefits. Social insurance benefits are provided to the elderly, invalids, and the ill (e.g. Medicare). In contrast, 'Supplemental Security Income' is a means-tested benefit providing supplementary assistance to the aged, blind, disabled, widow/ers and spouses; and also 'Aid to Families with Dependent Children' (relabelled 'Temporary Assistance to Needy Families' in 1996) is a 'stringently means-tested' flat-rate benefit for families with children (Goodin et al., 1999, p. 59). Social insurance benefits in the United States have 'low coverage rates and low benefit levels', which has 'left a large residual population which ... had to rely upon means-tested public assistance of a traditional poor-law sort' (ibid.). The British Poor Law of 1834 acknowledged a collective responsibility for the relief of deprivation. However, aid was not distributed as a right. And benefits were set at a level that was to discourage anyone from relying on public assistance when they still had the ability to provide for themselves through market employment. As means-tested benefits emphasize selectivity with respect to state-provided benefit, they

---

'Selectivity'	Residual state (selective, means-tested benefits).
	Charity (& rights of justice against theft and violence).
	Public services (e.g. education) without redistributive goals.

Figure 2.2   Utilitarian welfare state model 1: 'liberal market model'

also encourage self-reliance within the market as an alternative to the receipt of state benefits.

Consequentialism and utility

Mill's utilitarianism combines a theory of what we ought to do, consequentialism, and a theory of the good to be realized, welfarism. It is also assumed that the good can be quantified; that different people's utility can be measured and summed.

Consequentialism

Every moral theory has a value that is to be 'realized'. The value could be utility, but also it could be equality, liberty, freedom from exploitation, and so on. A 'theory of the right' states what we ought to do so as to realize what we value (Pettit, 1991, p. 230). For utilitarianism, the value to be realized is happiness, or utility. The question put to us then is, 'how can we best realize utility?' Consequentialism is the utilitarian theory of 'correct action' (Sen and Williams, 1982, p. 3). If there is a value to be realized, the best way to do so is by 'promoting' that value. However, non-consequentialists argue that utilitarianism has the following weakness.

> We could imagine circumstances in which a larger overall level of happiness . . . could be achieved in society but it would be secured by severe discrimination against a particular group of people.
>
> (Plant, 1991, p. 154)

If that is the case, then the utilitarian must conclude that such discrimination is permissible or even obligatory. The non-consequentialist argues that we ought to respect or honour the value to be realized, even when we could generate good consequences by *not* honouring that value in certain instances.

Because of this criticism, some utilitarians have refined consequentialism. If we discover that respecting certain rights best promotes happiness, then we ought to respect those rights. Further, we ought to do so in every instance. This is Mill's argument in defence of rights that protect liberty. Note, utilitarians have not renounced consequentialism here. They argue that we should respect only those rights that we have 'justified' by consequentialist reasoning. This is indirect, restricted consequentialism (Pettit, 1991, p. 236).

A similar point is made in defence of 'rule-utilitarianism'. However, non-consequentialists still are not satisfied. They argue that the dangers of consequentialism have simply been moved from the arena of everyday deliberation to that of theoretical justification. At the level of justification, utilitarians need not accept or accede to non-consequentialist principles of equitable distribution. As liberals complain, utilitarians 'are supposed to produce as much good as . . . [they] can, not worry about who wins and who loses in the distribution process' (Scarre, 1996, p. 153).

Welfarism and sum-ranking

Utilitarians defend a welfarist theory of the good, the value to be realized. An entitlement is justified if its enjoyment is likely to promote welfare, or utility. However, utilitarians must be able to define, identify, and measure utility. Is this possible?

Hedonists argue that utility is a matter of a person's 'desires': a set of goods is useful to me if they help satisfy my desires (Brandt, 1979). However, others argue that utility refers to 'preferences': I prefer to attain things other than that which gives me pleasure, and my utility should be defined to take preferences like these into account (Harsanyi, 1977; Hare, 1981). For instance, even though eating fatty foods gives me pleasure, I may refrain from doing so because I prefer to have a healthy diet. However, I do not always know what my preferences *should* be. For that reason, utility may be defined as 'true preferences' or 'welfare interests'. They are what I *would* prefer if I had perfect information, a strong will, and settled preferences (Goodin, 1991, p. 244). They are 'useful resources whatever people's particular projects and aims' (ibid.). A yet further approach is represented by Mill's 'ideal' utilitarianism. Utility is not what people merely desire or prefer, but 'the manner of existence which employs their higher faculties', that is, human perfection.

Utilitarians are to promote the good, however defined. It may be a very demanding morality if we are to 'maximize' the good. To produce as much good as possible requires that each person give equal consideration to the like interests *of all*, whether they are strangers or not. However, utilitarians are aware that often the best way to promote happiness is to promote the interests of those near and dear (Mill, 1861, p. 150). Moreover, for 'satisficing utilitarianism', one need only produce 'enough' good: one is not obliged to 'maximize' the good (Slote, 1992). In any case, utilitarians 'add up' individual utilities when they assess the consequences of actions (Sen and Williams, 1982, p. 4). That is, even if we are obliged only to produce 'enough' good, it must be the case that the good is something that can be measured. 'The good, whatever it is, must be an aggregative commodity, . . . so that moral decision can rest on a basis of comparative quantitative judgements' (Scarre, 1996, p. 133). It also follows that utilitarians must examine the way in which many different benefits are enjoyed (and burdens borne) and many different individuals are affected (for good and ill). They compare the utility derived from different goods, and also the utility experienced by different people.

It could be argued that comparison of goods and utilities is obligatory. It would be immoral to fail to compare goods and utilities. This is the case, for instance, when we decide whether or not to tax the wealthy and able-bodied *so as* to distribute goods to the poor and disabled. If we do not impose the tax, the poor and disabled will not receive goods that would (in all probability) better promote utility. If these goods do exhibit the quality of 'diminishing marginal utility', then the use of goods to ease disability and limit poverty will better promote utility than the use of the same goods by the able-bodied and non-poor. If we do impose the tax, it is likely that these benefits will accrue, but it is also likely that the wealthy and able-bodied will be burdened. Will that burden be justified? Utilitarians argue that we can only answer this question by 'comparing' the likely burden on the wealthy and able-bodied with the likely benefits enjoyed by the poor and disabled. (A further issue is what institution is to effect such a distribution of benefits and burdens, whether the state, market, family, charity, and so on.)

Is it possible to measure and compare different goods and utilities? We may argue that utility can be equated with pleasure, and experiences of pleasure can be quantified. This is the case for 'hedonistic utilitarians' like Richard Brandt (1979, pp. 255ff, 260ff). We can compare levels of desire satisfaction with regard to both the pleasantness of an experience and its duration, he contends. Then, for interpersonal comparisons, behavioural evidence can be used to identify when one person obtains more pleasure from an experience than others. However, such comparisons are highly problematic. As we cannot see into the minds and hearts of others, how can we quantify, measure, and then compare the pleasures of different people? We can ask the people concerned to report their feelings. But it is difficult to know how we can compare

the subjective expression of opinion about the experience of pleasure by one person with that of another. Some people are effusive
and others more reticent; and their subjective reports on their
experiences will reflect this difference in character (as well as differences in the experiences concerned).

There is a further objection to hedonistic utilitarianism. The
hedonistic utilitarian view of what is valuable does not prioritize
autonomy. In criticizing hedonistic utilitarianism, Robert Nozick
uses the example of the 'experience machine'. I could freely choose
to attach myself to a machine, and program it to stimulate my brain
to produce the sensations associated with, for instance, writing a
novel. 'What else can matter to us, other than how our lives feel
from the inside?' (Nozick, 1974, p. 43). Nothing else matters for the
hedonist, and this is just the problem. Nozick rejects hedonism
because it ascribes value only to pleasurable states of consciousness.
According to Nozick, humans actually want to do certain things (not
just feel the pleasures associated with doing them) and they want to
be a certain sort of person (e.g. someone who can and does write
novels).

Utilitarians instead can argue that utility refers to preferences.
Whose preferences should be promoted? Perhaps some preferences are irrational and anti-social. If that is the case then it does
not seem to make sense to argue that, morally speaking, we ought to
give those preferences priority over rational and socially responsible preferences. Instead of maximizing actual preferences, some
utilitarians argue we should promote an idealized version of those
preferences. John Harsanyi argues that 'true preferences' are those
a person 'would have if he had all the relevant information', rea-
soned with great care, and in a 'state of mind conducive to rational
choice' (1977, pp. 56–7). Nonetheless, some true preferences arise
from sadism, envy, resentment, or malice, and we are not obliged to
promote them. They are anti-social preferences. Harsanyi tends
towards abstraction, however, as he associates a person's utility
with what an 'ideal observer' would choose for him (Sen and
Williams, 1982, p. 14). Utilitarians had contended that the utility
of each is to count for one. The tendency to locate information about
utility in abstraction moves utilitarian deliberations further away
from the actual utility of each.

Utilitarians could respond to criticisms such as these. For Mill, it
is 'better to be Socrates dissatisfied than a fool satisfied' (1861,
p. 140). What people do desire and prefer can be compared with

Table 2.2 Utilitarianism and criticisms

	Utilitarian theory	Criticisms
Consequentialism	▪ Direct consequentialism. ▪ Indirect consequentialism.	Sacrificing entitlements of individuals may be required. Consequentialism vis-à-vis justification.
Welfarism	▪ Hedonism. ▪ Preference utilitarianism. ▪ True preferences. ▪ Ideal utilitarianism. ▪ Two levels of reasoning.	Do not always prefer what is pleasurable. Cannot compare pleasures. Some preferences irrational/anti-social. Idealization (not actual preferences). No respect for autonomy. No respect for autonomy.

what they ought to desire and prefer if they are to be happy. This is an objective theory of welfare. However, it raises fears about autonomy. Liberals contend that the utilitarian judgement of the worth of a life 'is based on assessments of value in life that are wholly foreign to [the person concerned]..., that he would reject even if fully informed of the ordinary facts' (Dworkin, 1981, p. 46). Can utilitarians employ an objective theory of welfare and also ensure respect for autonomy? Indirect- or rule-utilitarians argue that there are two different 'levels' of moral reasoning (Table 2.2) (Hare, 1981). We justify welfare entitlements as 'utilitarians', but in this way we justify a series of rules that we are then obliged to 'respect', such as Mill's principle of liberty. This may have paternalistic consequences as well, however. This would result were the population divided into utilitarian legislators on the one hand and the non-utilitarian populace on the other. Legislators would use utilitarianism to formulate society's basic rules, while everyone else would be required to act on those rules without knowing their utilitarian justification.

Utilitarianism, distributive principles, and rights

Utilitarianism does not start from (so-called) human rights or (so-called) universal rational principles. For that reason, the following questions are often posed. Can utilitarianism provide good reasons to defend one distributive principle over others? And can utilitarianism guarantee protection of individual rights?

(i) *Equality* – Utilitarianism is an egalitarian position in the sense that its dictum is 'everybody to count for one, nobody for more than one'. We are to give 'equal consideration' to the 'like interests' of each (Singer, 1993, p. 21). However, we may be obliged to treat people unequally so as to give equal consideration to like interests. Some goods exhibit the quality known as 'diminishing marginal utility' (Quinton, 1973, p. 76). Receiving these goods is more valuable the less of them you have. It follows, we are obliged to give extra benefits to those who are most deprived of the good in question. However, in doing so, in treating people unequally, we may well bring about greater equality with respect to the enjoyment of the good in question and also with respect to the experience of utility.

Ronald Dworkin has rejected 'welfare egalitarianism'. Welfare egalitarians claim that 'a distributional scheme treats people as equals when it distributes or transfers resources among them until no further transfer would leave them more *equal in welfare*' (Dworkin, 1981, p. 12). However, we cannot accept a system that would make people as equal as possible 'in the degree to which each person's preferences about his own life and circumstances are fulfilled' (ibid., p. 28). Equality of welfare is problematic as it equates what is just with whatever it is that best satisfies people's preferences. Rather, liberals argue, in forming and pursuing their life projects, people 'need some sense of what resources will be at their disposal' (ibid., p. 29). That is, a theory of distribution, which is independent of people's actual preferences, should provide boundaries to determine what projects people may pursue and what they may not; for instance, I can only pursue my preference for a life of indolence and leisure if I can justly (as determined by the independent theory of justice) receive the goods needed to do so.

(ii) *Need* – Utilitarianism requires us to act so as to promote utility. Is it possible to replace 'utility' with 'need'? This might be crucial if we are to compare the utility of different people. Then we could say that some experiences are clearly more significant than others as they are more closely tied to basic needs. Indeed, is this not what Goodin does when he talks of 'welfare interests'? As we saw, my welfare interests are what I *would* prefer if I had perfect information, a strong will, and settled preferences; *and* they are useful resources whatever my particular aims [see .pp. 32–5]. Similarly, what Singer calls 'important human interests' include avoiding pain, developing ability, satisfying basic needs for food and shelter, and being free to pursue projects without unnecessary interference (1993, p. 22).

However, Goodin rejects the needs-based approach. He rejects the contrast between real needs and mere wants (1988, p. 37). Goodin notes that a needs-based approach assumes some needs are 'intrinsic' or 'absolute': they are objectively required for a person to attain flourishing or avoid harm. Goodin insists that *objective* theories of need cannot justify this account of value, as all value judgements must be derived from 'wants', that is, *subjective* preferences and interests. Note, for utilitarians, all value is subjective, although actual preferences can be corrected for lack of information and imperfect reasoning. The value of need satisfaction is derivative of the value of want satisfaction, he argues (ibid., p. 37). Although the satisfaction of certain basic needs has 'temporal priority' (they must be satisfied first), this does not translate into value priority. For instance, we value good health, and the services that meet this need, *because* of the value we attach to the wants that can only be satisfied if we are healthy. However, *pace* Goodin, it would seem that an objective account of value is better suited for making his distinction between actual interests and 'welfare interests'. It would explain why some preferences can be discounted. They are irrational or anti-social *because* they are opposed to what is objectively valuable for human beings (Nussbaum, 2000a, pp. 126–7).

(iii) *Merit* – Utilitarianism obliges us to act so as to promote happiness. And Mill argues that 'nobleness of character' increases the happiness of the virtuous individual, and others (1861, p. 142). Therefore, perhaps we should distribute benefits (in part at least) in proportion to merit, where 'merit' is determined by capacity to produce happiness. Some argue that utilitarianism here provides a justification for the market system of distribution. This is what I referred to as the 'liberal market model' [see pp. 29–31]. In the market economy, people are rewarded according to the contributions they make to the overall economy: salaries are paid (by employers) to those who perform work that is considered valuable, and producers are rewarded (by consumers) for providing what is desired. However, we must be careful not to overstate the support Mill provides for the market model. Mill notes that the pursuit of wealth as an end in itself can diminish utility. The love of money, power, and fame, 'may, and often do, render the individual noxious to the other members of the society to which he belongs . . .' (ibid., p. 171).

Table 2.3 Utilitarianism and principles of justice

Principles	Utilitarianism
▪ Equality	Diminishing marginal utility. Obliged to make people equal in utility?
▪ Need	Synonym for utility. Requires objective theory of value?
▪ Merit	The liberal market model. Or is the desire for profit a vice?

The above-mentioned points have been summarized in Table 2.3.

It seems that utilitarianism is not tied to any one principle of distribution. This should not be surprising. The utilitarian will judge any principle on the basis of its likely consequences regarding the promotion of utility. However, stability of expectations is an important element of utility. Stability is undermined when individuals do not know what principle is employed to justify entitlements, as they will then be unable to tell what actions, on their part, will bring about benefits (or burdens). Nonetheless, it is not clear what principle of distribution utilitarianism lends support to. Utilitarianism may enjoin us to stick to the principle once we have chosen it, but can it offer any concrete help in choosing that principle?

Utilitarians defend welfare entitlements if they promote happiness. However, can utilitarianism provide a meaningful guarantee for welfare *rights*? In an important respect, utilitarianism is individualistic and egalitarian. Utilitarians give equal considerations to the like interests of all. They insist also that there are no interests higher than the interests of all individuals combined. Utilitarianism therefore seems to provide good grounds to insist that society should protect the interests of each. And Mill argues that rights make secure for us our fundamental interests. For liberals, however, utilitarianism is unacceptable as it gives utility priority over individual rights that protect autonomy. Rawls has argued that other people's rights are boundaries we must respect. One should *not* 'take men's propensities and inclinations as given, whatever they are, and then seek the best way to fulfill them' (Rawls, 1971, p. 31). Some people have 'preferences' that can only be satisfied by denying basic rights to others (the preferences of the Nazi can only be satisfied by denying liberty, opportunity, and resources to Jews, among others). Can utilitarianism be defended against the charge that it cannot guarantee rights that protect autonomy?

R.E. Goodin: Welfare interests and the welfare state

Goodin tries to respond to some of these liberal criticisms of utilitarianism. He defines utility as 'welfare interests' [see pp. 32–5]. He also argues that the state is a 'moral agent' that can perform each citizen's 'perfect' duties to others, namely the provision of an unconditional basic income as a 'right' that protects 'autonomy'.

Mill expects us to be 'as strictly impartial as a disinterested and benevolent spectator' (1861, p. 148). Perhaps in private life we ought to give priority to the interests of those who are near and dear. However, Goodin contends, utilitarianism 'can be a good normative guide to public affairs without its necessarily being the best practical guide to personal conduct' (1995, p. 4). We expect those who deliver welfare services to take 'the view from nowhere', as the 'essence' of 'public service' is to 'strive to attain neutrality' (ibid., p. 9). Utilitarian theory also can justify the state's role in a welfare state. Utilitarians 'have a strong moral duty to protect those whose interests are particularly vulnerable to our actions and choices' (Goodin, 1988, p. x). Moreover, the state is a 'moral agent'. An individual has a right to welfare if someone else has a 'perfect' duty to ensure the right is enjoyed. No one, as an individual, has a 'perfect' duty to guarantee welfare rights; Goodin contends, however, 'everyone collectively has a strong, perfect duty to see to it those things are done' (1995, p. 33). There are responsibilities 'peculiar to the group as a whole', and the state can ensure they are performed (ibid.). Moreover, the rights of individuals correspond to the duties of the group to protect those particularly vulnerable to our actions (1988, p. 6).

Goodin provides an argument in favour of one further model of the welfare state, the 'minimum welfare state' (MWS) (Figure 2.3). It guarantees to each individual, as a right, those goods that protect the vulnerable. Goodin here refers to provision of 'certain basic needs' (ibid., p. 8), but we should understand this, I think, as an argument with respect to 'welfare interests'. As we saw, my welfare interests are what I *would* prefer if I had perfect information, a strong will, and settled preferences; *and* they are useful resources whatever my particular aims [see pp. 32–5]. The MWS is set in the

Principles	Policies
▪ Rights of individuals (and duties as members of the group). ▪ Protect the vulnerable (vis-à-vis 'welfare interests').	1. State intervention in market economy. 2. To meet basic needs. 3. To meet needs directly.

Figure 2.3 Utilitarian welfare state model 2: 'minimum welfare state' model

context of a market economy (ibid., p. 7); it limits its provision to certain basic needs; and strives to meet people's welfare needs 'directly, rather than indirectly' (ibid., p. 10). Therefore, the MWS does not entail the revolutionary overthrow of capitalism. It limits, but does not eliminate, inequality, as it provides a 'national minimum' above which individuals are free to create inequality through their own efforts. A state may do more than this (and, for instance, strive for greater equality), but such policies require a justification that is not provided by this theory of the MWS. Moreover, while those who follow the liberal market model seek to restrict the state's welfare role, the argument for the MWS makes a positive case for at least this level of welfare provision (ibid., pp. 16–17).

Goodin's work can provide an argument for a third utilitarian welfare state as well (Figure 2.4). He concludes that a 'broadly egalitarian distribution' is called for. First, most people are pretty much alike in their ability to convert resources into utility. Other things being equal, an equal measure of goods will bring about equal utility (1995, p. 23). Secondly, resources display a 'diminishing marginal utility', 'so the more you have of something, the less utility you derive from the next increment of it you are given' (ibid.). Moreover, Goodin rejects the principle of merit. He notes, in a manner reminiscent of Mill, 'people sometimes would derive

Principles	Policies
▪ Equality. ▪ Non-perfectionism. ▪ Autonomy. ▪ Stability.	1. Unconditional Basic Income Guarantee. 2. Social insurance (contribution-based). 3. The Dutch Model: welfare without work.

Figure 2.4 Utilitarian welfare state model 3: post-productivism

satisfaction from something in a way that they do not presently recognize' (ibid., p. 14). However, Goodin does not make the kind of perfectionist judgement of value that we find in Mill. Goodin's point is that, while pleasures and preferences vary, 'basic interests . . . are (at least at some suitable level of generality) pretty standard across all individuals (at least all individuals in any given society at any given moment)' (ibid., p. 14).

It may be impossible to conceptualize 'desert', he argues, such that the people picked out as 'deserving' are in fact importantly different (ibid., p. 235). This is the case with means-tested and selective benefits ('categorical assistance') intended for the 'disabled'. An unconditional basic income is 'less presumptuous'. It is less likely to cause harm due to errors in moral conceptualization and in sociological evidence. Therefore, the same amount should be given to the disabled and the 'merely idle'. At least all the 'deserving' will get aid, even if others (the idle) do so as well (ibid., p. 241). So, Goodin rejects a merit-based conception of justice and he also rejects the conditionality that can be a feature of merit-based theories. Nonetheless, Goodin also defends social insurance schemes. A scheme in which contribution determines levels of reward is likely to 'buffer people' against sudden life changes, which are 'radically disruptive of what people ultimately find satisfying' (ibid., p. 25). However, proportional benefits are justified not because these lives are judged 'the most satisfying lives' (ibid.), but because it best promotes utility, that is, basic interests.

Promoting utility must not infringe 'personal autonomy' or disregard the 'separateness of persons' (ibid., p. 23). The utility of each has moral significance for the reason that each person is 'a distinct locus of value'. Moreover, dire economic necessity and interpersonal domination diminish autonomy. They prevent people from being self-legislating agents, form having the capacity to reflect upon and shape their lives (2001, p. 17). If a person's basic welfare interests are met, it is all the less likely that he or she could be used merely as a means for the ends of others. Further, welfare interests are best promoted by an unconditional basic income, and this is the approach of the Dutch welfare state. In the 'social democratic' regime, particularly in Sweden, welfare benefits are a citizen's rights, but it is the citizen's responsibility to make productive contributions (ibid., p. 14). It expresses the idea of 'welfare *and* work'. In contrast, the epithet of the Dutch model is 'welfare *without* work'.

Goodin believes the Dutch welfare state is the best example of 'post-productivism' [see pp. 186–9 and pp. 200–3]. The social democratic regime is associated with the value of equality, but also, as a productivist system, it is believed that a citizen must work so as to be equal. In contrast, post-productivism is associated with the value of 'autonomy' and it detaches welfare entitlements from work. 'Minimal conditionality' attached to entitlements 'impinge minimally' on freedom of action, preventing 'interpersonal domination'. They bring greater personal independence, as income is independent of three factors: labour market participation, household attachments, and the discretion of bureaucrats. Entitlements are enjoyed as 'rights'. Rights are guaranteed to a person as a separate individual, independent of the entitlements of other family members (children, spouses, parents); rights are not designed to encourage the recipient to seek work in the market; and discretion is removed from the hands of bureaucrats in determining the level and duration of benefits.

Unconditional basic income best promotes utility *because* it causes less harm and protects autonomy, Goodin argues. How can Goodin judge that one harm, or one infringement on autonomy, is more serious than another? He has rejected Aristotelian perfectionism. The Aristotelian argues that we should guarantee what is needed so as to pursue not just any life, but a good life, a life of virtue. In contrast, John Rawls argues that we have entitlements to goods that any one would need regardless of their system of ends [see pp. 46–51]. Rawls also argues that his approach will guarantee individual rights that protect autonomy. However, the Rawlsian argument is not an option for Goodin either. Rawls can make this argument (he claims) only because he also rejects utilitarianism. Right is prior to the good, Rawls contends, as we ought to respect the rights of others when we pursue what we take to be the good and when we try to promote the good of society.

Conclusion

In the next chapter, I turn to liberal theory. Before doing so I want to recap on some liberal criticisms of utilitarianism.

(1) *Utilitarianism cannot guarantee respect for individual rights*. Utilitarians interpret the right as maximizing or enhancing the good. Therefore, they can never avoid the conclusion that we ought

to infringe the rights of unpopular individuals if in doing so we will better promote utility.

(2) *Utilitarians cannot guarantee respect for autonomy.* For utilitarians, the value to be realized is utility, and utilitarians seek to promote that value. Although Goodin calls for benefits that protect autonomy, he does so on the grounds that this will better promote utility. Utilitarians cannot justify the demand that we ought to always respect and honour the autonomy of each, irrespective of the costs of doing so and irrespective of the possible benefits of not respecting autonomy.

(3) *Utilitarians cannot defend fair principles of justice.* This is the case because utilitarianism cannot establish principles as normative requirements that are independent of each person's pursuit of their utility. Also it cannot guarantee each person's *rights* to their share of a fair distribution.

Utilitarianism is not without its difficulties, as its liberal critics point out. Why then should we consider accepting utilitarianism?

Simplicity – Utilitarianism supplies a single criterion of moral judgement: actions are right in proportion as they tend to promote happiness. Further, utilitarian moral reasoning is in line with every-day reasoning (Pettit, 1991, p. 238). If I want to attain some good, for example better health, I do so by thinking and acting in an instrumental manner: a course of action is rational if it is likely to make me healthier. Other normative theories try to introduce forms of rationality that are in conflict with instrumental reason. (As we shall see in the next chapter, liberals like Rawls ask us to reason as if we did not know our advantages and preferences, among other things, when we reason about justice.) They are therefore unnecessarily complex.

Common sense – Utilitarian reasoning conforms to our every day, or common sense, instrumental mode of reasoning. Further, as it places welfare at the heart of moral reasoning, it is a straightforward, direct way to reason about welfare entitlements. Other theories not only depart from everyday reasoning, but also come to well-being by a circuitous route. They give priority to different issues such as 'right', or 'community', or 'equality'.

Universality – We are asked to be 'as strictly impartial as a disinterested and benevolent spectator', and show equal consideration for the like interests of all. The conclusions of utilitarianism, therefore, are in the interests of each. Welfare entitlements are shaped by their context or 'regime'. However, if the conclusions of utilitarianism are universalizable, they apply to any and all situations.

Critique – Although utilitarianism is the common-sense approach, it is also 'critical', as it sees through prejudices constructed around morality that serve powerful interests. 'Many on most occasions conform to the [utilitarian] principle', but they are inconsistent, as 'few embrace it and many quarrel with it' (Bentham, 1789, I.12). Utilitarianism shows us that the fundamental feature of morality is concern for other humans, not fear of divine retribution or social conformity. It also shows us that each is to count for one. The utility of each is of equal value in our deliberations.

CHAPTER 3

Liberalism

The work of John Rawls offers certainly the most influential and perhaps also the most sophisticated contemporary defence of liberalism. Before looking in detail at his work, it should be noted there are a number of historical sources of Rawls's liberalism. The 'social contract' approach, of John Locke [1632–1704] in particular, is an important influence. For Locke, political obligation is based on the consent of equal and independent persons, and political society is constructed by its members forming a social contract (1683, Bk. 2, II. 6). The social contract is hypothetical (although it may call for instances of actual consent, such as the election of representatives). The social contract approach states that the members of a society ought to obey the rules of that society *if* rational individuals *could* agree to such rules as the social contract establishing that society. As we shall see, Rawls provides his own version of the social contract approach. Individuals are asked to make judgements about justice in the 'original position', from behind a 'veil of ignorance'; that is, they must think and act *as if* they did not know, among other things, their own particular aims and advantages (1971, pp. 136–7).

Rawls and other liberals offer a thorough critique of utilitarianism. However, John Stuart Mill's 'harm principle' is, to an important extent, also a source of liberalism. It states, 'the sole end for which mankind are warranted ... in interfering with the liberty of action of any of their number is self-protection' (Mill, 1859, p. 68). Rawls agrees that society must protect each person's liberty and that to do so it must guarantee the basic rights of each person. However, Rawls concludes that utilitarians cannot protect liberty or guarantee rights. This is the case as utilitarians are bound to protect liberty and guarantee rights *only in so far as* to do so best promotes the general happiness. If it turns out (liberals argue) that the general happiness is better promoted by allowing the rights of certain individuals to be infringed, or by suspending everyone's rights in one area, then utilitarians will be compelled to infringe or suspend those rights.

My concern in this chapter is with liberal *political* philosophy. Liberalism as a political project must be distinguished from liberal ethics. Liberal political philosophy provides ways in which to reason about moral issues that arise in politics, and liberals make proposals about the distribution of benefits and burdens by major social institutions. However, liberals believe that we can accept these political goals without being committed to a liberal viewpoint in personal ethics. Liberal politics, it is argued, does remain impartial between competing conceptions of the good, and it does not promote or reward any one conception (Rawls, 1971, p. 94). Nonetheless, it does not follow that we must remain impartial as individuals, that we must not develop a partial commitment to our own conception of the good. We can be single-minded in our devotion to a goal (a career, a hobby, a relationship, and so on) so long as we do not thereby infringe the rights of others.

I will be concerned in this chapter with Rawls's 'welfare' liberalism. I also look at a number of possible corrections to his approach and his conclusions. It is worth noting as well that, as we shall see, Robert Nozick's 'libertarianism' not only shares many characteristics with liberalism but also offers a radical critique of Rawls [see pp. 65–7].

The two principles of justice

Rawls sets out to discover the principles of justice we could agree to accept if we occupied a hypothetical initial situation. (This is a development of the social contract approach [see pp. 57–8].) If the individuals concerned do not know what position they will occupy in society, then it is rational for them to agree that each should receive a 'fair' distribution of 'primary social goods'. These goods include equal liberty, fair equal opportunity, and a share of income and wealth determined by the difference principle (Figure 3.1). Rawls defends the following two principles of justice.

- Apply to the basic structure.
- Order of Priority: liberty, fair equal opportunity, difference principle.
- Values: liberty, equality, utility, fraternity, need.
- Natural (dis)advantages do not count as reasons to receive social benefits.

Figure 3.1 The two principles of justice

First Principle
Each person is to have an equal right to the most extensive total system of equal basic liberties compatible with a similar system of liberty for all.

Second Principle
Social and economic inequalities are to be arranged so that they are both:

(a) to the greatest benefit of the least advantaged, consistent with the just savings principle, and
(b) attached to offices and positions open to all under conditions of fair equality of opportunity.

(ibid., p. 302)

Henceforth, the first principle will be referred to as (1), and point (a) of the second principle as (2a) and point (b) as (2b). An important characteristic of the two principles is that they are applied to society's 'basic structure'. This refers to 'the way in which major social institutions distribute fundamental rights and duties and determine the division of advantages from social cooperation' (ibid., p. 7). At the same time, in 'a well-ordered society', 'each person understands the first principles that govern the whole scheme as it is to be carried out over many generations; and all have *a settled intention to adhere to these principles in their plan of life*' (ibid., p. 528; emphasis added). That is, Rawls does *not* want principles of justice to apply, in the first instance, to individual actions and characters, but nonetheless the individual members of a just society *do* adhere to its principles of justice. If the basic structure is established in accordance with valid principles of justice, and if the members of that society do what, as publicly stated, is required of them to receive benefits, then they have entitlements to those benefits. The state and the market are also part of this so-called 'basic structure'. Citizens can be aware of what entitlements the state will guarantee. But it must also be the case that the market does not override, or infringe, basic liberties, fair equal opportunity, and a distribution of income and wealth determined by the difference principle.

These principles are in an order of priority. Rawls assumes that we are not free to violate liberty (1) so as to enhance opportunity. Further, we may not infringe rights of fair equal opportunity (2b) so as to raise the income and wealth of the least advantaged (2a). Rawls here gives priority to 'negative liberty'. Negative liberty refers to an 'area' in which a person 'is or should be left to do or be what he is able to do or be, without interference by other persons' (Berlin, 1958, p. 141). This is freedom *from* constraint. It is not 'positive freedom', which 'can only be made intelligible in terms of a conception of human agency', and such agency 'cannot be formulated without reference to human abilities, needs, capacities' (Plant, 2003, p. 4). For Rawls, civil and political rights protect negative liberty, and poverty is not a constraint on this liberty. However, Rawls argues, lack of means does affect the 'worth of liberty' to persons and groups, which 'is proportional to their capacity to advance their ends within the framework the system defines' (1971, p. 204). Fair equal opportunity and the difference principle 'maximize the worth [of liberty] to the least advantaged' (ibid., p. 205).

Rawls's 'difference principle' (2a) states that 'the higher expectations of those better situated are just if and only if they work as part of a scheme which improves the expectations of the least advantaged members of society' (ibid., p. 75). Rawls appeals to a number of moral principles here. As we saw, Rawls believes that the second principle maximizes the 'worth of liberty', while maintaining the priority of negative liberty. He calls this 'a reconciliation of liberty and equality' (ibid., p. 204). Rawls's version of equality is 'prioritarian equality', 'a policy of rendering the worst off people as well off as possible' (Cohen, 2000, p. 162). Rawls also includes consequentialist considerations of 'utility'. He assumes that inequality is justified if it acts as an incentive to the 'talented' to engage in productive work, which improves the position of the worst-off (1971, p. 102).[1] Moreover, Rawls makes a connection between the difference principle and 'fraternity'. He believes that it corresponds 'to the idea of not wanting to have greater advantages unless this is to the benefit of others who are less well off' (ibid., p. 105). The final moral consideration is 'need'. While competitive markets ensure free choice of occupation and an efficient use of resources, what he calls the 'transfer branch' of government takes responsibility for 'the social minimum'. It 'takes needs into account and assigns them an appropriate weight with respect to other claims' (ibid., p. 276).

Rawls does not defend a merit-based conception of justice. He argues that pluralism is a fact. We 'must allow for a diversity of conflicting, and indeed incommensurable, conceptions of the meaning, value, and purpose of human life' (1987, pp. 424–5). 'Justice as fairness' does not 'try to evaluate the relative merits of different conceptions of the good' (1971, p. 94). According to Rawls, 'a just scheme gives each person his due: that is, it allots to each what he is entitled to as defined by the scheme itself' (ibid., p. 313). However, simply because some person has received what he or she is *entitled* to, it does not follow that he or she is morally *deserving* of that benefit. I may have an entitlement to monetary rewards simply because the use of my abilities, skills, and training in productive work is economically beneficial to the community (and to the worst off in particular).

Rawls rejects a merit-based conception of justice for a further reason. As natural gifts and social privileges are not chosen, exercising these advantages does not by itself generate an entitlement to receive further benefits. We should reject a scheme of justice that 'permits distributive shares to be improperly influenced by these factors so arbitrary from a moral point of view' (ibid., p. 71). However, *pace* Rawls, it may be noted that in fact we can freely develop natural abilities. For this reason, it could be argued, the person who chooses to acquire skills and training has a greater claim to 'deserve' entitlements than the person who could have done so but instead chose to live a life of indolence. However, Rawls contends that individuals are not responsible for the character traits that lead to such efforts of self-improvement (or self-indulgence and self-neglect): 'for . . . character depends in large part upon fortunate family and social circumstances for which he can claim no credit' (ibid., p. 104). Rawls assumes that, as social forces influence our character, and as we cannot be responsible for our social environment, we also cannot be responsible for our character and that which is attributed to our character.

Justice as fairness does not allow natural advantages to count as reasons to receive social primary goods. However, it also does not let natural *dis*advantages count as reasons to receive social goods. In one sense, Rawls's position is set up to ensure that those with natural disadvantages are not further disadvantaged with respect to their social goods. It 'would allocate resources in education, say, so as to improve the long-term expectations of the least favored' (ibid., p. 101). However, Rawls conceptualizes the position of the 'worst off' with reference to social goods alone. *Natural* primary goods refer to health and vigour, intelligence and imagination. However, 'although their possession is influenced by the social structure, they are not so directly under its control' (ibid., p. 62). Rawls's position is problematic to the extent that a person's natural disadvantages may diminish the real value of his or her social goods:

if X and Y are equal in their income and wealth, but X has a serious medical condition requiring expensive treatment, and must spend a great deal of his social resources on medical bills, and Y has no comparable disadvantage, then the real position of X is inferior to that of Y.

Before moving on, let us take note of one further elaboration of the 'liberal market model' [see pp. 29–31]. Rawls rejects what he calls the 'system of natural liberty' (ibid., p. 66ff.). It guarantees equal liberty and formal equality of opportunity. This is the ideal of meritocracy (Figure 3.2). It removes formal and informal constraints preventing individuals from applying for courses, posts, and offices. However, it does not diminish the social inequalities that influence people's chances of attaining enrolment or employment, and it does not diminish the income received as rewards, or attempt to redistribute income to the benefit of the least advantaged (Barry, 2005, p. 114).

In his critique of meritocracy, Brian Barry nonetheless defends the principle of equal opportunity. If two students, *Able* and *Charlie*, have the same personal resources (e.g. ability), and if *Able* spends half his time in the pub and half studying, while *Charlie* spends all his time in the pub, *Able* will with all likelihood pass his exam and *Charlie* will fail. This result will be fair. Because they have been provided with the same starting gate, the outcome is fair (ibid., p. 43). However, a third student, *Baker*, would have to spend twice as much time studying to pass his exams. This provides a low incentive to work, and so he is much more likely to drop out of the course. Barry does not conclude that *Baker* not getting his exams is unfair. However, he does conclude that *Able*'s claim to greater material rewards, as a consequence of his passing these exams, is limited by, in part, the fact 'that his success depended on his starting with an advantage over Baker' (ibid., p. 44). At the same time, so as to further equalize starting positions, society must spend money to reduce social inequalities that affect the development of abilities, cognitive and others (ibid., p. 114). Another requirement is the

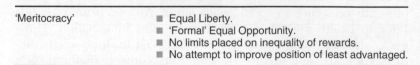

'Meritocracy'   ■ Equal Liberty.
                       ■ 'Formal' Equal Opportunity.
                       ■ No limits placed on inequality of rewards.
                       ■ No attempt to improve position of least advantaged.

Figure 3.2 Liberal market model (2): meritocracy

provision of more generous teaching resources to children with learning difficulties (ibid., p. 22).

Welfare liberalism

I want to draw attention to three basic features of Rawls's position, which I refer to as 'welfare liberalism' (Figure 3.3).

(i) Rawls assumes that *the right is prior to the good*. Rights are not justified for the reason that they promote utility. Rawls does not remove all consideration of utility from his theory of justice. As we saw, he assumes that a just distribution of benefits and burdens will provide sufficient incentives to elicit productive efforts from the 'talented'. However, for Rawls, in striving to improve the condition of the least advantaged, we may never infringe the liberties or opportunities of any individual. Moreover, we are, as private individuals, restrained in the sorts of goals we may pursue. When we plan and pursue our 'good life', we must accept that principles of right and justice 'impose restrictions on what are reasonable conceptions of one's good' (Rawls, 1971, p. 31). Rights provide a 'framework' within which alone we may conceptualize and pursue our conceptions of the good.

(ii) Liberals reject utilitarianism (in part) because they believe consequentialists cannot ensure *respect for autonomy*. According to liberals, utilitarians will feel obliged to sacrifice autonomy, if such a policy best promotes happiness. In contrast, for Rawls, autonomy must be respected, that is, it must be honoured irrespective of the likely consequences of doing so. Rawls owes a great deal here to Immanuel Kant [1724–1804]. Kant argued that any proposed norm can be assessed to determine whether or not it conforms to the 'categorical imperative'. He gave four formulations of the categorical imperative (1785, § 55–79). I want to mention just two.

First, 'Act only on that maxim through which you can at the same time will that it should become a universal law' (ibid., § 51).

1 Right is prior to the good.	Against utilitarian consequentialism.
2 Respect rights that protect autonomy.	Kant's categorical imperative.
3 Fairness.	Primary social goods, Impartiality.

Figure 3.3 Rawls's welfare liberalism

Second, 'Act in such a way that you always treat humanity, whether in your own person or in the person of any other, never simply as a means, but always at the same time as an end' (ibid., § 66–7).

Does Rawls's 'difference principle' satisfy the requirements of the categorical imperative? A Rawlsian society may impose taxes, and use those taxes to finance a welfare system that primarily benefits others, the 'least advantaged'. The taxed person is used as a means, but he or she is not used *simply* as a means if the system of taxation can be justified by valid principles of justice. Rawls's different principle satisfies this requirement, he claims, as any individual in the original position could agree to it. 'The parties arrive at their choice as free and equal rational persons . . .' (1971, p. 252).

(iii) Rawls refers to his position as 'justice as fairness' (ibid., p. 11). He starts from the observation that humans have different and unequal natural and social advantages, and if each individual is left to do as he or she wishes, great inequalities will result. This is a factual observation about the relationship between advantages and resulting inequalities. Rawls also makes the moral claim that, as we do not deserve our initial social and natural advantages, we also do not deserve the inequalities to which they give rise (ibid., p. 72). A system of distribution is fair if it is in the 'interests' of each person, irrespective of their social and natural advantages. Rawls also argues that a fair distribution must be 'neutral' (or impartial) with respect to competing moral doctrines and conceptions of the good life. That is, liberalism does not judge and rank different forms of life. Indeed, the goods distributed by Rawls's position would be of value to 'every rational man' as these 'goods normally have a use whatever a person's rational plan of life' (ibid., p. 62).

The original position

I want to look at some of the key features of Rawls's approach in a little more detail. Rawls develops the social contract approach (ibid., p. 11). Social contract theorists started from the assumption that a legitimate political society is one that could be based on the consent of its members, and then they went on to specify what sort of society that would be. On Rawls's account, a society is legitimate if it institutes 'justice as fairness' in its basic structure. He also describes the hypothetical situation of consent-giving (the 'initial position of equality') as the 'original position' (Figure 3.4) where reasoning occurs

■ Veil of ignorance	No knowledge of own natural assets, social class, psychological dispositions, generation, and global position of society.
■ Circumstances of Justice	Mutually disinterested, moderate scarcity.
■ Moral justification	Universality, generality, publicity, finality, rational ordering of claims.

Figure 3.4 The original position

behind a 'veil of ignorance' (ibid., pp. 11–12). In the 'original position' we put to one side knowledge of our natural assets, social class, and psychological dispositions, along with the generation to which we belong and the global position of our society (ibid., pp. 136–7).

As David Hume [1711–1776] argued, justice is necessary as external resources are relatively scarce, and our sympathy is not unlimited (Hume, 1739–1740, III. 2, § ii). These are the 'circumstances of justice'. In Rawls's terms, people in the original position are 'mutually disinterested' (1971, p. 128). While they 'do not know their conception of the good, they do know . . . that they prefer more rather than less primary goods' (ibid., p. 93). They are not free to promote their own interests, and they are not motivated by envy (ibid., p. 143). But also they are not motivated by sympathy for any specific persons, as utilitarians would require (ibid., p. 190). Rather, each person tries 'to win for themselves the highest index of primary social goods', without knowing what life they do lead (ibid., p. 144). Nonetheless, the 'combination of mutual disinterest and the veil of ignorance achieves the same purpose as benevolence' (ibid., p. 148). That is, it forces each person in the original position 'to take the good of others into account' (ibid.).

Rawls argues that deliberation in the original position also satisfies the requirements of 'moral justification'. A principle of justice must be 'universal' and 'general'. It cannot be 'rigged' so as to benefit some one group (ibid., pp. 131–2). In contrast, the following principle is universal but *not* general: 'Give all superfluous resources to male Caucasians.' As it is designed to benefit white men, it is not general. Note that, according to Rawls, racists and sexists are 'irrational' (ibid., p. 149). As they do not know their race or gender in the original position, it is irrational to accept principles that benefit some because of these natural differences. It may be argued that the fanatical racist would accept, or even demand, his or her own subjugation if it turned out that he or she belonged to the stigmatized race. We could imagine the committed Nazi reacting in this way to the discovery of his or her own racial 'impurity'. However, in the original position we also do not have knowledge of our conception of the good, and so we cannot be motivated to act from such an ideological commitment.

The difference principle, in contrast, is both universal and general. It ensures anyone who does enter into the position of the worst-off does have an entitlement to goods; and this is a principle from which anyone could benefit. Principles of justice also must satisfy the requirement of 'publicity'. Not only must all 'understand and follow a principle', this fact itself must be 'widely known' (ibid., p. 133). A principle of justice can then be used to ensure 'finality' and place a 'rational order' on conflicting claims. It is known and accepted that 'those who ... have done what the system announces it will reward are entitled to their advantages' (ibid., p. 103).

The so-called 'free-rider' is aware that others follow a rule, but he or she chooses not to follow it when in doing so he or she can receive some benefit and avoid the punishment owed to those breaking such rules. Rawls contends it is 'irrational' to be a free-rider. As the requirement for each person's good life has been taken into consideration in the original position, each person's self-interest has counted (if indirectly) in the decision that a principle is justified (ibid., p. 135). Note, Rawls assumes that the consideration of self-interest must figure in any rational argument. The parties are 'rational' in the sense that they are (at least in part) self-interested utility maximizers.

Rationality and the original position

Rawls assumes that rational objective answers can be given to questions posed about justice. However, to be rational and objective, such answers must be given from within the original position.

The maximin rule

In a situation of ignorance, it is rational 'to adopt the alternative the worst outcome of which is superior to the worst outcome of the others' (ibid., p. 153). This is the 'maximin rule'. Rawls asks us to consider three hypothetical outcomes, and he argues that, in the original position, it is rational to make the third decision (d3). In each of the three situations we know three possible circumstances. Under d1, the worst possible outcome is the loss of $700, someone will gain $800, and the best possible outcome is a gain of $1200. Under d2, the worst possible outcome is the loss of $800, someone will gain $700, and the best possible outcome is a gain of $1400. Under d3, finally, the worst possible outcome is a gain of $500, someone will gain $600, and the best possible outcome is a gain of $800. Under d3, even if you turn out to occupy the worst possible situation, you will gain $500. The worst-off person under d2 would loose $800, and in d1 he or she would loose $700. It is also rational to choose d3, even though the potential gains from d1 and d2 are much greater: $1200 and $1400 respectively.

We are not told the probabilities of the different outcomes. Note also that the sum of all three outcomes from d3 ($1900) is greater than the sum of the outcomes from d1 ($1300) and also from d2 ($1300). However, this is *not* the reason why, for Rawls, it is rational to choose d3. The choice of d3 is rational as, Rawls assumes, we are 'risk averse'. The

> person choosing has a conception of the good such that he cares very little ... for what he might gain above the minimum stipend ... It is not worthwhile for him to take a chance of a further advantage, especially when it turns out that he may lose much that is important to him.
>
> (ibid., p. 154)

The possibilities of losing $700 or $800 are 'outcomes that one can hardly accept. The situation involves grave risks' (ibid.).

However, not everyone is 'risk averse' in the way Rawls assumes (Barry, 1973, Ch 9). Also, not everyone 'cares very little' for what they might gain above the minimum. This consideration returns us once again to the argument in defence of the 'liberal market model' (Figure 3.5).

For such a position, it *is* rational to take the risk of occupying a position of great poverty for the opportunity of attaining a position

---

Rationality of risk-taking	Justice requires that we accept the costs for failure and the benefits for success determined by the market mechanism.

Figure 3.5 Liberal market model (3): risk-taking

of great wealth. This is just the sort of opportunity, and risk, offered by the capitalist market. The capitalist market imposes costs on those who fail to do what is socially valued, and it distributes benefits to those who do or produce what is valuable. On this view, Rawls offers a mistaken account of human psychology: his account of a conservative, risk-averse reaction to uncertainty is not the only rationally compelling account. Rawls's position is also too egalitarian, according to this view. The fact that they are disadvantaged is no reason why the worst off should, morally speaking, receive more than they do. (I will return to Nozick's version of just such a critique later [see pp. 65–7].)

Reflective equilibrium

Deliberation about principles of justice is a search for 'reflective equilibrium'. In reasoning we 'work from both ends', Rawls argues, with respect to 'considered convictions of justice' and the principles of justice chosen in the original position (1971, p. 20). If there is a conflict between the two, we 'can either modify the account of the initial situation or we can revise our existing judgements' (ibid.). 'Considered judgements are simply those rendered under conditions favorable to the exercise of the sense of justice', that is, when we have 'the ability, the opportunity, and the desire to reach a correct decision' (ibid., p. 48). What considered judgements does Rawls himself employ? He assumes that each person possesses an inviolability founded on justice (ibid., p. 3). This is the priority of the right over the good. Rawls also appeals to a basic egalitarian principle. 'All social values . . . are to be distributed equally unless an unequal distribution of any, or all, of these is to everyone's advantage' (ibid., p. 62). Rawls, in search of reflective equilibrium, alters these convictions to conclude that we cannot depart from equal liberty for the sake of equal opportunity and an equalization of income and wealth, and also that inequalities in income and wealth are justified if they are to the benefit of the 'least advantaged'.

Is this a convincing account of our deliberation in political philosophy? Some argue that Rawls does not do justice to the irreducible plurality of moral principles. Rawls takes account of many different basic values: liberty, equality, fraternity, utility, and need. However, Rawls believes that the purpose of a political theory is to place such values in 'order of priority'. Political debate can always be resolved by appealing to an independent set of theoretical rules that determine the relative importance of any given consideration. For David Miller, in contrast, there is a plurality of distributive principles and forms of allegiance: the principles of need, desert, and equality in, respectively, solidaristic communities, instrumental associations, and citizenship (1999, p. 26ff). Others argue that Rawls is simply mistaken with respect to our basic intuitions about justice. This is the case in particular as Rawls excludes considerations of merit from social justice. Most people have a strong conviction that desert does create entitlements to benefits (and burdens): a person is more deserving if he or she has worked harder, or produced more things of value, or has shown greater moral worth [see pp. 145–50].

The social contract approach

Rawls's social contract approach gives priority to what individuals take to be their interests (although it states that a society is just only if it is in the interests of all equally). Rawls seems to equate rationality with self-interested utility maximization. He assumes it is rational to want more rather than less primary goods. In the original position we know that a 'person's good is determined by what for him is the most rational long-term plan of life given reasonably favourable circumstances' (1971, p. 93). This is the case as we prefer 'the greater means for realizing our aims, and the development of wider and more varied interests' (ibid., p. 413). Rawls wants to provide an account of rationality that does not presuppose commitment to one moral doctrine rather than another. However, it could be that the adherents of other moral doctrines cannot accept that rationality simply consists in self-interested utility maximization. For Aristotelians, the utility maximizer is not thinking or acting in a rational way, and this is so because he or she equates goals and aims with mere desires. Instead, rationality requires placing one's desires in a rationally determined order, the order that best contributes to the human good [see pp. 145–50].

However, Rawls does not simply reduce rationality to self-interested utility maximization. He also argues that, in choosing principles of justice, we must be 'reasonable'. Reasonable citizens not only view one another as free and equal, and offer each other fair terms of social cooperation, but also 'they agree to act on those terms, even at the cost of their own interests in particular situations, provided the other citizens also accept those terms' (1997, p. 578). Reasonable people do not think of their terms of cooperation as a mere *modus vivendi* (ibid., p. 589), but a social contract approach does seem to be based on each person's self-interest. Therefore, perhaps there is a conflict between 'reasonableness' and 'rationality' (Bufacchi, 2005, pp. 26, 27). Also, perhaps there is a conflict between Rawls's search for reflective equilibrium and his social contract approach. As communitarians argue, one basic intuition is that adults enter communities that have already-established goals and norms, communities to which we also owe a debt for years of care, education, and security (MacIntyre, 1999, p. 98ff.). Therefore, it is not rational to simply put one's own self-interest ahead of the interests of others.

In the original position, right is prior to the good, and we prefer an equal distribution of social values. Rawls also argues that the difference principle is 'strongly egalitarian'. It is based on the intuition that 'unless there is a distribution that makes both persons better off... an equal distribution is to be preferred' (ibid., p. 76). However, justice as fairness does not guarantee a *right* to a basic minimum of social goods. The least advantaged are entitled to receive only whatever will 'improve' their expectations in a given context. Rawls makes the following warning against an overly generous social minimum distributed by the difference principle: it will either prevent investment for future generations or undermine incentives in the present (ibid., p. 286) (Figure 3.6). Further, justice as fairness also does not justify the public provision of income and wealth at all times. A market distribution, in certain circumstances, may be of greater benefit to the least advantaged, Rawls assumes (ibid., p. 78).

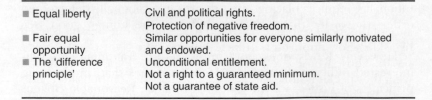

■ Equal liberty	Civil and political rights.
	Protection of negative freedom.
■ Fair equal opportunity	Similar opportunities for everyone similarly motivated and endowed.
■ The 'difference principle'	Unconditional entitlement.
	Not a right to a guaranteed minimum.
	Not a guarantee of state aid.

Figure 3.6 Rawls and welfare entitlements (including the 'difference principle')

Fairness: Ronald Dworkin and natural primary goods

Is Rawls's theory 'fair'? For Ronald Dworkin, a theory of justice should respect the difference between 'chance and choice'. Fairness requires that individuals be held responsible for their choices (in particular, choices concerning work and leisure), but they ought not to be penalized for what has resulted from chance (whether natural disability or inherited social deprivation). However, as Rawls's position measures the position of the least advantaged with reference to their social goods, it does not compensate natural disadvantages (or at least, it does not do so sufficiently), and it does not reward (and penalize) people for the consequences of their freely made choices.

'Suppose a number of shipwreck survivors are washed up on a desert island that has abundant resources and no native population' (Dworkin, 1981, p. 66). Suppose also they accept that these resources should be divided equally. The resulting distribution should pass the 'envy test'. No 'immigrant would prefer someone else's bundle of resources to his own bundle' (ibid., p. 67). An (hypothetical) auction will also ensure that the bundles of resources distributed are not 'arbitrary', that is, no one would prefer what he or she would have received under another system of distribution. In the auction, each person is given an equal share of money (clamshells in the example) and the 'auctioneer proposes a set of prices for each lot and discovers whether that set of prices clears all markets, that is, whether there is only one purchaser at that price and all lots are sold' (ibid., p. 68). Each person will start with an equal share and each will be responsible for the resources they received (and so cannot reasonably envy the goods of others) and each will play a part in determining the set of bundles actually chosen (and so the composition of the bundles will not be arbitrary).

The *market* character of the auction is at the centre of the ideal of equal resources, according to Dworkin. In a market, 'the true measure of the social resources devoted to the life of one person is fixed by asking how important, in fact, that resource is for others' (ibid., p. 70). Those whose preferences turn out to be expensive, because what they prefer is not easily attained, will not be compensated. This leads to the distinction Dworkin makes between 'brute luck' and 'option luck'. 'Option luck is a matter of how deliberate and calculated gambles turn out . . . Brute luck is a matter of how risks fall out that are not in that sense deliberate gambles' (ibid., p. 73). We should compensate for brute bad luck. At the same time, those who gamble and win deserve their gains (e.g. those who invest in successful commercial enterprises); and those who chose not to gamble do not have an entitlement to compensation (1985, p. 193). This is the case as the 'price of the safer life . . . is precisely forgoing any chance of the gains whose prospect induces others to gamble' (1981, p. 74). So, this is like the 'liberal market model' in one sense. Individuals will be allowed to take great risks in the hope of attaining great gain, and they will be forced to accept their losses. However, the freedom to retain their gains is limited by redistributions required to compensate for natural disadvantages.

Dworkin wants to employ the idea of an insurance market to justify compensation for natural disadvantage. Now, many people are born with handicaps, or develop them before they can insure against such a risk.

> If (contrary to fact) everyone had at the appropriate age the same risk of developing physical or mental handicaps in the future . . . but the total number of handicaps remained what it is, how much insurance coverage against these handicaps would the average member of the community purchase?
>
> (ibid., pp. 77–8)

Dworkin accepts that not everyone is risk-averse to the same degree, and not everyone would accept monetary payment as a sufficient compensation for handicaps. However, he also assumes 'that most people would make roughly the same assessment of the value of insurance against general handicaps, such as blindness or the loss of a limb' (ibid., pp. 78–9). The purpose is not to make people equal in ability. (This is the goal of Sen and Nussbaum, according to Dworkin (2000, p. 286) [see pp. 62–5].) The question is 'how far the ownership of independent material resources should be affected by differences that exist in physical and mental powers' (1981, p. 80).

Why should we compensate those who have serious handicaps but not compensate those whose tastes are expensive?

> Someone who is born with a serious handicap faces his life with what we concede to be fewer resources, just on that account, than others do. This circumstance justifies compensation . . . and though the hypothetical

insurance market does not right the balance – nothing can – it seeks to remedy one aspect of the resulting unfairness.

(ibid., p. 81)

Dworkin's position rests upon a distinction between persons and circumstances. He assigns tastes and ambitions to the person, and physical and mental powers to circumstances.

According to Dworkin, Rawls's approach fails to be both 'ambition-sensitive' and 'endowment-insensitive' (Kymlicka, 2002, p. 75). Rawls concedes that primary goods include the 'natural' resources of imagination and intelligence, and health and vigour. However, 'although their possession is influenced by the basic structure, they are not so directly under its control' (Rawls, 1971, p. 62). For that reason, Rawls identifies the least advantaged only with respect to 'social' goods. As a result, natural handicaps do not by themselves generate the right to compensation (ibid., p. 101). At the same time, 'justice as fairness' does not force the individual to pay for his or her own expensive choices. Rawls's difference principle does not make any distinction between chosen and unchosen inequality, as entitlements are generated by 'social position'. This means that Rawlsian entitlements will be unconditional; they will not be granted for a limited time period only, and nor will they have as their goal to encourage the recipients to enter or re-enter market employment. In this way, Rawls's approach differs from the 'selectivity' of the 'liberal market model'; and in contrast, Dworkin has emphasized the market character of his hypothetical auction.

Is Dworkin's scheme 'ambition-sensitive', as he claims? As individuals can freely develop natural assets, it is important to show that re-distribution from the endowed to the unendowed is not an unjustified violation of autonomy. However, Dworkin concedes that it is not easy to distinguish advantages that are 'natural' (and undeserved) from advantages that arise from choice. In attempting to make this distinction we 'will be thwarted by the reciprocal influence that talents and ambitions exercise on each other' (1981, p. 91). As a 'second-best theory', Dworkin proposes to tax the *socially* advantaged and transfer resources to the *socially* disadvantaged. However, Dworkin's scheme is then open to the same charges he has made against Rawls. As it responds only to social deprivation, it does not compensate for natural disadvantage and it shows insufficient concern for autonomy.

Impartiality: Sen and Nussbaum's capabilities approach

Amartya Sen and Martha Nussbaum share Rawls's commitment to impartiality (Figure 3.7). However, while Rawls and Dworkin call for the distribution of primary goods alone (social and/or natural), Sen and Nussbaum are concerned with 'capabilities'. If a liberal theory of justice is to be truly impartial, they argue, it must ensure all have entitlements to the resources needed to pursue their conception of the good. However, one cannot pursue a genuinely good life if one does not also develop certain capabilities. And people have different requirements when converting resources into capabilities.

The following is an abridged version of Nussbaum's 'list of capabilities': *Life*, 'being able to live to the end of a human life of normal length...'; *Bodily Health*, 'being able to have good health, including reproductive health...'; *Bodily Integrity*, 'being able to move freely from place to place, having one's bodily boundaries treated as sovereign...'; *Senses, Imagination, and Thought*, 'being able to use the senses, to imagine, think, and reason...'; *Emotions*, 'being able to have attachments to things and people outside ourselves...'; *Practical Reason*, 'being able to form a conception of the good and to engage in critical reflection about the planning of one's life...'; *Affiliation*, 'being able to live with and for others,... to be able to imagine the situation of the other and to have compassion for that situation...'; *Other Species*, 'being able to live with concern for and in relation to animals, plants, and the world of nature...'; *Play*, 'being able to laugh, to play, to enjoy recreational activities...'; *Control over One's Environment*, 'being able to participate effectively in political choices that govern one's life,... being able to hold property...' (Nussbaum, 2000a, pp. 78–80).

Dworkin on fairness	Sen & Nussbaum on impartiality
Choice: risks allowed.	Concern with capabilities (not resources).
Chance: compensate natural disadvantages.	
Similar to liberal market model?	Utilitarian and consequentialist?
Only responds to social disadvantage?	Perfectionist commitment? Social democratic?

Figure 3.7 Welfare liberalism revised

Consider what happens to the person who lacks these capabilities. He or she would not be in the position to flourish in a meaningful sense. People may come to take pleasure from lives that are 'degrading' or 'unworthy' (Nussbaum, 1980, p. 403). This deprivation may be the result of previous infringements on 'bodily integrity', or an education that stifled 'imagination', or else insecure, aggressive, and violent personal relations. Moreover, although people need networks of relationships in which to develop 'affiliation', if the ties of community are too strong they may stifle independence and critical thinking. For Nussbaum, individual 'separateness' is a key element of the human good. 'A person's self-respect must come to him in virtue of his own activity as a planner of a life' (ibid., p. 410). Therefore, justice is concerned with capabilities, not resources. Sen also argues that 'goal-rights' are those that 'characterize a relation between a person...and some capability to which he has a right' (1982, p. 16). Sen and Nussbaum belong to the strand of liberalism that offers a 'substantive' conception of autonomy and well-being (Raz, 1986, pp. 369–90; Van den Brink, 2001, p. 93; Plant, 2003).

In one sense, Sen and Nussbaum have not strayed far from Rawls's position. Rawls contends that distributive justice does not address the uses to which resources are put. Liberalism does not rely on or promote a general and comprehensive moral doctrine, and yet the liberal theory of justice does rest on an evaluative commitment. Rawls assumes that his theory of justice rests on a 'thin theory of the good'. That thin theory claims that people in the original position 'should try to secure their liberty and self-respect, and that, in order to advance their aims, whatever these are, they normally require more rather than less of the other primary goods' (Rawls, 1971, p. 397). Rawls defines self-respect as

> a person's sense of his own value, his secure conviction that his conception of the good, his plan of life, is worth carrying out [and]...a confidence in one's ability, in so far as it is within one's power, to fulfill one's intentions.
>
> (ibid., p. 440)

Do Sen and Nussbaum remain within liberalism? Is it possible to defend impartiality and also argue that rights must bring about good consequences? Sen argues that goal-rights should bring about capabilities. However, he emphasizes that rights cannot be infringed in the process. The 'realization of rights' itself is incorporated in the 'evaluation of a state of affairs' (Sen, 1982, p. 13). However, Dworkin insists that Sen must choose between a liberal argument for 'equal resources' and a utilitarian argument for 'equal welfare' [see pp. 35–9]. If an individual suffers a metabolic disorder that creates the need for expensive food, it is right that he or she should be compensated. However, it does not follow that society should 'fine-tune' the individual's metabolic needs, so that individuals are 'made equal' with regard to their 'capacity to achieve' happiness (Dworkin, 2000, p. 301). To do so would extend social control and state power at the expense of individual autonomy.

Alternatively, it may be argued that Sen and Nussbaum cannot justify their conception of capabilities if they do not make a 'perfectionist' value judgement about the good life. Nussbaum agrees with Aristotle 'that human life is worth the living only if a good life can be secured by effort, and if the relevant sort of effort lies within the capabilities of most people' (Nussbaum, 1986, p. 320). Aristotle does provide a perfectionist conception of well-being, and he derives moral principles from a life of moral virtue in the Athenian city-state [polis]. Nonetheless, Nussbaum is careful to stress that her account of capability is not derived from the ethical views of any given community. As I mentioned, she gives individual 'separateness' priority over the demands of the collectivity, as the 'flourishing of individuals one by one' is 'normatively and analytically prior' (2000b, p. 62) [see pp. 141–3].

Finally, at one stage, Nussbaum defended what she called Aristotelian *Social Democracy* (1990). Since then, Bo Rothstein has defended universal and unconditional entitlements on the basis of an impartial (non-comprehensive) conception of capabilities. First, the state should guarantee to each citizen 'the right to certain basic capabilities enabling them to make well-considered choices' (Rothstein, 1998, p. 218). Secondly, the state should not dictate to citizens when they make life choices; and it should allow citizens to choose between private, public, and cooperative suppliers of welfare. Finally, he argues that means-tested selectivity in the provision of benefits would tend to violate the 'principle of equal concern and respect' (a Rawlsian principle made explicit by Dworkin). It is discriminatory for public service providers to exclude recipients on grounds of status, just as it would be to exclude on grounds of race, religion, or gender (ibid., pp. 211–12). And if the charges for privately provided services are too high, and if private providers do not take their fair share of the 'difficult cases', this will introduce means-testing 'through the back door' (ibid., p. 211). Public producers will be unable to 'compete on equal terms, and will gradually become an inferior alternative' (ibid.) [see Chapter 5].

Means–ends distinction: Robert Nozick's libertarianism

Robert Nozick defends the 'libertarian' version of liberalism. It departs dramatically from Rawls's position as it does not restrict inequalities. However, Nozick's position, like Rawls's, arises from an interpretation of the Kantian injunction that we must never treat humanity simply as a means.

For Nozick, rights are not end-oriented, but 'side-constraints'. They are not justified because they bring about an end, such as the greatest possible gains to the least advantaged. They are rights we must respect whatever ends we do in fact pursue, and they guarantee freedom from interference (Nozick, 1974, p. 32). This follows, Nozick claims, from Kant's second formulation of the categorical imperative: you should 'always treat humanity, whether in your own person or in that of any other, never simply as a means but always at the same time as an end' [see pp. 51–2]. However, rights are not constructed in the original position, according to Nozick. Rights of non-interference are 'inherent'. They are owed to those who have the qualities of rationality, free-will, and moral agency, and the ability to regulate and guide a life in accordance with some overall plan (ibid., p. 49).

Nozick contends that we have entitlements to not only our person and powers, but also the external possessions we produce or acquire through their use. He defends the 'classical liberal notion of self-ownership' (ibid., p. 172) and therefore argues that 'entitlements to holdings' entail 'rights to dispose of them' (ibid., p. 166). Rawls does not call for the elimination of natural distinctions, but he does conceptualize 'the distribution of natural assets as a common asset' (Rawls, 1971, p. 101). However, Nozick concludes, such Rawlsian 'taxation of earnings from labour is on a par with forced labour' (1974, p. 169). It creates a 'partial property right in persons' (ibid., p. 172). Rawls's difference principle does not respect the difference between persons, Nozick claims: Rawls assumes the greater benefit to the least advantaged justifies the losses suffered by the better off. The difference principle also does not ensure each is treated as an end: Rawls's approach uses one individual's person and powers simply as a means to improve the expectations of the least advantaged. Both of these criticisms of Rawls are particularly sensitive for it is on these same grounds that Rawls rejects utilitarianism.

Nozick's 'entitlement theory of justice' is 'historical' and 'non-patterned'. Any distribution is just if, first, the acquisition of property leaves no one 'worse off' and, secondly, the transfer of property is 'voluntary'. To determine whether a distribution is just, we only 'need consider how the distribution came about' (ibid., p. 154). Nozick gives the example of the popular American basketball player Wilt Chamberlain (ibid., p. 161). Imagine resources have been distributed according to the difference principle so as to rectify past injustices. Individuals are then free to exchange those resources as they wish. Also imagine that, in addition to paying the admission price, each one of Chamberlain's fans chooses to give an extra 25 cents to Chamberlain, who quickly becomes very wealthy. Is Chamberlain entitled to the goods he has received? Some people in society may be poor as a result of these and other voluntary exchanges. And Chamberlain may of course agree to voluntarily transfer some of his property to the needy. However, he is not bound by a perfect duty to do so: no recipient can claim these goods as a right. This is the case as 'your being forced to contribute to another's welfare violates your rights', and 'someone else's not providing you with things you need greatly . . . does not influence your rights' (ibid., p. 30).

Nozick's position is deeply problematic on its own terms, however. Its vision of political morality is attenuated and socially corrosive. It does not allow the development of any collective welfare obligations not based on consent. However, the question to ask is, *could* a free and rational person agree to Nozick's libertarianism? That is, *should* they, morally speaking, accept a broader range of duties as members of a community concerning the welfare of others? There is a moral case that can be made against libertarianism: morality requires us, at the very least, to improve the position of the least advantaged (and also guarantee basic rights and opportunities).

Liberalism is a broad church indeed if it includes both Nozick and Rawls. However, it makes sense to talk of these two quite different models of the welfare state as both are, in their own ways, 'liberal'.

The 'liberal market model' [see Figure 3.8] is based on the assumption that the market is the most efficient mechanism to

| (1) Selectivity. | (3) Rationality of risk-taking. |
| (2) Meritocracy. | (4) Libertarian property rights. |

Figure 3.8 Four features of the liberal market model

distribute and produce resources. It may also be assumed that the market is inherently valuable. This is the case as it protects negative liberty, freedom from constraint. Moreover, as Max Weber noted, capitalism has been associated with the social ethic of the Protestant Reformation. The English Puritans praised as virtues both 'industry', diligent application to one's occupation, and 'thrift', prudent investment of income to finance future industry (1904–1905, p. 76). However, this is not the only model of liberalism. According to T.H. Marshall, in the first stage of modern citizenship, 'civil citizenship', individuals are guaranteed freedom of conscience and expression, and geographical and occupational freedom as workers (1949, p. 77). However, in the twentieth century, citizens gain not only political freedom but social rights as well. The twentieth-century welfare state is, then, an approximation of Rawlsian welfare liberalism.

Conclusion

John Rawls's welfare liberalism has been the central focus of this chapter. He argues that principles of justice are fair if they are constructed in the 'original position'. They distribute a fair distribution of 'primary social goods', which does not presuppose any one conception of the good life, and does maintain the priority of the right over the good. Finally, his 'difference principle' states that an equal distribution of income and wealth is preferable, unless an unequal distribution is to the benefit of the least advantaged.

Rawls's difference principle calls for redistribution from the advantaged to the least advantaged. However, according to Nozick, this uses the advantaged *simply as a means* so as to improve the welfare of the least advantaged, and therefore it creates a partial property right in other persons. Does the difference principle violate the Kantian injunction to never treat humanity simply as a means? It does not, if it is reasonable to expect people to accept this duty to make the position of the worst off as best as possible. Dworkin argues that Rawls's position will not compensate people with natural disadvantages, as it measures disadvantage with reference to social goods only, and it will not force people to pay for expensive choices, as it guarantees everyone entitlements based on their social position. Sen and Nussbaum are concerned instead with 'capabilities'. They quite rightly show that people have different requirements for converting resources into capabilities.

However, it seems that welfare liberalism has failed to show that we do not need consequentialism and/or perfectionism and/or social democracy. Rawls's difference principle states that the higher expectations of the better off are justified if they lead to good consequences, namely improved expectations for the least advantaged. Further consideration is also called for regarding the correct account of the good. Is it a matter of capabilities, as Sen and Nussbaum argue, or is it a matter of the higher pleasures, the manner of existence that employs our higher faculties, as Mill argued? Finally, are universal and unconditional (social democratic) entitlements just, and are they the best mechanism to bring about such good consequences?

CHAPTER 4

Conservatism

Conservatism is an approach that, in important respects, differs from liberalism and utilitarianism. Conservatism arose as a critical response to modernism. This is the case with the Irish philosopher Edmund Burke [1729–1797], the French sociologist Emile Durkheim [1820–1895], the French writer and analyst of American society Alexis de Tocqueville [1805–1859], and the German philosopher Georg W. F. Hegel [1770–1831]. Robert Nisbet describes the conservative 'picture of modernism' in the following terms:

> Egalitarianism and centralized power based on the people are perhaps the leading elements of the picture, but they are closely joined with others: the substitution of feeling and passion – in religion and politics and art – for the disciplined restraints of tradition and piety; the replacement of non-rational, sacred values by impersonal and ephemeral norms of contract and utility; the decline of authority, religious and social as well as political; the loss of liberty – which the conservatives chose to define in the medieval sense of this word, as connoting not so much freedom, which signified disengagement and license, as principled *right* within divine law and tradition; the debasement of culture...; and... the progressive-deterministic mentality that insisted upon regarding past, present, and future as iron categories of ethically bad, better, and best.
>
> (1967, p. 14)

According to Nisbet, conservatives define liberty as 'principled *right* within divine law and tradition'. Liberty does not equate with individualism. Indeed, liberty is threatened by modern commercial life, that is, greater individual economic freedom. In the market, money provides an incentive to abandon traditional modes of life, should they be less economically valuable. Conservatives do not reject the capitalist market, but, they argue, the market must always be embedded in the social bonds of community. Secondly, conservatives criticize rationalism, which, in Nisbet's terms, involves the 'replacement of non-rational, sacred values by impersonal and ephemeral norms of contract and utility'. Modern society becomes more rationalistic as religion, in particular, looses its force in people's lives and in philosophy. Further, for conservatives, practical reasoning involves an awareness of one's place within a tradition, and also one's readiness to acknowledge and recognize authority.

Building on its critique of individualism and rationalism, conservatives challenge 'radicalism'. Radical power is both egalitarian and statist. Conservatives offer 'premonitions of social chaos surmounted by absolute power once individuals had become wrenched from these [traditional] contexts by the forces of liberalism and radicalism' (Nisbet, 1967, p. 11). According to conservatives, the state's bureaucracy is based on instrumental rationality. It replaces communally specific norms and goals with uniform 'rational' standards and rules of efficiency. It also has egalitarian consequences (Tocqueville, 1835–1840, p. 555; Oakeshott, 1962). It does not acknowledge inequalities in experience and wisdom, as it bases rationality on rule-following. It also does not acknowledge inequalities in merit among persons, as all are equal as citizens.

Conservatives reject the so-called universal principles of modernism, the principles of individualism, rationalism, and radicalism. But conservatives also appeal to their own universal norms, such as those of natural law. This is the case with Christian social thought in particular [see pp. 88–9]. However, conservatives try to show that genuine universal principles must always be applied to quite distinct communal and traditional contexts. Unlike the social contract approach of Rawls, according to conservatives, rights are justified by their historical legacy and by their place within a community with certain shared norms and goals. Rights are socially established. Now, utilitarians also reject the social contract approach. But conservatives do not accept utilitarianism. Utilitarians are subjectivists as they take people's desires and preferences as given, whereas conservatives contend that social order and virtue provide the authority needed 'for the restraint of men's passions' (Nisbet, 1986, p. 35). So, conservatism offers a comprehensive critique of utilitarianism and liberalism. Moreover, the influence of conservatism can be seen still in welfare policies in the United Kingdom, the United States, Germany, and Japan (Esping-Andersen, 1990).

Robert Nisbet: Nineteenth-century conservatism

According to Robert Nisbet, nineteenth-century conservatives assumed that reason and 'prejudice' are not antithetical, and this is the case as tradition is the foundation of reason and morality. Also, the scope of the state's welfare responsibilities is to be restricted. Welfare, by and large, is to be distributed as charity, and it is to be distributed by non-state groups. This is the case as conservatives not only give precedence to established property rights, but also emphasize the 'family character' of property.

Property and community

'The conservative position, set forth eloquently by Tocqueville, is that intermediate associations are valuable as mediating and nurturing contexts for individuals...' (Nisbet, 1986, p. 49). Conservatives emphasize the importance of groups such as family, church, and local community, and this 'is in practice a stress too upon the several social roles which exist perforce in these groups' (ibid., p. 49). Liberty and communal order are mutually necessary. Conservatives believe in a 'manly, moral, regulated, liberty' (Burke, 1790, p. 89). Liberals are mistaken when they equate liberty with freedom from constraints, or separateness. Rather, liberty refers to the quality of the social roles that can be performed, the quality of one's immersion in a community. One way to characterize this approach is to say *conservatives do not give the right priority over the good of the community*. They defend rights that protect liberty. However, right and liberty are concepts that are derived from community.

The family is the most significant intermediate association, and this is due by and large to 'the historic affinity between family and property' (Nisbet, 1986, p. 52). Through the family, genetic, cultural, *and* material advantages are transmitted. And conservatives wish to protect such intermediate associations against 'the ever-mesmerizing power of the social democratic state and its creed of equality' (ibid., p. 49). As we saw, Rawls insisted that inequalities are justified only if they improve the condition of the least advantaged, and such equality is compatible with liberty. For conservatives, however, egalitarian redistribution 'cripples' liberties, 'especially the liberties of the strongest and the most brilliant' (Nisbet, 1986, p. 47). Equality is a levelling doctrine. It erases the communal contexts, and inequalities, necessary for liberty. Burke called social and political equality a 'monstrous fiction'. He characterizes inequality in the conservative society as follows:

> protected, satisfied, laborious, and obedient people, taught to seek and to recognize the happiness that is to be found by virtue in all conditions; in which consists the true moral equality of mankind, and not in that monstrous fiction, which, by inspiring false ideas and vain expectations in men destined to travel in the obscure walk of laborious life, served only to aggravate and embitter that real inequality.
>
> (1790, p. 124)

Liberty requires the enjoyment of property rights. However, property is not 'the uncertain, possibly transitory, possession of the individual alone' (Nisbet, 1986, p. 57). Conservatives defend 'the *family* character of property' (ibid., pp. 56–7). This represents the feudal idea that social roles both justify and limit the market, an idea that can be seen in the German *social* market economy as well [see pp. 88–9]. In contrast, the American constitution guarantees *inherent* individual rights. Inherent individual rights do not protect liberty, according to conservatives, for the reason that they encourage egoism and individualism (ibid., p. 58). The character of Caleb Garth, in George Eliot's *Middlemarch*, is a clear example of the virtues praised by conservatives. 'Though he has never regarded himself as other than an orthodox Christian, . . . his virtual divinities were good practical schemes, accurate work, and the faithful completion of undertakings: his prince of darkness was a slack workman' (1871–1872, Ch 24, p. 251). Eliot is quick to clarify that Caleb is not motivated by a desire for gain as such; he does not treat profit as an end in itself: 'he could not manage finance: he knew values well, but he had no keenness of imagination for monetary results in the shape of profit and loss' (ibid.).

Conservatives do not defend property as libertarians do: they do not claim that persons have *unconditional* rights to their life, liberty, and external possessions [see pp. 65–7]. Nonetheless, Nisbet describes Burke as 'an apostle of *laissez-faire*' (1986, p. 58). That is, for Burke, government must not interfere in the economic, social, and moral affairs of its people. For instance, indigence is to be relieved by charity, and charity is an obligation of church, family, village, and neighbourhood, 'but never of the government' (Nisbet, 1986, p. 59). Government is not without a role. Government is 'to look to the conditions of strength of these *groups*, in as much as they are by virtue of ages of historical development the best fitted to deal with the majority of problems in individuals' lives' (ibid., p. 62). This is similar to the selective, means-tested view of welfare entitlements that we discussed while analysing the 'liberal market model' [see pp. 15–18 and 29–31.]: recipients are means-tested; receipt of entitlements is conditional on performing certain duties; benefit levels are low; and benefits last only for a short duration.

Tradition and prejudice

Conservatives do not give individual rights priority over the community. They also stress the importance of the tradition of a community. They do not accept 'the progressive-deterministic mentality' according to which the present must be better than the past (Nisbet, 1967, p. 14). They also point out that a democratic society puts community and tradition in danger. Democracy is egalitarian, and so it is a levelling doctrine. According to de Tocqueville, the citizens of a democracy are too quick to accept 'a single and central power which governs the whole community by its direct influence' (1835–1840, p. 551). Moreover, democracy encourages 'simple and general notions', such as 'a great nation composed of citizens all formed upon one pattern and all governed by a single power' (ibid.). The commitment to equality is also a commitment to uniformity.

> As every man sees that he differs but little from those about him, he cannot understand why a rule that is applicable to one man should not be equally applicable to all others. Hence the slightest privileges are repugnant to his reason.
>
> (ibid.)

In contrast to democratic egalitarianism, conservatives contend that rights are established. It is rational to accept that rights are not prior to the good of the community. This is the case as we reason with 'prejudice'. For Burke, ' "prejudice" is a distillation of a whole way of knowing, of understanding, and of feeling' (Nisbet, 1986, p. 29). It is something *common* among individuals in a nation' (ibid., p. 30). Burke refers to what he calls 'inherited freedom'. That is, we are 'always acting as if in the presence of canonized forefathers' (Burke, 1790, p. 121). In Hans-Georg Gadamer's [1900–2002] terms, we

cannot reason without an 'horizon', an historically determined series of presuppositions or prejudices. However, we are then forced
to put those prejudices in question, and seek a 'fusion of horizons'.
We are 'continually having to test all our prejudices. An important
part of this testing occurs in encountering the past and in understanding the tradition from which we come' (Gadamer, 1975,
p. 306). This is, of course, in sharp contrast to Rawls's argument
that we reason from behind a veil of ignorance.

The prejudice and tradition of community are also necessary for
personal liberty. Nisbet notes that, for Burke, liberty could not exist
without 'order and virtue'. Both are necessary 'for the restraint of
men's passions' (Nisbet, 1986, p. 35). Unlike utilitarians, conservatives do not take people's given desires and preferences as the
ultimate standard of what is valuable. Desires and preferences
indicate what is good and right only when they have been restrained
in the appropriate manner, and they are restrained by order and
virtue. However, Nisbet quickly passes over the role played by
virtue, and instead he emphasizes order: 'the walls of authority
represented by traditions and social codes' (ibid.). Intermediate
associations are 'structures of authority . . . which all require a substantial degree of autonomy – that is, a corporate freedom – in order
to perform their necessary functions' (ibid.). 'The problem of freedom . . . is inseparable from a triangle of authority' (ibid.). Authority
is shared between the individual, the state, and intermediate
groups. For this reason, conservatives call for both *laissez-faire* policy
and decentralization of power. The state must not infringe on the
authority and functions of intermediate groups, in particular concerning the provision of welfare on the basis of established rights
and duties.

So, conservatives begin from a concern with personal liberty,
and conclude that the autonomy of communal groups must be
protected from state interference. Conservatives also stress the
importance of communal duties with respect to the poor, but
they assume that, by and large, intermediate associations carry
out such duties.

Justice and charity

Conservatives tend to equate justice with merit or desert. People get
what they are due when they get what they deserve. This is most
clearly the case, conservatives assume, when we look at punishment.

Utilitarians like Bentham assume that, if punishment is a disincentive, a deterrent, it better promotes happiness (Plamenatz, 1963, vol. 2, p. 3). However, the utilitarian approach can lead to the following perverse conclusion: perhaps the best way to promote happiness is to punish innocent people so as to deter them, and others, from committing crimes in the future. For conservatives, punishment is justified only if the perpetrator is punished, and only if the punishment is proportionate to the crime. Similarly, when it comes to the distribution of benefits, conservatives believe that those who have contributed most should receive the greatest rewards. Entitlements are based on 'contributions', and contributions are measured with respect to one's role-performance in intermediate associations.

However, conservatives do not always conceptualize the distribution of welfare in terms of the recipient's just deserts. For Burke, as we saw, indigence is to be relieved by 'charity', and charity is an obligation of church, family, village, and neighbourhood, as these groups are the best fitted to deal with the majority of problems in individuals' lives. For Benjamin Disraeli [1804–1881], poverty prevented the poor from enjoying full membership of the community, or 'nation'. Poverty creates a division between 'Two Nations, governed by different laws, influenced by different manners, with no thoughts or sympathies in common' (1845, Ch 8). However, 'Disraeli's answer to the existence of "two nations" was not a social revolution but a stronger sense of *noblesse oblige* among the landed aristocracy' (Barry, 2005, p. 24).

Why are the wealthy and able-bodied bound by a 'duty of charity' to relieve poverty? On the one hand, conservatives assume that property ownership entails duties of care to other members of a community, and these duties are sustained by traditional norms and religion. On the other hand, the indigent should be given what they need. However, conservatives are concerned to ensure that, in the future, the poor (if they are able-bodied) should play a full role as independent members of the community. Once again we can see the importance for conservatives of one's contribution to the community. Neediness is understood with respect to what a person requires so as to regain full membership of the community. And for that reason, this conservative approach to poverty cannot do without a distinction between the 'worthy' and the 'unworthy' poor. The worthy poor are indigent through no fault of their own, or they are willing to do what is required to become full members of society once again. While conservatives distinguish merit-based justice from charitable duties

■ Established rights	Family character of property.
	Liberty is opposed to equality.
■ Against abstract theory	'Prejudice' (against rationalism).
	Order and Virtue (necessary for liberty).
■ Principles of justice	Merit: contribution-based entitlements.
	Need: charity (plus 'worthy' and 'unworthy' poor).

Figure 4.1 Nisbet's account of nineteenth-century conservatism

to the needy poor, they also tend to see charity through the lens of merit and desert, or worthiness (Figure 4.1).

The state must play a residual role in welfare provision, and conservatives call for *laissez-faire* policy and decentralization. On Nisbet's account, the state must play *some* role. The government is 'to look to the conditions of strength' of the groups that do provide welfare. However, it may be anachronistic to claim that the family is the primary welfare provider. Many who defend the state's role as a welfare provider argue that social institutions such as the family and church can no longer perform their traditional welfare functions (Wilensky, 1975). Finally, is equality incompatible with liberty and excellence? Must we accept Burke's conclusion that talking of equality is merely 'inspiring false ideas and vain expectations in men destined to travel in the obscure walk of laborious life'? Rawls has tried to show just the opposite, namely that an egalitarian distribution can nonetheless allow and encourage justified inequality, inequality that is not simply the outcome of social and natural advantages.

Francis Fukuyama: Contemporary American conservatism

In his book *Trust* (1995), Francis Fukuyama contends that a preexisting moral community is necessary for trust, which in turn is needed for well-being and economic prosperity. However, while Nisbet gave the family and social order precedence, Fukuyama emphasizes non-kinship communities and also argues that social virtues are just as significant as the order imposed by intermediate associations.

Trust

A 'nation's well-being, as well as its ability to compete, is conditioned by a single, pervasive cultural characteristic: the level of trust inherent in the society' (Fukuyama, 1995, p. 7). In an earlier work, Fukuyama had heralded the 'end of history': a global convergence on the 'liberal' institutions of representative democracy and capitalism (1992, pp. 39–51). He made this argument after the final demise of Soviet state socialism. However, by stressing the importance of trust, Fukuyama is departing from neo-classical economics (Becker, 1964; Buchanan, 1994). Fukuyama concedes that markets are, 80% of the time, efficient allocators of resources, and that giving free reign to self-interest does generate economic growth (1995, p. 17). Yet, we are not solely 'rational utility-maximizing individuals', he argues (ibid., p. 21). 'Social, and therefore moral, behaviour co-exists with self-interested utility-maximizing' (ibid.). What is more, sometimes efficiency is achieved by 'groups of individuals who, because of a preexisting moral community, are able to work together effectively' (ibid.).

Fukuyama equates moral behaviour with social behaviour, co-operation for shared goals. He also notes that moral behaviour is necessary for (at least 20% of) economic success. Fukuyama wants to reject not only the assumption that the economy is a self-enclosed or self-sufficient system, but also the assumption that we must choose between moral well-being and economic prosperity.

Trust requires 'social capital', 'the ability of people to work together for common purposes in groups and organizations' (ibid., p. 10). Social capital in turn 'depends...on the degree to which communities share norms and values and are able to subordinate individual interests to the interests of larger groups' (ibid.). That is, the social virtues are necessary for social capital. We could imagine a Robinson Crusoe figure exercising the 'individual virtues' associated with the rise of capitalism: industry, thrift, innovativeness, and openness to risk. These are the virtues Max Weber associated with the first years of capitalism in seventeenth century English society (1904–1905). However, as we have seen, conservatives argue that authority is necessary for individual liberty. Authority may refer not only to an external source of order, but also to the self-imposed discipline of virtue. For Fukuyama, 'social virtues' are required for the exercise of individual virtues. Fukuyama lists the social virtues as honesty, reliability, cooperativeness, a sense of duty to others (1995, p. 46), and loyalty and dependability (ibid., p. 27). Social virtues give rise to 'social capital'. While 'human capital' refers to skills and expertise an individual may acquire, social capital is 'the proclivity for sociability' and is 'based on ethical habit' (ibid.). It 'requires habituation to the moral norms of a community' (ibid., pp. 26–7). The 'liberal market model' involved an argument for meritocracy, the freedom to develop and deploy talents and skills (human capital). For Fukuyama, equal opportunity is not sufficient. Social capital is needed for both prosperity and well-being.

American community

Between Fukuyama and Nisbet, a number of differences in approach can be identified. This may be the result of differences in context: Fukuyama is exploring the phenomenon of trust in contemporary American society; Nisbet is analysing the nineteenth century heritage of conservative thought. However, Fukuyama's approach does, in the long run, come much closer to Nisbet than was first obvious, and this is most clearly the case when Fukuyama discusses the poverty of African-Americans.

Nisbet emphasized the family, and the family character of property. In contrast, Fukuyama insists that 'non-kinship' communities are more compatible with large-scale firms, modern professional management, and efficient and satisfying work relations (ibid., p. 28). Fukuyama also argues that American culture exhibits high levels of social virtue, social capital, and trust. This stands in stark contrast to de Tocqueville's assessment, discussed by Nisbet, that American culture, at least in the nineteenth century, was individualistic and egalitarian. Fukuyama describes the United States as a society 'with a high degree of generalized social trust and, consequently, a strong propensity for spontaneous sociability' (ibid., p. 29). The American commitment to community is evident in political campaigning, charitable work, church attendance, and so on. Americans have strong anti-statist feelings, and, Fukuyama concedes, they call themselves 'individualists'. 'But such people are often simultaneously in favor of the strengthening of the authority of certain social institutions like the family or the church' (ibid., p. 279). Communitarians need not be statists, he argues. State and community need not be co-extensive. Americans are 'nonstatist communitarians' due to their willingness 'to subordinate their interests to those of intermediate social groups' (ibid.).

Fukuyama argues that the exercise of social virtues is the most important factor explaining the existence and strength of community and also that non-kinship community is the most appropriate to

■ **Role of the state**	African-American poverty explained by atomization, caused by unconditional benefits (and consequences of slavery).
■ **Social virtues and their effects**	Social virtues > Social capital > Trust > Effective organization (*this represents a causal chain*).
■ **US culture is not individualistic**	Non-statist, but also communitarian.
■ **Explanation for poverty**	Demise of non-kinship community (but emphasizes weakness of African-American family).

Figure 4.2 Fukuyama's American conservatism

modernity. However, he also argues that Americans are communitarians in so far as they favour strengthening the authority of the family and the church. The latter brings Fukuyama's contemporary American conservatism (Figure 4.2) very close to Nisbet's nineteenth century conservatism. This is clear when Fukuyama discusses the welfare entitlements of poor African-Americans. Fukuyama's chief concern is for the character and communal relations of the poor, and he also assumes that the state is not suited to remedy indigence. In this way he might be said to apply Edmund Burke's views in a contemporary setting.

Poverty can be caused by a lack of social virtues and trust among the poor, according to Fukuyama. The origin of African-American poverty lies in the history of slavery, which continued in the United States until the 1860s. Slavery robbed African-Americans of individual dignity and also 'social cohesiveness as well by discouraging cooperative behaviour' (ibid., p. 303). It is sometimes argued that individual self-interestedness is necessary for personal economic success and that poverty is explained by the absence of such motivation. However, the continued marginalization of poor African-Americans, according to Fukuyama, is caused by excessive individualism, not its absence.

> The contemporary black underclass in America today represents what is perhaps one of the most thoroughly atomized societies that has existed in human history. It is a culture in which individuals find it extremely difficult to work together for any purpose from raising children to making money or petitioning city hall.
>
> (ibid.)

Note the importance attributed to the family: welfare payments to unmarried, unemployed mothers 'became the mechanisms that permitted entire inner-city populations to raise children without the benefit of fathers' (ibid., p. 314).

The ending of legal discrimination against African-Americans (and others) was 'One of the great and necessary victories of American liberalism' (ibid.). However, in the US 'culture of rights', 'rights have an absolute character that is not balanced or moderated' by 'duties to the community or responsibilities to other people' (ibid., p. 315). As a result, welfare rights, and the state that enforced them, became the enemy of smaller communities. The expectations of the poor have continued to expand, the state has continued to satisfy those demands, and as a result African-American life has become increasingly atomized.

The real problem is unconditional rights to welfare. The state must be cut back, as it tends to undermine community. Before doing so, it must 'regenerate civil society' (ibid., p. 320). However, Fukuyama's thesis entails the state must not only encourage the exercise of social virtues. It must ensure the family, once again, becomes autonomous and a source of authority. Each family must take greater responsibility for the welfare of its own members. Therefore, Fukuyama gives the family a primary explanatory role when he accounts for the spread of rights culture and the subsequent demise of local communities. If there is good reason to think that Nisbet's argument about the centrality of family-based community is anachronistic, Fukuyama's position is open to this charge as well.

Conservatism *contra* the liberal market model

We saw [Chapters 1 and 2] that the 'liberal market model' has the following four features: (i) selective, means-tested benefits, and also the distribution of welfare through charity; (ii) a meritocratic conception of equal opportunity, where society does not equalize social inequalities between individuals; (iii) allowing individuals to take risks and keep the rewards of success, and forcing them to accept the costs of failure; and (iv) inherent individual rights to property that are unconditional and absolute, and so individuals are free to dispose of their property as they see fit, and they have no non-contractual duties to aid those in need. Is the conservative position different from the 'liberal market model' in any meaningful sense?

The answer is represented in Figure 4.3: (i) The conservative position does employ selective, means-tested benefits. Conservatives also distinguish the worthy from the unworthy poor in the

Liberal market model	Conservatism
Selectivity	Selectivity concerning the needy. But also contribution-based entitlements and criterion of merit.
Meritocracy	Formal equal opportunity is necessary. But social capital is needed as well (human capital is insufficient).
Risk-taking	Not hostile to market mechanism. But long-term view as well.
Inherent property rights	Established rights (not inherent), which bring with them duties, including duties to the poor.

Figure 4.3 Conservatism *contra* liberal market model

distribution of charity to the needy. However, conservatives defend a merit-based conception of justice as well, and therefore they defend contribution-based benefits. (ii) Conservatives do accept the ideal of formal equal opportunity. However, they are not only concerned with the equal opportunity to develop human capital. We also need to develop social capital, which is based on the exercise of social virtues. (iii) Conservatism is not hostile to monetary gain and reward. However, it encourages a long-term view with respect to social aims; in particular, the development of social capital. (iv) Conservatives also defend property rights. However, such rights are 'established' rather than inherent, and they bring with them social duties (including duties to the poor) as well.

Conservatism: The key themes

I want to summarize the key themes of conservatism. In doing so, however, I will draw attention to some important differences within conservatism.

(1) *The right is not prior to the good of the community* – Conservatives emphasize the moral significance of 'established rights'. Rights are 'established' when they are enjoyed in conjunction with playing roles in communal groups like the family, church, neighbourhood, profession, corporation, or nation state. For the conservatives discussed above, by and large rights attach to property, and the family (and perhaps the church) is the most significant communal association. However, as we shall see presently, Harold Perkin contends that rights may attach to human capital, to skills and training,

and, in particular, to professional expertise [see pp. 89–90]. And professional associations are a crucial type of community. One implication is that, as rights attach to skills and training, state spending on education could guarantee those rights to ever more people.

(2) *Pluralism* – Many communities exist in the area between the individual and the state. These are 'intermediate' or 'secondary' associations. The most important political question is, how is the state to relate to the 'plurality' of communities? Many conservatives believe political power should be decentralized and plural. At the same time, some conservatives see the state as a moral agent. Perhaps the most ambitious claims made on behalf of the state by a conservative are those of Hegel. And they may well have authoritarian implications. The 'freedom' of the individual, he argues, will be completely compatible with the state's coercive powers once the state has attained a final stage in its historical development:

> The state is absolutely rational inasmuch as it is the actuality of the substantial will... This substantial unity is an absolute unmoved end in itself, in which freedom comes into its supreme right. On the other hand this final end has supreme right against the individual, whose supreme duty it is to be a member of the state.
>
> (1821, § 258)

(3) *Merit-based justice* – Justice is based on the principle of merit or desert, according to conservatives. A person's merit is determined not only by the history of his or her past actions, but also by his or her social context and the legitimate expectations it creates. There are two different ways in which conservatives think about merit. Fukuyama defines as meritorious those qualities that contribute to the good of the community. This is the case with the 'social virtues'. This 'conventional' conception of merit may be tied to the distinction made between the worthy and the unworthy poor. However, merit may be conceptualized in a way that is 'ideal'. People ought to be rewarded according to their deserts, even if this is not the case at present. This conception of merit can be used to challenge the existing distribution of benefits and burdens and also their moral justification.

(4) *Individual liberty does not entail liberal individualism* – Conservatives assume that liberty and community are mutually necessary. As liberal individualism is a threat to community, it is also a threat to individual liberty. For Fukuyama, 'individualism

means the unwillingness or inability to subordinate one's individual inclinations to larger groups...' (1995, p. 303). Liberty requires an ordered social context. Emile Durkheim agrees, and argues that if people's appetites are 'boundless and insatiable' there will be no peace in their hearts or in their interactions (1957, pp. 11, 16). However, as we shall see, Durkheim concludes that we cannot undo what the individual has become in modern society, namely 'the exalted object of moral respect' (ibid., p. 56). Now, the 'cult of the human person' is a central part of our shared norms and goals.

Emile Durkheim: Professional ethics and civic morals

Emile Durkheim's work offers a different perspective within conservatism. He tries to show that professions are the most significant form of community and that professions encourage the exercise of virtues that sustain community. Unlike Fukuyama, however, Durkheim does not resort to the anachronistic claim that, at the end of the day, the family is the most important community. Durkheim also argues that political authorities must redistribute property to help sustain and develop professions.

Moral particularism

Durkheim agrees with other conservatives that the right is not prior to the good of the community, and also that liberty and order are mutually necessary. Community is a 'moral power' as it is 'common to all', a 'collective power', 'which stands above the individual and which can legitimately make laws for him' (1957, p. 7).[1] We claim and enjoy rights by virtue of our membership in a community to which we are duty-bound. This is not an empirical observation that only existing communities can enforce rights. Liberals perhaps could agree with that. Durkheim is also claiming that communal authority is required for the justification of those rights. He also argues, 'it is by reference to the sanction that all rules of law and morality are defined' (ibid., p. 2). This is the case with property rights. Theft is punished not because it is a violation of a natural law, but only because an individual has broken a rule of conduct. Some moral rules are universal due to our 'intrinsic human nature' (ibid., p. 3). Nonetheless, Durkheim focuses on moral principles that 'depend . . . on particular qualities not exhibited by all men' (ibid.). This is the area of 'moral particularism'. He agrees with Aristotle that 'to some degree, morals vary according to the agents who practice them' (Durkheim, 1957, p. 4).

Communal authority is exercised over the individual and also it encourages virtue. For Durkheim, 'there must be a group about us to call it [a sense of duty] to mind' (ibid., p. 12). We are reminded of Fukuyama when Durkheim states that the professional group encourages the virtues of self-restraint, disinterestedness, selflessness, and sacrifice (ibid.). These are social virtues, dispositions to contribute to social aims, and without them, people will experience 'ceaseless mistrust' (ibid., p. 24). Durkheim also shows how community can be built up within the economy. Professions could socialize economic activity, and permeate it with 'ideas and needs other than individual ideas and needs' (ibid., p. 29). Professions are 'to become so many moral *miliuex*'; they have the goal 'of bringing men's minds into mutual understanding' (ibid.). It follows, 'economic functions are not an end in themselves but only a means to an end', namely 'a harmonious community of endeavours' (ibid., p. 16).

Durkheim gives social aims priority. He situates the market within a social context, and assumes that exercising virtue contributes to social aims. What he calls 'moral particularism' includes the realms of the family and citizenship. However, although moral particularism 'makes its appearance' in the family, it 'goes on to reach its climax in professional ethics' (ibid., p. 5). So, Durkheim (like Fukuyama) equates virtue with the pursuit of social aims. However, although Durkheim does not neglect the family as a community, and therefore a realm of moral practice, he assumes that, in modernity, the most developed form of moral particularism is found in professions.

Political authorities and the limits of property rights

Dukheim and Fukuyama can agree that professions exercise authority over individuals and encourage the social virtues. However, Durkheim's conservatism departs from Fukuyama's position on two important issues: the role of political authorities and the limits of property rights. Durkheim believes that professionalism can be sustained only through legal compulsion. However, he also believes the central state would be *unable* to carry out this function, 'overburdened as it is with various services, as well as being too far removed from the individual' (ibid., p. 40). Professional associations are not overburdened with the state's functions, and they are not too far removed from the individual. Professions must be regulated by professional associations, then, which are subsidiary, intermediate groups, although organized nationally.

Durkheim also calls for the redistribution of property. Property rights are 'limited by the claims of the moral aims, in which a man has to co-operate' (ibid., pp. 122–3). A property right does *not* imply 'the right of each to his (or her) own faculties, to what he can produce by them, and to whatever he can get for them in a fair market' (ibid., p. 122). Fukuyama would agree that property rights are not absolute claims. Nonetheless, Fukuyama does not accept that the political authorities may legitimately redistribute property for the sake of social aims. Durkheim's argument is that, if we are bound to exercise virtues for the sake of the community (which Fukuyama claims), we are also bound to give some portion of our property to the community.

> We do not belong to ourselves entirely: we owe something of ourselves to others, to the various groups we form part of. We give them and are bound to give them the best of ourselves; why should we not be equally bound . . . to give them the material product of our labours?
>
> (ibid., p. 122)

Durkheim, Hegel, Kant (and Rawls)

Durkheim contrasts his view of political society with that of Hegel and Kant. On Hegel's account, the state is to carry out a social aim that is superior to all individual aims and unrelated to them (Durkheim, 1957, p. 54). Durkheim concedes that the role of the state has expanded because society has grown in scope and complexity (ibid., p. 90). Nonetheless, 'we cannot undo the individual having become what he is' (ibid., p. 57): 'the exalted object of moral respect' (ibid., p. 56). Modernity is marked by a 'cult of the human person'. Nonetheless, Durkheim also rejects the 'individualism' of Kant. The basis of individual right is, according to Durkheim, the 'way society puts the right into practice, looks upon it and appraises it' (ibid., p. 67). The individual is, in some respects, 'the product of the state' (ibid., p. 58).

Durkheim refers to the Hegelian approach as 'the mystic solution' (Durkheim, 1957, p. 54). Hegel's argument is that we pass from absorption in the family to a condition of individual negative freedom, and therefore division, in the market. The purpose of the state is to overcome that division, to re-establish unity, but not the unity of a family (Hegel, 1821, § 157). Because of the sentiment towards the state found in virtuous individuals, 'self-consciousness . . . finds in the state . . . its substantive freedom' (ibid., § 257). Moreover, as 'poverty leaves them [the poor] more or less deprived of all the advantages of society', public authorities must also take responsibility for poverty (ibid., § 241). The state's function is to pursue a common ethical goal as a way in which to overcome conflicting interests, including the social divisions that result from economic inequality. Durkheim accepts that political authorities should exercise a collective responsibility to remedy indigence. However, he criticizes the Hegelian approach for its inattention to the exalted moral standing of the modern individual.

Durkheim's conservatism has some affinities with Rawls's Kantianism. Both assume that the community can redistribute what individuals produce through the use of their natural and social advantages, and also, neither would eliminate natural differences. Therefore, they not only accept the division of labour, and inequalities of power and rewards in the division of labour, but also defend a redistribution of social assets. Durkheim claims that social and economic inequality must be reduced to ensure that those who have the appropriate aptitude and capacity are chosen for available posts. There must be 'absolute equality' in what Durkheim calls 'the external conditions of the struggle' (1902, p. 313). As a result, each social value 'is not distorted in one direction', but 'is appreciated at its true worth' (ibid.). That is, social advantages must not determine one's value to employers and therefore one's income, status, and power.

There are three important differences between Durkheim and Rawls, however. First, Rawls argued that social advantages are 'arbitrary from a moral point of view', and Durkheim agrees that social advantages should not determine employment. However, Rawls believed that natural advantages are arbitrary from the moral point of view as well. In contrast, for Durkheim, it is right that 'social inequalities express precisely natural inequalities', that is, that 'no obstacle whatever prevents them [individuals] from occupying within the ranks of society a position commensurate to their abilities' (ibid., p. 313). Secondly, Rawls assumes that it is never just to infringe individual rights so as to promote the common good.

For Durkheim, the duty of the state is to provide 'the milieu' (i.e. the professions) in which individuals can develop their abilities, and also to protect individuals against the tendency to be absorbed or subjugated by social groups such as professions (1957, p. 64). The state is to 'provide the milieu in which the individual moves, so that he may develop his faculties in freedom' (ibid., p. 69). But Durkheim does not show that such benefits will be received by those who do not play a productive role in the community: those who do not now, or do not have the ability to, participate productively in professions. Finally, Rawls also argued that inequalities in income and wealth are justified only if they best maximize the position of the 'least advantaged'. Durkheim also insists that the community can redistribute the fruits of each person's labours. However, he does not defend redistribution on the egalitarian principle of maximizing the position of the least advantaged (Figure 4.4).

Durkheim's conservatism provides a way in which to respond to a noted weakness in Fukuyama's position. Durkheim does not resort to Fukuyama's anachronistic argument, which, in the final analysis, gives priority to family-based community. Durkheim also contends that, just as political society has a role to play in fostering professions, it also may redistribute property to attain that goal. Therefore, Durkheim places real limits on property rights, and he provides a justification for more extensive welfare provision by the political society. However, due to his pluralism, Durkheim limits the role played by a central state. Moreover, Durkheim's position does not create rights individuals may enjoy irrespective of their place within a community. In any case, redistribution does not have the

■ Selectivity or contributory?	No guarantee to worst-off. Rights tied to past contributions.
■ Meritocracy or social capital?	Social inequalities should express precisely natural inequalities. This will require social spending to reduce social inequalities.
■ Risk-taking or long-termism?	Provide the milieu for freedom (i.e. professions and professional associations).
■ Unconditional or established rights?	Redistribution of wealth for the sake of social aims. No mention of rights of individual (recipient).

Figure 4.4 Durkheim and welfare

(Rawlsian) egalitarian goal of ensuring the position of the least advantaged is as good as possible.

A conservative welfare state?

Durkheim's position is indicative of the fact that conservatism is amenable to a more comprehensive and extensive state welfare policy. But what are the limits of this development towards a *conservative* welfare state? Can conservatism go well beyond selectivity and means-tested welfare?

Tories and Christian Democrats

Two historical instances show that conservatives have found good reasons to support a welfare state. In England during the twentieth century, the 'Tory' Party, under Harold Macmillan's leadership, defended 'moderate state collectivism' (Ritschel, 1995, p. 63). This was a 'Middle Way' between socialism and unregulated capitalism. It accepted that every citizen must be provided with an irreducible minimum standard of living (ibid.). However, welfare provision by the state was accepted only because it was seen to be the best defence of both enterprise and tradition (ibid.). Tories warned against excessive state welfare. They therefore emphasized the duties of welfare recipients (George and Page, 1995, p. 50). Moreover, rights were tied up with the roles people do, or ought to, play. State welfare is excessive to the extent that it infringes established rights, makes traditional roles redundant, and undermines the authority of traditional communal groups.

German Christian Democracy is based on the idea of a social market economy. The market is both justified and limited by social roles. And the state provides welfare entitlements tied to past participation in social roles. Entitlements are 'passive' and 'transfer-oriented' (Van Kersbergen, 1995, p. 4). Individuals have rightful claims based primarily on their past contributions to a scheme of social insurance, and entitlements do not greatly alter social structures. Moreover, the religious convictions of elites explain the emergence of this conservative welfare state: a 'spirit of social capitalism' (ibid., p. 197; see Dierickx, 1994, p. 22). For instance, Catholic thinkers argued that the working class was becoming more alienated from the Church *because* of miserable social conditions created by the industrial revolution (Van Kersbergen, 1995, p. 217). The state was to introduce social changes whose purpose was a moral rejuvenation of social life.

Harold Perkin: Professional society and the professional ideal

Can a conservative welfare state be justified? Harold Perkin shares many of Durkheim's views on political theory and welfare entitlements, but also he gives the central state an extensive role in welfare provision. However, Perkin may also move outside the boundaries of conservative thought, as he gives priority to human capital rather than social virtues, and he argues that the moral exhortation of individuals is (in large part) made redundant by effective social organization.

Perkin can agree with Fukuyama that professions are increasingly important. Professionalism is an ideal that members of all classes now strive towards. Even the manual working class can demand many of the characteristics of professional employment: security of income, a rising salary scale, fringe benefits (such as holidays and sick leave), and pensions (Perkin, 1989, pp. 307–14). What Perkin calls the professional 'social ideal' is also more significant. According to this ideal, justice is based on the principle of merit. Rewards are justified by the professional's contribution to both 'social efficiency' and the 'avoidance of waste': that is, effectively solving social problems and employing human capital (ibid., pp. 8–9). The ideal has been applied to all grades in society:

> it implied a principle of justice which extended to the whole population the right to security of income, educational opportunity, decent housing in a clean environment, and, some professionals would say, the right and obligation to work.
>
> (ibid., p. 9)

However, for Perkin, professionalism is based on human capital, skills and expertise an individual may acquire, not social capital as Fukuyama claimed. It could be said that Perkin provides a non-moralized account of professions. That is, Perkin merely argues that, if professions do exercise the human capital needed to perform their professional responsibilities, then they will contribute to social efficiency and they will avoid waste, and for these reasons they will be due rewards (income, status, and power). Perkin does *not* contend that if professionals exercise their human capital in this way then they exercise moral virtues as well.

The professional society provides a new way to conceptualize property. Property simply refers to 'a right to a flow of income', according to Perkin (ibid., p. 377). Professional expertise can be defined as property, then, to the extent that it entails a right to a flow of income. Nineteenth century conservatives were concerned with landed property, which was embedded in traditional roles and norms and closely linked to the family. According to Perkin, professional service can be transformed into an income-yielding property. The service must be based on specialized training. However, the profession must also control the market, creating 'artificial scarcity' in the supply of the service (ibid., p. 7). Therefore, Perkin is not naïve concerning the social conditions required by professions. Professional society is 'quasi-feudal'. There is a danger of exploitation if elites become 'would be absolute owners' of human capital (ibid., p. 389). However, as professional 'property' refers only to human capital, not social capital, it can be disseminated to the disadvantaged with greater ease. Professionals do try to attain 'social closure', and limit access to their profession, but social policy can make professional training more widely available.

The state and the welfare state

The state plays an important role in the development of professions. Perkin assumes (like Durkheim) that modern society is becoming more complex and interdependent (ibid., p. 22) (Figure 4.5). Where there is ever-greater specialization, greater integration is required. This in turn creates a need for an expansion of government and the state's delivery of services. And this expansion of government serves the interests of professionals. However, the changing nature of society is kept from view by the persistence of class-based ideologies. Public professions in the welfare state are given a working class, socialist justification. They are justified as the providers of services to the working class. Early pioneers of the welfare state, such as W. Beveridge [see pp. 108–9] and R.H. Tawney [see pp. 111–15.], assumed that professional elites should be employed to help bring about social reform so as to improve the material and spiritual well-being of the working class. However, 'What they did not bargain for was the extent to which the welfare state would come to exist as much for welfare professions as for their "clients", the ostensible beneficiaries' (ibid., p. 344).

■ **Selectivity or contributory?**	Professional judgement of 'neediness' (but public universalistic services).
■ **Meritocracy or social capital?**	Professional working conditions (and benefits). Parallel hierarchies of unequal height. Fair equal opportunity (i.e. redistribution required).
■ **Risk-taking or long-termism?**	Social efficiency & Avoidance of waste. Implies a critique of market waste (deprivation).
■ **Inherent or established rights?**	Non-moralized conception of entitlements (a 'professional solution'). Danger of excessive professional power (i.e. unrestricted 'property' rights).

Figure 4.5 Perkin and welfare

Perkin quotes Richard Titmuss's (1958, p. 27) conclusions that

As the social services become more complex, more specialized, and subject to a finer division of labour they become less intelligible to the lay councilor or public representative. A possible consequence is that, collectively, more power may come to reside in the hands of those interests.

(Perkin, 1989, p. 344)

Services in education, social work, and town planning are organized around professional skills rather than clients' needs alone, Perkin concludes. Nonetheless, although the welfare state serves the interests of professionals, it is also justified by the professional ideal.

[T]he rise of the welfare state was a practical expression of the professional ideal. It was initially an attempt to extend to those as yet excluded from professional status the basic security and conditions already enjoyed by the established professions.

(ibid., p. 9)

The basic principles of a professional welfare state are 'humanitarian concern' and the 'avoidance of waste'. Professional society is to raise every citizen to minimum acceptable standards of life. It is not an egalitarian society, however. It is to secure 'a collection of parallel hierarchies of unequal height', each with its own career ladder (ibid., p. 9). However, perhaps it is inaccurate to say that the professional society is not egalitarian. It could be called a society based on fair equal opportunity (providing the resources needed to ensure that all who are similarly motivated and endowed also have similar opportunities). In addition, professionals employed by the central state will deliver entitlements to the least advantaged. In this respect it is more egalitarian than Durkheim's position.

Further, the professional welfare state does not focus on what Perkin calls 'individual', 'moral' considerations. From the perspective of professionals, social problems are the product of social organization, not individual inadequacies. They call for collective, professional solutions, not moral exhortation.

> Problems thus defined as institutional and societal rather than moral and individual cried out for collective, professional solutions rather than moral discipline or exhortation. And once the legislative and administrative treatment began, the process of professionalization and feedback set in, by which the welfare professionals uncovered new problems which demanded further legislative and administrative solutions and the recruitment of still more welfare professionals.
>
> (ibid., p. 357)

He also argues that elites should accept a fair distribution of rewards *not* for the sake of social justice but so as to purchase 'willing cooperation' which is the hallmark of a 'stakeholder society' (1997, p. 37). Nonetheless, Perkin himself gives a normative defence of 'public sphere' professionalism. He claims that 'functional service' represents a 'higher moral justification' of property (1989, p. 389). He also criticizes societies that move away from his 'stakeholder' model and do not protect against 'monopoly and extreme exploitation' (1997, p. 38). Moreover, professionals will have to make moral judgements themselves. They must determine how to both respect the autonomy of clients and protect the expertise of professionals.

Perkin defends fair equal opportunity, as he supports the social spending needed to ensure that everyone similarly motivated and endowed has similar opportunities. However, Perkin also goes beyond Durkheim's position as he defends the entitlements of the least advantaged and argues that the central state should distribute these goods. But can Perkin offer a conservative moral justification for the professional welfare state? Like Durkheim and Fukuyama, Perkin believes professions are a prominent source of community in modern society. However, Durkheim and Fukuyama assume that professions are 'moral *milieu*', as they encourage social virtues and the subordination of individual interests to the interests of the group. Perkin does not conceptualize the profession as a social and moral milieu. Perkin sees the profession as an association of individuals who have developed human capital, and he assumes that moral considerations are made redundant by greater professional efficiency. His defence of public sphere professionalism, and the role of the central state within a welfare state, requires a moral justification. It is not clear that a conservative view of professions provides that justification.

Conclusion

What are the strengths of conservatism? First, it provides a compelling, because demanding, substantive and perfectionist view of autonomy and well-being. It is assumed that we are only free, and only attain well-being, if we strive for a higher, social goal: primarily, the exercise of social virtues. It provides a socially embedded and perfectionist conception of the person. In contrast, liberalism and utilitarianism seem unable to explain why we would be motivated to act in the ways that morality requires. Secondly, conservatives can combine this substantive and perfectionist view with a commitment to state welfare and individual rights. This is the case with Durkheim and Perkin, while nineteenth century conservatism limits the role of the state and sees welfare as, primarily, an issue of charity. In either case, poverty is thought of as a problem for the whole society, not just for the poor, as it puts in question the claim that there is one community in which we all live.

Nineteenth century conservatism is problematic because it seems anachronistic. Even Fukuyama gives the family a primary explanatory role when he accounts for the spread of rights culture and the subsequent demise of local communities, in particular, among the African-American urban poor. The alternative conservative positions also have shortcomings. Durkheim limits the role played by a centralized state. Moreover, Durkheim's position does not create rights that individuals may enjoy irrespective of their place within a community. And although Durkheim is committed to reducing social inequality among those who are equal in ability and capacity, he is not committed to making the position of the least advantaged as good as possible. Perkin's attempt to avoid such conclusions is not completely successful. He sees the profession as an association of individuals who have developed human capital, and he argues that moral exhortation has been made redundant by more efficient social organization. Perkin has difficulty combining this non-moralized approach with his own normative commitments. His defence of public sphere professionalism, and the role of the central state within a welfare state, is left without a clear moral justification.

CHAPTER 5

Socialism

Socialism is often misunderstood, both by its supporters and by its detractors. For that reason, I want to begin by making three general points. First, socialism is a theory of *modern* societies. Like conservatism, socialism arose in response to the demise of feudalism, and the emergence of industrial production, liberal democracy, and the class division between the bourgeoisie and the proletariat (wage-workers). For that reason, it is unlike pre-modern examples of communism. For instance, in *The Republic*, Plato [427–347 B.C.] argues that 'guardians' ('philosopher kings') should live communally, that is, without property or family (Rep, V. 462b2). However, Plato defended a class division between the guardians (who would be given the opportunity of living a truly good, virtuous life) and manual workers. In contrast, socialists emphasize that reforms are needed most urgently among workers and also that it is by and large workers who evince socialist virtues. Plato tended to equate virtue with 'good birth'. Nonetheless, socialists need not be hostile to such substantive or even 'perfectionist' views of the human good. Richard Tawney [1880–1962], like many socialists, simply claims that the pursuit of human excellence is not incompatible with social, economic, and political equality.

Secondly, socialists need not be hostile to liberal democratic ideals. Karl Marx [1818–1883] contended that the ruling ideas of capitalist society (including the justifications for civil and political rights) were the ideas of the ruling class, the bourgeoisie. Under capitalism, a person can attain only the appearance of emancipation, as 'man frees himself from constraint . . . in an abstract, narrow, and partial way' (Marx, 1843, p. 32). Equality and freedom remain empty and abstract now, while socialism makes such concepts concrete by applying them to everyday life, and, in particular, to work (ibid., p. 46). Under socialism, each person is free to develop his or her abilities in a spontaneous way, and society distributes benefits according to each person's needs. Therefore, the term 'socialism' need not refer to the Soviet system (USSR). Soviet leaders, in particular Lenin, insisted that they were simply applying the ideas of Marx. However, many socialists, including Marxists, reject the Soviet model as a totalitarian system that denied personal freedom and moral equality (Cohen, 2000, p. 20ff.).

Finally, Marx defined human nature as 'conscious life activity' and also 'productive life' (1844, p. 113). The true well-being of an individual involves more than being rationally autonomous (*pace* liberalism); it requires the free development and exercise of creative powers. Moreover, socialism is to bring about good consequences that promote the interests of all, but it is not true that socialism is just another version of utilitarianism. Utilitarians equate 'utility' with a person's given desires and preferences. That is, utilitarians do not believe that individuals are systematically deceived about their interests. In contrast, socialists assume that the prevailing social structure is not only unjust and inefficient, but may also cause an ideologically distorted view of interests.

This final point is of particular interest. Marxists assume that the ruling ideas of capitalist society are the ideas of the ruling class. The ideas that justify socialist society, in contrast, will be appreciated and accepted as valid only under a socialist system, once the bourgeoisie have been removed. It would seem then that, for Marxists, moral ideas are rational 'relative to' a given circumstance: capitalist ideas are compelling under capitalism, socialist ideas under socialism. Of course, Marx assumed that socialism represents an advance over capitalism, but he cannot explicitly state that, morally speaking, we *ought* to bring socialism about. In contrast, other socialists *do* argue that we ought to bring socialism about. That is, they appeal to non-relative, universal moral principles.

Classical Marxism: Historical materialism, exploitation, and alienation

First I look at classical Marxism, the work of Karl Marx and Friedrich Engels [1820–1895]. According to Marx and Engels, capitalism is inefficient, as it does not meet real human needs. However, although they eschew moral argumentation, I hope to show that they themselves rely on a moral critique of capitalism and a moral defence of socialism.

Historical materialism

On the basis of a socialist science, 'historical materialism', Marx and Engels contend that capitalism is inefficient as it does not meet real human needs. They try to provide an objective, scientific explanation of why socialism will replace capitalism (Engels, 1892). Their position is not based on a value commitment to socialism, they argue. It is an objective analysis of the material causes of historical change and progress. Other socialist theorists (for instance, Henri Saint-Simon [1760–1825]) are merely 'utopian' as they base their arguments on nothing more than moral sentiments.

According to Marx, 'productive forces' determine the rogress from feudalism to capitalism and on to socialism. The term 'productive forces' refers to the technology used in a society and the ways it is implemented in the sphere of work. No social system (for instance, capitalism) will perish 'before all the productive forces for which there is room in it have developed' (Marx, 1859, p. 426). Marx is claiming here that, in historical development, 'material' features of society (productive forces) are the causal factors. In this way he is reversing the conclusions of the 'idealist' Hegel, who claimed that human consciousness was the cause of historical development (Hegel, 1807). According to Marx, capitalism will not be superceded until it has exhausted its potential to develop its productive forces: 'new, higher relations of production never appear before the material conditions of their existence have matured in the womb of the old society itself' (1859, p. 426). What is more, 'The mode of production of material life conditions the social, political, and intellectual life processes in general' (ibid., p. 425). This is the reason why socialists cannot make a 'moral' argument to justify socialism. The moral ideas available to us are determined by the very system that socialism will replace. Marx has the following to say of a society undergoing a period of transformation from one system to another. 'Just as our opinion of an individual is not based on what he thinks of himself, so can we not judge of such a period by its own consciousness; on the contrary, this consciousness must be explained rather from the contradictions of material life' (ibid., p. 426).

How do we get from capitalism to socialism? We must wait until the productive forces can no longer expand under the capitalist system. Capitalism is based on industrial production and the class division between property owners and property-less wage-workers. It replaced rural craft production and the relationship of master craftsman to apprentice. Although the intellectual condition of the pre-industrial worker was 'not worthy of human beings', nonetheless, the industrial system made 'the workers machines pure and simple, taking from them the last trace of independent activity' (Engels, 1845, p. 309). The capitalist class and capitalist ideas were 'revolutionary'; it was one of the 'progressive epochs' (Marx, 1859, p. 426), but this was true only when feudal productive forces were becoming redundant. In turn, socialism is revolutionary now that capitalism is increasingly inefficient. What is more, capitalism is 'the last antagonistic form of the social process of production' (ibid.). Productive forces could meet the needs of all, but the division of labour, and the division between property owners and property-less workers, creates evermore material misery.

'With the division of labour . . . is given simultaneously the distribution . . . of labour and its products, hence property' (Marx and Engels, 1846, pp. 184–5). As the division of labour begins in the family, so 'the wife and children are the slaves of the husband', for he has 'the power of disposing of . . . [their] labour-power' (ibid., p. 185). In a socialist society property will be held in common, and workers will be free to do a variety of tasks. There will be no private property *or* division of labour. Under a socialist system the ideas that justify socialist relations will be seen to be reasonable, even though they seem antithetical to conventional morals under capitalism. On the one hand, socialism does not respect an individual's property rights, but only in the specific sense that it does not allow individuals the freedom to dispose of property in whatever way they desire. On the other hand, socialism does not respect equal opportunity, but again only in that it does not guarantee to any individual the right to become a specialist in some field and to 'dispose of the labour-power of others'.

Capitalism and morality

I do not think that Marx's critique is 'scientific' and value-free, as he had claimed. First, his argument relies on a moral judgement that labour is 'life's prime want' (1875, p. 347) and under capitalism the worker is 'alienated' (1844, pp. 112–14). He is alienated from (i) the products of his labour; (ii) himself; (iii) his 'species being'; and (iv) his fellow humans. This is all due to the 'enslaving subordination to the division of labour' and the antithesis of mental and manual labour (1875, p. 347). As a worker, I am alienated from my human nature, 'conscious life activity' or 'productive life' (1844, p. 113). When tasks are specialized, I work *so as* to survive. I treat my human nature not as an end, something intrinsically valuable, but as a mere 'means of individual life' (ibid., p. 112). The division of labour turns my work into an objective force that is hostile to me. I become 'enslaved' to my work as I cannot continue to live without working and yet I cannot work in a way that is creative (ibid., p. 109). This experience of alienation is also externalized into class relations. Capitalists are a hostile external force who own whatever I produce. Moreover, my fellow workers are competitors and mere 'machines'.

Here is an implicit moral argument, namely that conscious life activity or productive life should be treated as 'an end in itself'. Like Kant (and Rawls), Marx seems to believe that humanity is intrinsically valuable and that autonomy must be respected. However, Marx conflates autonomy with material creativity. In contrast, Kant assumes that the world of work is antithetical to freedom; it is governed by laws of material causation. Kant equated humanity with the 'rational' capacity to legislate for oneself and adhere to those 'moral' laws: 'freedom belongs universally to the activity of rational beings endowed with a will' (1785, Ch III, § 100).

I turn now to the second moral strand of Marx's critique of capitalism. Employers 'exploit' their employees. The worker is allowed to work and 'therefore to live' only 'if he works a certain amount of time without pay' (1875, p. 352). Wage-labour is, then, 'a system of slavery' (ibid.). Profits are generated only in so far as owners extract 'surplus value' from the productive efforts of workers. That is, the level of profit is the difference between the value workers actually create and the wage or salary that is then paid to them. Further, the 'worker becomes an ever cheaper commodity the more commodities he creates' (1844, p. 107). The more productive workers are, the greater the surplus value that can be extracted from them, but the more profitable capitalism is, the greater the power of employers over workers. Exploitation will become more severe, and therefore, the proletariat will become more deprived.

Marx also identified a group of people completely excluded from, and below, the prevailing class structure. Marx used the term 'lumpenproletariat' to refer to those whose labour is not in demand in the capitalist system (Marx and Engels, 1848, p. 253).

The lumpenproletariat exists on the margins of mainstream society, and subsists through work in the black market. Marx's lumpenproletariat has some affinities with contemporary discussions of an 'underclass', which is composed of the unemployed, criminals, and single-parent families [see pp.196–203]. Also, there is a certain overlap here between the ideas of Marx and the 'liberal market model'. In both cases it is assumed that the market is the primary source of welfare for workers, and that those who rely on other sources of welfare are a marginal and deprived group. However, Marxism is based on the conviction that the 'liberal market model' will be superceded by a form of society radically different.

Socialism and morality

It has been my argument that Marx offers something like a moral critique of capitalism. Marx also offers something like a moral defence of socialism. First, 'communism' enables each person to attain the human good. It creates abundance where capitalism created misery. As communism abolishes the division of labour, individuals can then realize their human nature, 'conscious life activity' and 'productive life'. As a result, 'labour has become not only a means to life but life's prime want'.[1] Further, 'the productive forces have also increased with the all-round development of the individual, and all the springs of co-operative wealth flow more abundantly' (1875, p. 347). That is, when workers can freely engage in it, work will be the basic human need, but also it will be more enjoyable and therefore more productive; and the products of workers co-operating together can be enjoyed as benefits throughout society.

It is fair to say that Marx here provides an 'ethical' vision of a 'good society'. It abolishes the division of labour and private property. The basis of community then is solidarity and 'the free development of all, and . . . the universal character of the activity of individuals on the basis of the existing productive forces' (Marx and Engels, 1846, p. 207). The 'free development of all' is possible if each person can work in a 'universal' way. This is an egalitarian notion that each person may engage in both manual and intellectual labour. Each person can then pursue his or her own 'all-round development'. Of course, it is not possible to attain this level of free development without solidarity. The class division is an obstacle to freedom, as the immediate interests of capitalists are served instead by the enslavement of workers to the division of labour. That is, equality is a prerequisite of freedom, and freedom requires solidarity.

Secondly, Marx's communism is based on principles of justice. There are two stages of socialism. In the lower stage, society is in transition from capitalism. It is 'still stamped with the birth-marks of the old society from whose womb it has emerged' (Marx, 1875, p. 346). In this society, rewards ought to be distributed in proportion to desert, and desert is measured by past contribution, that is, by the value created through labour (ibid.). This principle is called for because, under capitalism, although workers produce what is of value, employers extract, or steal, that value. Therefore, the principle of merit is a radical, or ideal, principle in this context. However, for the higher stage of socialism, communism, Marx does not accept an exclusively merit-based view of justice. He does not assume that every worker should have a right to receive rewards that are proportionate to his or her contributions. Such a system would tacitly recognize and reward unequal natural ability. Although Marx argues that this 'right is thus in its content one of inequality, *just like any other right*' (ibid., p. 347; emphasis added), he proposes a specific principle of distribution for a 'higher phase of communist society': 'From each according to his abilities, to each according to his needs!' (ibid.).

This is a combination of two principles of justice. First, the principle of merit: individuals ought to contribute to society in proportion to their ability to do so. However, benefits are not distributed in proportion to past actions, and therefore, they are not seen as rewards for productive efforts. Rather, benefits are distributed on the basis of a second principle: the principle of need. The distribution of benefits then reduces the inequalities that arise because of differences in ability (Figure 5.1).

Does Marx offer a 'moral' justification for socialist welfare entitlements? Marx argues that communism will institute a specific principle of distribution, and it will be an egalitarian society of universal free development and solidarity. Marx *does* defend a moral position, then. His real objection seems to be to those who follow 'bourgeois economists' in their 'treatment of distribution as something independent of the mode of production' (ibid., p. 348). What he does is apply the principles of merit, need, and equality to the sphere of work. However, Marx does *not* offer a justification for the welfare state. The state cannot truly emancipate any citizen now,

■ **Capitalism**	Alienation vis-à-vis conscious life activity and productive life. Exploitation of workers through labour-theft.
■ **Socialism**	Ethics: equality, solidarity, freedom, and universal character of activity. Justice: Every right is a right of inequality. But criteria of merit and need under the higher stage of socialism.

Figure 5.1 Marxism and morality

as such an individual still treats others as means and 'degrades himself to the role of mere means' (1843, p. 34). Also, the functions of the state may not be needed in a communist society. Communism would convert the state from an organ 'superimposed' upon society to one completely 'subordinated' to it (1875, p. 354). In the stage of transition away from capitalism, Marx calls for a 'revolutionary dictatorship of the proletariat' (ibid., p. 355; 1852, p. 58). Coercive power must be used to wrest property from the hands of the bourgeoisie. However, once communism is attained, order will arise spontaneously, without the use of coercive force.

Three objections to Marx's socialism can be noted. First, he seems to assume that principles of distribution are pointless *unless* they are made concrete in work relations. However, many people who play no part in work (the severely disabled, children, those who are ill, the elderly, parents working in the home, and so on) do make valuable contributions and/or do have needs that must be met, and a theory of justice must be able to help decide what they 'ought' to receive. Secondly, in communism, the state will be subordinated to society. Blurring the division between state and society in this way may lead to one of two very different outcomes: either anarchy, where the state is powerless to impose its decisions; or totalitarianism, where individuals have no freedom to resist the state. In Marx's communist society, order arises spontaneously, but a 'dictatorship of the proletariat' is required in a transitionary stage to communism. Finally, there is perhaps a contradiction between, on the one hand, Marx's refusal to give a moral justification for socialism on the basis that productive forces condition morality and, on the other, his belief that socialism is the better society as it is a 'kingdom of freedom', a society free from 'irrational determining forces' (Popper, 1966 vol. 2, p. 201). This contradiction can be resolved, it seems, only if we reject

Marx's basic methodological position and enter the realm of moral debate and moral justification.

G.A. Cohen: 'Against the Marxist Technological Fix'

G.A. Cohen agrees that Marxists have always relied on moral assumptions that have been given no explicit justification. According to Cohen, Marx also fails in his attempt to show that, due to great abundance, moral exhortation will be unnecessary under socialism.

Against historical materialism

In an earlier work, Cohen had defended 'historical materialism' (1978, pp. 134–65). It claimed to show that Marxism was *historically necessary*. It also assumed the working class will be 'driven to socialism' (1995, p. 154). Workers are in the majority, and they are the most exploited, the most productive, and the most needy. This means that workers have 'nothing to lose', and should choose revolution (ibid.). However, in a later work, Cohen conceded that classical Marxism also relied on an implicit moral judgement (ibid., p. 6). Revolution is in the interests of the workers, and, because of the characteristics of workers, revolution is *necessarily just*. As it is in the interests of the majority, it can be justified on democratic grounds; as it overcomes exploitation, it satisfies the Kantian categorical imperative to always treat humanity as an end; as it recognizes the productivity of workers, it rewards merit; and finally, as workers are the most deprived, socialism also meets the most urgent needs.

At one time, Cohen had assumed that as 'so many principles justify socialism...any person of good will would be moved by at least one' (ibid., p. 8). There was 'no call to do normative political philosophy for socialism's sake...because...only sub-intellectual reasons, reflecting class and other prejudice, could persuade a person against it' (ibid., p. 3). However, the classical Marxist position proved untenable. First, the working class has changed, in part due to social improvements brought about by the welfare state. Although many workers are exploited, they are not always needy, or the most needy: a 'sadly infirm capitalist' may, because of a physical disability, be more needy than many workers (ibid.,

p. 150). Secondly, it is not true, if it ever was, that as technical knowledge grows, productive power (the capacity to turn nature into use-value) will expand with equal speed or progress (ibid., p. 7). Rather, the phenomenon of environmental degradation shows that we cannot hope for a society of unlimited abundance. We cannot infer that socialism is justified by every available moral principle. As we cannot presume abundance either, we must make decisions about the distribution of scarce resources, enforce those decisions, and justify them with moral criteria.

Self-ownership

Cohen rejects what he calls the 'Marxist technological fix' (ibid., p. 125). Communists 'do not put to people the moral demand: love one another, do not be egoists, etc.' (Marx and Engels, 1846, p. 199). However, the higher phase of communism will implement a principle of distribution: 'from each according to his ability, to each according to his need'. Marx seems to assume that this principle requires no justification, and can be implemented without having to make and enforce moral demands. This is due to what Marx assumes will be 'the high material level of abundance' of communism. For Marx, it is not necessary to coerce anyone 'to lend his ability to the community, for the sake of equality of condition' (Cohen, 1995, p. 126). This is the case as 'labour has become life's prime want: the unconstrained exercise of the ability of each not only allows but also promotes satisfaction of the needs of all' (ibid.). Further, economic inequality will not be needed as 'incentives' (ibid.). Effort will be made simply because work is itself what people want. It is unnecessary to make and enforce moral demands if, as a result of technologically determined abundance, it is not necessary either to deny anyone unequal rewards or to force anyone to create needed goods. Issues of distribution simply do not arise. This is the 'technological fix'.

Cohen goes on to argue that, in fact, classical Marxism relies on n implicit moral commitment, one that is given no rational justification (Figure 5.2). Marx defines exploitation as 'appropriation, without recompense, of surplus product' (Cohen, 1995, p. 120). Wage-labour is 'labour-theft' (ibid., p. 145).[2] It follows, Marx must have assumed that workers have entitlements arising from 'self-ownership'. This is the thesis 'that each person is the morally rightful owner of his own person and powers' (ibid., p. 67). Workers

Moral assumptions (unacknowledged, unjustified, & unacceptable)	1. Socialism is necessarily just. Values of autonomy, need, merit, and democratic consent. 2. No need for moral exhortation or coercion under socialism. Due to abundance & generosity. 3. Self-ownership. But even the welfare state will involve labour-theft.

Figure 5.2 Classical Marxism according to Cohen's critique

must, morally speaking, 'own' their labour and what it produces. However, Cohen argues, Marx did not elaborate on or justify these moral assumptions. What is more, the idea of self-ownership is associated with libertarianism [see pp. 65–7]. Marxists and libertarians can agree that 'forced dispossession' involves exploitation (Cohen, 1995, p. 120). However, Marxists assume that *all* capitalist relations are exploitative, even if they do not arise from violence, theft, or fraud.

What is the normative basis for the differences between libertarianism and Marxism? Marxists are (implicitly again) committed to equality and community as well as self-ownership. Libertarians, of course, reject egalitarian distribution, and they also conceptualize justice solely in terms of the entitlements of individuals. Marxist society pursues solidarity, universal free development, and equality, along with the principles of merit and need. For Marxists, self-ownership does not justify 'unlimited original rights in virtually unrestricted unequal amounts of external natural resources' (Cohen, 1995, p. 118). However, according to Cohen, classical Marxism is in danger of reaching the same conclusions as libertarianism. The Marxist must assume that, morally speaking, taxation to finance welfare state spending aimed at eliminating poverty is an illegitimate infringement of self-ownership (ibid., p. 151). Like capitalist wage-labour, taxation is a theft of the worker's labour. And this is just the conclusion that Nozick reached.

Socialism: The key themes

I want to draw attention to a divisive issue within socialism. Some commentators contend that the term 'socialist' should refer to 'revolutionary' Marxists alone. 'Reformists' should be referred to

■ **Equality**	Distribution according to need.
	Equality within the sphere of production (free development of all).
■ **Creativity**	Freedom/autonomy as workers (conscious life activity and productive life).
	Merit of labourer recognized (e.g. industrial citizenship).
■ **Community**	The right is not prior to the good of the community.
	Solidarity that transcends class inequality.
■ **Morality**	(i) Relativism (Morality conditioned by productive forces).
	(ii) Universalism (Conventional morality).

Figure 5.3 Four themes of socialism

as social democrats instead (Cf. Esping-Andersen, 1985; Przesworski, 1985). 'Reformists' are willing to participate in liberal democratic political institutions. They seek support for their policies beyond the working class. They also assume that capitalism can be reformed. 'Revolutionaries' reject all these assumptions. For instance, Marx assumed that, because welfare spending brings some improvements to their lives, it may in fact undermine workers' determination to pursue socialism. However, in this chapter, I will not conflate socialism with Marxism. It is not so easy to retain a clear division between reform and revolution. The so-called 'reformers' hope not only to significantly improve the conditions of workers, but also to place limits on capitalism. This is the case with Beveridge [see pp. 108–9], Castles [see pp. 109–11], Crosland [see pp. 115–18], and Tawney [see pp. 111–15]. On the other hand, some revolutionary socialists willingly concede that a welfare state can be justified. Entitlements, in the short term, can suspend the operation of the capitalist market and, in the long term, can help bring about a non-capitalist society (Esping-Andersen) [see pp. 109–11]. 'Socialist' theories of the welfare state share a number of features. The four key themes of socialism are given in Figure 5.3.

1. *Equality* – Socialists apply the principle of equality not only to the distribution of goods, but also to the sphere of production. Marx called for a distribution of goods on the basis of need because a distribution on the basis of contribution (merit) would lead to greater inequality. Marx also called for the equal freedom to pursue self-development, that is, equality within work. He also assumed that equality could be attained only after a revolutionary overthrow of capitalism. But others defend a socialist welfare state put in place

alongside a capitalist economy, and entitlements in this socialist welfare state have an egalitarian goal. The socialist conception of equality is controversial. Welfare liberals start from the conviction that all persons are morally equal. However, Rawls concludes that material incentives are justified if they help improve the condition of the least advantaged. Further, conservatives argue that unequal authority is necessary and justified. The practical knowledge required in everyday life is imparted and acquired through relations of authority, for instance between apprentice and master (Oakeshott, 1962, p. 11).

2. *Creativity of workers* – For Marx, workers create what is of value, but receive less in remuneration. This is 'labour-theft'. Further, as socialism does away with the division of labour, work itself can be 'life's prime want'. Marxism will guarantee freedom from alienation and exploitation. However, in a socialist (non-Marxist) welfare state, one purpose of welfare entitlements is to guarantee worker creativity. Workers can enjoy what are known as industrial or economic rights of citizenship [see pp. 109–11], which ensure a just distribution of powers and responsibilities within work. However, liberals do not accept the socialist account of human nature, in particular Marx's 'productive life'. Not everyone *wants* to be a worker. For Isaiah Berlin, at the heart of socialist theories of 'self-realization' is the idea that we can 'coerce people for their own sake' (Berlin, 1958, p. 151). Berlin contends that socialists equate what a person would choose, if he or she were something he or she is not, with what that person actually seeks and chooses (ibid.).

3. *Community* – Socialists do not give the right priority over the good, unlike liberals. They agree with conservatives about the significance of community. However, unlike conservatives, socialists promote a historically unique form of community. After all, Marxism comes about after the 'revolutionary' overthrow of capitalism. The socialist welfare state is associated with a unique type of community as well. Universal and unconditional benefits, provided through the public sphere, are distinctive features of a socialist community. It is based on a solidarity that, in one way or another, transcends class boundaries. For its critics, however, the socialist community is a fictional entity. According to individualists, a community is nothing more than the individuals who compose it. In promoting the so-called 'good' of the community, socialists do not respect the desires and preferences of existing individuals, in particular, capitalists.

4. *Socialist morality* – According to his critics, Marx assumed that 'moral ideas are weapons in a class struggle', that one must decide whether to adopt the moral system of the present or the future, and also that this decision is 'not a choice that is itself moral' (Popper, 1966, vol. 2, pp. 203–4). It is a choice between moralities, a choice outside morality. Although he is a universalist to the extent that he wants to show that socialism is a necessary stage of historical development, Marx is a relativist concerning morality. In any case, others are quite explicit in their attempt to justify socialism from within conventional morality. They appeal to the norms of need, equality, and merit. But if such an argument does provide a justification for socialism, then the moral basis of that argument is universal rather than relative. This is the one categorical difference between non-Marxism and Marxism (at least, official Marxist methodology).

Two models of a socialist welfare state

Cohen has argued that classical Marxism cannot justify a welfare state. I have also pointed to a non-Marxist strand of socialism as well. I turn now to the question of whether any actual welfare state provides a model or paradigm for socialism.

Post-war British Welfare State

According to Ramesh Mishra, Britain developed a 'collectivist' approach to welfare during the 1930s, due to the high density of trade unionism and also due to the influence of a socialist political movement (1981, p. 116). At the time, the Labour Party was strongly influenced by the ideas of 'guild socialism' and 'corporatism' (Foote, 1995, pp. 151, 179). While corporatists pursued a policy of nationalization (state ownership) simply so as to maximize well-being and protect workers' standards of living, guild socialists assumed that workers should exercise direct economic and political power so as to overcome 'wage slavery' (ibid.). However, people like William Beveridge and T.H. Marshall, some of the most important figures in the development of the British welfare state, were not socialists as such, but rather social liberals. Beveridge identified five 'evils' that the welfare state was to eliminate (Beveridge, 1942). Contributory social insurance, along with a non-contributory safety-net, was to eliminate 'want' caused by loss of earning power;

the National Health Service was to eliminate 'disease' or ill health through the free provision of health care to all citizens; the public provision of education was to eliminate 'ignorance'; town planning was to eliminate 'squalor'; and a policy of full employment was to eliminate 'idleness' (Clarke, et al., 1987, p. 87).

Like Beveridge, T.H. Marshall did not reject liberal democratic principles. Marshall simply wished to extend the civil and political rights of liberal democratic citizenship to include 'social' entitlements [see pp. 65–7]. Further, Beveridge's reforms would only 'modify' the free market as a mechanism for the distribution of income and commodities (Ginsburg, 1992, p. 141). Beveridge did not hope to replace the market with an alternative means of distribution. Socialists commend Beveridge's model because it guarantees unconditional rights to social welfare. However, Gosta Esping-Andersen also believes that Beveridge's reforms stopped short of socialism. Its universal services provided only 'an equality of minimal needs', and it allowed members of the middle classes to purchase welfare privately (1990, p. 64). As a result, the middle classes have secured many privileges through occupational and private insurance (Titmuss, 1965, p. 122). Further, its use of non-contributory income maintenance is 'discretionary'. Recipients are expected to show that they are seeking work. Those who do not 'co-operate' are denied eligibility for the receipt of benefits (Titmuss, 1970b, p. 243).

The Scandinavian model

The Swedish welfare state, the 'Scandinavian model' as it is known, is seen by many as a paradigm of socialism or social democracy (Figure 5.4). For Francis Castles, social democracy involves the public provision of 'health, education, community services, etc.', and it is 'to reallocate benefits from wage earners to non-wage earners through child, unemployment, and sickness benefits as well as old-age pensions' (1978, pp. 52–3). However, Marxists like Frank Parkin (1971) argue that these welfare entitlements merely help perpetuate the prevailing social structure, and its in-built class inequalities. Marxists ask, 'whether Social Democratic ideology can lead to a fundamental transformation of the reward structure of capitalism?' (Castles, 1978, p. 50). According to Castles, however, we should ask, 'has social democracy made a fundamental improvement in the condition of the working class?' (ibid.). The answer is

British (Beveridge, Marshall)	Scandinavia 1 (Castles)	Scandinavia 2 (Esping-Andersen)
■ Universal services to citizens. ■ Means-tested safety-net. ■ Contributory social insurance.	■ Fundamental improvement in condition of working class.	■ De-commodification: emancipate from market & reach frontier with socialism.
Critique: Market mechanism is left unrestricted. It is merely an extension of liberalism.	**Critique:** Does not alter structure of distribution & production.	**Critique:** 'Liberal' emphasis on autonomy & freedom from work.

Figure 5.4 Two socialist models

that it has. Social democracy changes the way goods are distributed so as to favour workers, but without overturning the market mechanism. Social democrats can also provide an egalitarian justification for welfare entitlements, Castles argues. Their aim is an equal 'level-of-living' (ibid., p. 79).

Standards of living can be measured along various dimensions: (a) health; (b) nutrition; (c) housing; (d) family origins and relations; (e) education; (f) work and its milieu; (g) economic resources; (h) political resources; and (i) leisure-time pursuits (ibid.). Average quality of life should be as high as possible in each dimension, and individuals should be in a position to enjoy an equal measure in each. (This is similar to Goodin's utilitarian defence of equality with respect to welfare interests [see pp. 39–42].) Entitlements must also counter the 'cumulative impact' of inequalities. Unequal levels of living in one category must not cause inequalities in others. Finally, in addition to T.H. Marshall's three levels of citizenship (civil, political, and social), Castles adds a fourth: industrial and economic citizenship. Such rights protect individuals against 'an undesirable work milieu, inability to participate in decisions affecting one's own life chances and absence of political resources' (ibid., p. 90). Castles thus shows how the principle of equality can be applied to work as well as the distribution of resources.

Esping-Andersen offers an alternative view of the Scandinavian model. Socialists must respond to what he calls 'commodification'. This refers to 'the process by which both human needs and labor power became commodities and, hence, our well-being came to depend on our relation to the cash nexus' (1990, p. 35). In a capitalist society we cannot meet basic needs if we do not have the power to command commodities, and we do not have that power without property or employment. Karl Polanyi had argued that, although labour is thought of as a commodity, the labourer would perish without the 'protective covering of cultural institutions' (1944, p. 73). For Esping-Andersen, such protection results in 'de-commodification'. It is a measure of 'the degree to which distribution is detached from the market mechanism' (1989, p. 186). In the short term, it will 'substantially emancipate individuals from market dependence' (ibid.), but also, in the long term, it is 'a potential power resource that defines the frontier between capitalism and socialism' (ibid., p. 177). Therefore, *pace* Castles, welfare entitlements must alter the structure of capitalism. They must create 'welfare time' where 'workers exercise their own choices under the [work] contract...The appropriate empirical case here is paid absence from work' (1990, p. 149).

Esping-Andersen's concept of de-commodification is not without its problems. First, de-commodification is the freedom to remain *away* from work. It is not clear that de-commodification involves a fundamental transformation of capitalist work relations, therefore. Secondly, he accepts that Swedish socialist policies arose from a conservative agenda, to increase the population and improve the health of citizens, but now, in contrast, it 'is a peculiar fusion of liberalism and socialism' (1989, p. 26). It now reflects a 'liberal' concern for individual independence, in particular women's autonomy. However, perhaps the convergence between socialism and conservatism is not merely a historical contingency. Both arose from a critique of the de-humanizing effects of unregulated capitalism. As we shall see, Tawney's ethical socialism has much in common with Durkheim's conservatism. In particular, both call for the redistribution of property, and both give priority to social aims over individual rights.

R.H. Tawney: Ethical socialism

Richard Tawney is perhaps the most important advocate of *ethical* socialism.[3] The institutions that satisfy basic needs and bring about equality are only valuable as instruments. They are to help attain certain shared goods, the 'social purpose' of a 'functional' society.

For that reason, Tawney emphasizes the principle of contribution and the criterion of merit, and welfare entitlements are conditional.

A socialist ethic

Tawney makes a distinction between a 'social purpose' and the means used to attain it. 'Property, wealth, and industrial organization' are only instruments, while their purpose should be 'the growth towards perfection of individual human beings' (1938, p. 84). The socialist social purpose includes the egalitarian idea of 'the dignity of man' (ibid., p. 81). And, showing the importance of the principle or merit, Tawney argues that the goal of 'civilization' entails that we should 'recognize genuine superiority and submit to its influence' (ibid., p. 86). That is, 'socialism' itself refers to a society where the members share an ethic and, for that reason, are committed to the 'goods' of human dignity and civilization. Moreover, in contrast to Marx, Tawney bases his argument for socialism on the following universal moral considerations.

John Locke had argued that a man's rights over things removed from nature were justified on the basis that 'he has mixed his labour with it' (Tawney, 1921, p. 55). Tawney insists that labour does justify property rights, but only rights that are 'an aid to creative work, not an alternative to it' (ibid.). Therefore, not all property involves 'theft' (exploitation of workers by non-workers); but it follows that property rights are conditional. A person may claim rights to what is needed to secure the basic requirements for life and for creative work. Property is justified on the basis of need and merit, therefore. Tawney also draws on the ethics of modern professions, as Durkheim did [see pp. 83–8], for professional ethics demands 'creative' work. Professionals should maintain the standards of their profession and also provide a 'service to the public' (ibid., p. 151). Conditionality is important here. Workers can demand greater powers and rewards, but such entitlements are conditional on making contributions to the common good and also striving to sustain standards of excellence within the activity. Finally, Tawney's combination of egalitarianism and conditionality is based on Christian ethics.

> By affirming that all men are the children of God, it insists that the rights of all men are equal. By affirming that men are men and nothing

more, it is a warning that those rights are conditional and derivative – a commission of service, not a property.

(ibid., p. 185)

Equality

What is Tawney's conception of equality? A socialist community is based on a shared purpose. As fellow citizens, we should acknowledge that a 'measure of communism is needed to ensure that inequalities of personal capacity are neither concealed nor exaggerated by inequalities which have their source in social arrangements' (1938, p. 132). That is, socialists should willingly restrain their self-interest for an egalitarian goal. *Economic* equality does not involve identical levels of reward or authority, according to Tawney. Inequality of economic power is justified *if* it is 'based on differences of function and office' (ibid., p. 61). This in turn requires 'the very easy movement of individuals, according to their capacity, from one point on the scale to another' (ibid.). Tawney calls for *social* equality as well. It includes 'not equal ... intellectual attainments, but equal opportunities of cultivating the powers with which Nature has endowed them' (ibid., p. 171).

Up to this point, Tawney has not departed from Durkheim's position. They both assume that, in a just society, each is free to develop talents, positions are filled on the basis of ability, and social inequalities are not obstacles to the development of natural abilities. However, unlike Durkheim, Tawney makes an explicit egalitarian commitment to improve the condition of the least advantaged. Social equality entails 'equal access' to fresh air, warmth, rest, and food, for without them people 'will be too enfeebled to exercise them [legal rights] effectively' (Tawney, 1938, p. 164). Society 'is to provide for the contingencies of life, and thus to mitigate the insecurity which is the most character- istic of the wage-earner's disabilities' (ibid., p. 180). Therefore, social equality encompasses a healthy environment, education, and economic security. However, they 'are the source of a social income, received in the form, not of money, but of increased well-being' (ibid., p. 150). A 'social income' is composed of 'inte- gral, or social, ends' rather than 'divisible or individual ends' (ibid., p. 149). He conceptualizes social equality in terms of not individual rights, but 'equality of environment'. He goes so far as to say that claiming rights is divisive, while duties are a 'principle of union' (1921, p. 80).

Perfectionism

For Tawney, human welfare is closely related to an ethical conception of creativity, a perfectionist ideal of human nature (Figure 5.5). Members of the socialist community must exercise certain virtues, as we have seen: (i) they should be committed egalitarians, and willingly restrain their self-interest; (ii) they should recognize genuine superiority and submit to its influence; (iii) they should maintain their professional standards; (iv) they should provide a service to the public; and (v) they should be good Christians as well.

Starting from the criterion of *need*, Tawney argues that people should have the possessions necessary for health and comfort (ibid., p. 83). On the basis of the criterion of *merit*, he argues that people should have rights to the materials needed to provide society with needed services. As property is 'an aid to creative work', welfare entitlements include the access to productive materials and skills. Finally, Tawney also assumes that *all* work *can* be creative. Workers can rightly demand 'stronger organization, fuller responsibility, larger powers' (ibid., p. 145). Tawney is therefore optimistic about the possibility for social reform. However, he also insists that social

---

■ **Socialist ethic**   Conditionality: service to community and maintain standards of profession.
Need: entitlement to property needed for basic requirements of life.
Merit: creative work to be rewarded.
Equality: willingly restrain self-interest for a measure of communism.

■ **Equality**   Economic equality:
Unequal rewards and powers must be based on differences in function.
Recruitment must be based on capacity.
Social equality:

 (i) Equal opportunity to develop abilities.
 (ii) Equality of environment: security, education, health.

■ **Perfectionism**   Virtues:
Egalitarianism, recognize authority, professionalism, service to community, Christianity.

Figure 5.5 Tawney's ethical socialism

reforms bring duties as well as rights. The worker must accept the duty to serve the public and maintain professional standards.

Critics of ethical socialism contend that it is far too concerned with virtue. It is hostile to what it sees as the 'militant hurry' to bring capitalism to an end (Miliband, 1969, p. 182). Rather, it seems that Tawney shows how a virtue-based approach can also be critical and radical. According to Tawney, 'a considerable reconstruction of society' is required (1921, p. 10) and the worker can rightly demand 'stronger organization, fuller responsibility, larger powers' (ibid., p. 145). Admittedly, this sounds very similar to Durkheim's conservatism. They both assume that professions must be subject to moral regulation, and compelled to contribute to social purposes. Both are unenthusiastic about individual rights, and see welfare distribution as a 'social' aim. Unlike Durkheim, however, Tawney *does* make an explicit egalitarian commitment to improve the conditions of the least advantaged. Nonetheless, like Durkheim, Tawney has not shown any greater enthusiasm for social 'rights'.

Anthony Crosland: Liberal socialism

Tony Crosland's [1918–1977] version of socialism would improve social welfare and social equality, as Tawney also insisted. However, Crosland does not call for substantial structural changes to work relations or greater economic redistribution, and he does not expect citizens generally to evince socialist beliefs and aim for common goods. For that reason, to an important extent, this strand of socialism comes close to the welfare liberalism of Rawls.

Three socialist aspirations

According to Crosland, the term 'socialism' should be based 'explicitly on an ethical view of society, a belief in a certain way of life and certain moral values' (Crosland, 1956, pp. 101–2). Socialism refers to certain aspirations, not the means used to attain them. However, as a result of social progress, two socialist aspirations (both were important for Tawney) simply are no longer relevant: 'protest against the material poverty and physical squalor which capitalism produced' and 'protest against the inefficiencies of capitalism as an economic system, and notably its tendency to mass unemployment' (ibid., p. 103). However, three socialist aspirations are still relevant: (i) 'a rejection of competitive antagonism, and an ideal of fraternity and cooperation'; (ii) 'a wider concern for "social welfare" '; and (iii) 'a belief in equality and the "classless society" ' (ibid.).

Crosland and Tawney agree that the ideal of solidarity is still relevant and also that professionals lessen class conflict. Conflict between owners and wage-labourers has lessened. 'Business leaders are now, in the main, paid by salary and not by profit, and owe their power to their position in the managerial structure, and not to ownership' (Crosland, 1956, p. 34). Nonetheless, if Tawney's socialism is 'direct' and 'ethical', Crosland's is 'indirect' and 'mechanical'. For Crosland, socialism can be brought about 'without having to create egalitarian citizens' (Plant, 1996, p. 173). Crosland does not assume that socialism will or must promote solidarity in personal and work relations. This is the case as open competition for posts is required by both 'democracy' and the socialist goal of 'equalization of opportunities for advancement' (Crosland, 1956, p. 106). Moreover, 'differential rewards for differential efforts' may now be 'good for economic growth and the standard of living' (ibid., pp. 106–7). Material inequality is a necessary incentive, as Rawls has argued. In such a context, we cannot expect or demand 'other regarding instincts' (ibid., p. 108). It should be noted that Tawney also believed in open competition for posts and selection based on merit, but that both were compatible with a willingness to restrain self-interest.

The second relevant socialist aspiration, for Crosland, is 'a wider concern for "social welfare" '. Welfare spending and the reform of capitalism have eliminated long-term unemployment and extreme deprivation ('primary poverty'), but social welfare must tackle 'secondary poverty'. 'The main object of social expenditure' should be the 'elimination of this squalor': 'ugly towns, mean streets, slum houses, overcrowded schools, inadequate hospitals, under-staffed mental institutions, too few homes for the aged, indeed a general, and often squalid, lack of social amenities' (ibid., p. 113). In contrast to Tawney, Crosland does not justify social welfare provision with the principle of equality. His arguments 'are humanitarian and compassionate, not egalitarian' (ibid.). The criterion of need, not equality, justifies welfare entitlements. This is the case as 'we have now reached the point where further redistribution would make little difference to the standard of living of the masses' (ibid., p. 190). As the 'extremes of wealth are so much less marked' (ibid., p. 191), redistribution would gather little from the rich while simply penalizing the middle classes.

The final aspiration is 'social equality'. It refers to style of life, accent, education, non-pecuniary benefits in work, decision-making in work, and influence over policy. Crosland contends that 'social strife' is caused when workers receive an increase in income but are still thought of as *merely* labour (ibid., p. 198). Social equality would diminish 'social antagonism' (ibid., p. 206). Social equality is also the 'just' distribution of privileges and rewards. First, 'wealth should be a reward for the performance of a definite service or function', and secondly, each person should have an equal opportunity to 'that position in the social scale to which his native talents entitle him' (ibid.). For Crosland, thoroughgoing economic democracy is mere 'fussing' and 'interfering' (Whitemore, 1991, p. 133). Nonetheless, social equality increases the power of the worker at the point of production (Crosland, 1956, pp. 210–11). These points are summarized in Figure 5.6. Tawney was committed to similar goals: reduced status distinctions, 'fair' equal opportunity (in Rawls's terms), selection based on ability, rewards for service, greater worker power, and a social income to be received by all. However, Crosland does not presume or demand fraternal motives (ibid., p. 111).

Criticisms of Crosland

It seems fair to contrast Crosland's 'liberalism' with Tawney's 'conservatism'. They could agree that inequality is justified if it arises from 'fair' equal opportunity, if it is based on differences in 'native talents', and also if social policy effectively tackles deprivation. Further, although Crosland does not call for greater economic redistribution, he does argue that if inequality of incomes is too great, then, even with equal opportunity for posts, an excessive gap

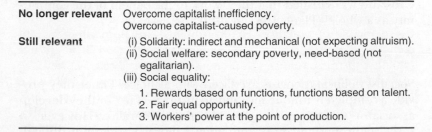

No longer relevant	Overcome capitalist inefficiency.
	Overcome capitalist-caused poverty.
Still relevant	(i) Solidarity: indirect and mechanical (not expecting altruism).
	(ii) Social welfare: secondary poverty, need-based (not egalitarian).
	(iii) Social equality:
	1. Rewards based on functions, functions based on talent.
	2. Fair equal opportunity.
	3. Workers' power at the point of production.

Figure 5.6 Crosland's liberal socialism

may emerge between elites and non-elites (ibid., p. 236). Nonetheless, Tawney rejects the notion of unconditional individual rights, and he calls for fraternal and egalitarian commitments. Tawney could agree with conservatives who call for a subordination of individual aims and interests to social aims and interests. In contrast, Crosland defends the rights individuals may claim *against* society. He is writing in a time of affluence, which prioritized 'liberty' and 'gaiety' in private life (Daniel, 1997, p. 16). He does not think it likely or necessary to foster other-regarding, fraternal motives.

Crosland's position is open to a number of objections. First, he contends that contemporary society is 'post-capitalist'. It is the case that professional managers play a greater role and that state intervention in the economy has increased. However, it does not follow that shareholders, managers, and senior civil servants are not members of the one class, the new economic elites (Miliband, 1969, pp. 10–11). Secondly, Crosland does not believe that citizens must adhere to socialist principles. However, this leaves socialism exposed to challenges from opposing belief systems that are more confident about their 'salience to the values of society' (Plant, 1996, p. 174). Crosland simply 'declined to offer an argument', choosing instead to rely on 'the moral predilections of the reader' (Daniel, 1997, p. 18). Third, Crosland defends a version of socialism that guarantees individual rights against society. Crosland himself said that Rawls's work was the closest approximation of the views he had striven to convey (1976). However, while Crosland emphasizes fair equal opportunity, he does not stress the importance of re-distribution of income and wealth to the least advantaged. In contrast, Rawls defends the 'difference principle' because economic deprivation is still relevant. While Rawls believed inequalities must be shown to improve the condition of the least advantaged, Crosland was satisfied that they 'work to the benefit of the community as a whole' (Plant, 1981, p. 142).

Conclusion

Socialist political theorists are faced with a choice. Either they provide a completely unique morality to justify welfare, or they develop a socialist interpretation of conventional morality. However, if socialists propose a completely unique morality, then it is difficult to see how this can be justified. If Marxist morality does not rely on accepted principles or accepted methods of moral argumentation, then it does not provide any way in which its conclusions can be shown to be either reasonable or unreasonable. Other, non-Marxist, socialists accept that they should try to develop socialism from within conventional morality. Francis Castles comes close to the utilitarian argument that justice maximizes happiness and ensures its equitable distribution. Other socialists approach a conservative position. Tawney argues that a socialist society exists only if its members exercise socialist virtues, and that socialism brings about not equal rights but shared goods such as equality of environment. Finally, some socialists fall back on a liberal position. Crosland concluded that citizens of a socialist society need not adhere to socialist values and that each individual's rights against society can be defended.

In each instance, what began as a distinctive socialist theory seems to collapse back into one of the theories already discussed. This need not be problematic. Any one of these theories may help better understand welfare and arrive at a sound theory of welfare entitlements. But it does put in question the need for a 'socialist' political philosophy. However, this chapter has discussed socialist political philosophy without mentioning the most pervasive contemporary critique of socialism, the New Right. The next few chapters will address issues that, in recent times, have put to the question each of the theories discussed so far. We will then be in a better position to understand the New Right critique and assess its cogency. The final chapter in this book will return to various attempts made to defend extensive state provision of unconditional entitlements.

CHAPTER 6

Political Liberalism

Mainstream political philosophy has faced serious challenges recently. They arise as part of a broader problematization of modern political philosophy and modern welfare states. Modern theorists, it seems, presupposed the existence of a national economy, a nation state, and a national society. It was assumed that the state, society, and economy were 'co-extensive within the same national boundaries' (Habermas, 1999, p. 48). According to some commentators, this is no longer a tenable assumption (ibid.). This is of interest to us as a national bond could be the central feature in the motivation for, and justification of, the welfare state. In a changed context, however, the following question is posed: *does the state still have the moral authority to intervene in economic relations and guarantee welfare entitlements?* Must the welfare state be based on a substantive moral consensus no longer available in an increasingly diverse and cosmopolitan society? However, it could be argued that John Rawls's liberalism did not rely upon a substantive moral consensus. Rawls accepted a plurality of moral doctrines and conceptions of the good, and yet, he claims, welfare liberalism provides a way to respond to that plurality such that a moral justification can be given to the welfare state. That is, if we accept 'the priority of the right over the good', we should also be able to agree on a theory of justice that guarantees each person's basic rights irrespective of their conception of the good.

In this chapter, I explore Rawls's later work, 'political liberalism', which is a response to his communitarian critics. Communitarians have argued that Rawls's liberalism relies on a sense of community that it in fact undercuts. This critique of Rawls arises due to the way in which Rawls responds to pluralism. Michael Sandel's argument is that Rawls is rationally committed to a 'philosophy of common purposes' which 'justice as fairness' then undercuts. The difference principle must presuppose a prior moral tie as it treats natural advantages as common assets. 'Otherwise, it is simply a formula for using some as means to others' ends ...' (Sandel, 1984a, p. 22). That sense of community is undermined by Rawls's insistence on 'impartiality'. Communitarians respond to Rawls by questioning whether justice implies the priority of the right over the good. They also question whether justice is always the primary moral consideration.

This chapter also introduces feminist thought. Rawls tends to equate rationality with self-interested utility maximization. 'While the persons in the original position do not know their conception of the good, they do know ... that they prefer more rather than less primary goods' (Rawls, 1971, p. 93). Feminists contend that Rawls undervalues the emotions, and women's caring role. As a result of this critique, some feminists call into question both mainstream theoretical analysis as well as the primacy given to justice. 'Ethic of care' feminists identify two moral projects, one concerned with rights and justice, another concerned with care and the emotions (Gilligan, 1982; Baier, 1987). The latter, they argue, can motivate a feminist approach to welfare that will adequately account for the experiences of women.

After discussing the feminist and communitarian critiques of Rawls, I then look at Rawls's 'political liberalism' (Rawls, 1987, 1993, 1997). He still defends the two principles of justice (including the difference principle). However, a 'political' conception of justice is defended not as morally true, but as the reasonable basis of stable cooperation. Then I look at Martha Nussbaum's attempts to develop political liberalism as a theory acceptable to feminists (2000a, b). Political liberalism overcomes unjustified gender inequality as it guarantees women's (*and* men's) 'capability', and it gives due weight to the emotions (*and* rationality).

Michael Sandel's communitarian critique of Rawls

Michael Sandel made an important contribution to the communitarian critique of Rawls. Sandel rejects Rawls's justification for welfare entitlements simply because it gives priority to justice and the right and presupposes a conception of moral agency unacceptable to non-liberals.

The 'unencumbered self'

Sandel's objection to 'justice as fairness' begins with an analysis of Rawls's conception of moral agency. Rawls contends that the right is prior to the good and the right is independently derived. In contrast to utilitarianism, 'individual rights cannot be sacrificed for the sake of the general good' (Sandel, 1984a, p. 13). However (and more to the point for communitarians) in opposition to Aristotelianism, Rawls assumes, '...principles of justice specify these rights cannot be premised on any particular vision of the good life' (ibid.). Rawls's principles of justice 'do not presuppose any particular ends' (ibid., p. 18). They are not tied to any one substantive view of the *telos* or purpose of human beings. However, 'What they *do* presuppose is a certain picture of the person,...of the unencumbered self...' (ibid.). There is 'always a distinction between the values I *have* and the person I *am*'; there is 'some subject "me" standing behind' those values, 'and the shape of this "me" must be given prior to any of the aims or attributes I bear' (ibid.). The self is also unencumbered in the 'original position'. Rawls wants us to put to one side 'contingent' facts, our natural and social advantages, our conception of the good, our psychological dispositions, and so on. The moral agent is independent of, and prior to, historically specific aspects of his or her identity.

According to Sandel, Rawls assumes an 'antecedently individuated self' (1982, p. 62) (Figure 6.1). Rawls provides no account of membership in a 'constitutive' community, a community that 'would engage the identity as well as the interests of the participants...' (Sandel, 1984a, p. 19). In a constitutive community, a person's identity or self is 'at stake'. Rawls assumes that we retain control of our identity, whatever community we belong to. Sandel also introduces the idea of 'intra-subjective' and 'inter-subjective' conceptions of the self (1982, p. 62). For the *inter*-subjective conception, 'in certain moral circumstances, the relevant description of the self may embrace more than a single, individual human being' (ibid., p. 63). This happens when responsibility is attributed to a family or community or nation. Alternatively, for the *intra*-subjective conception of the self, the appropriate description 'may refer to a plurality of selves within a single, individual human being', for instance, when we account for 'moments of introspection in terms of occluded self-knowledge...' (ibid.). That is, as a person, I am never simply an isolated self, and also I am always a member of communities in a variety of ways.

Rawls (according to Sandel)	Unencumbered self	A distinction between the values I have and the person I am.
	Agency is voluntaristic	Radically free choice of ends.
Sandel	Inter-subjective self	Description of the self includes more than one individual.
	Intra-subjective self	Plurality of selves within one individual.
	Agency is cognitive	Understanding ends that are already given.

Figure 6.1 The self in Rawls (on Sandel's interpretation) and Sandel

Sandel also gives priority to 'cognition', while Rawls emphasizes the 'will'.

> Where the ends of the self are given in advance, the relevant agency is not voluntaristic but cognitive, since the subject achieves self-command not by choosing that which is already given (this would be unintelligible) but by reflecting on itself and inquiring into its constituent nature, discerning its laws and imperatives, and acknowledging its purposes as its own.
>
> (ibid., p. 58)

'The relevant question is not what ends to choose, for my problem is precisely that the answer to this question is already given' (ibid., p. 59). We achieve 'self-command' by understanding ends that are 'already given'. This has the troubling connotation of intensive social conditioning and programing. However, Sandel goes on to note that the question is 'who I am, how I am to discern in this clutter of possible ends what is me from what is mine' (ibid.). Truly valuable ends are not created by an act of will; they are common purposes and ends. Nonetheless, there are many common purposes and ends, and, within this 'clutter', 'I' must decide 'what is me'.

A philosophy of common purposes

'Justice as fairness' is impartial with respect to different conceptions of the good, Rawls claims. However, according to Sandel, Rawls's position would entail that conceptions of the good are subjective and arbitrary. On the one hand, in the Rawlsian scheme, I need not analyse whether I should have the desires and wants I happen to have. Rawls assumes that a life is good if it is well planned, but Rawls does not provide any way to rationally assess whether the ends of such a plan are themselves any good. On the other hand, 'the good...includes as ingredients various contingencies which are arbitrary from a moral point of view, while the right is free from such arbitrariness' (Sandel, 1982, pp. 155–6). Sandel is referring here to Rawls's own distinction between reasons that are relevant for receiving entitlements and those that are not (those that are 'arbitrary'). Rawls assumes that the distinctive features of one's life (one's psychology, conception of the good, natural and social advantages, etc.) do not count as reasons to receive entitlements, and are, therefore, 'arbitrary'.

Although Sandel rejects impartiality, his is not an intolerant or prejudicial account of human goods. For instance, rights of privacy for homosexuals can be defended because, like heterosexual marriage, this 'practice' realizes a 'human good' (1989, p. 83). Privacy is defended not as the inherent rights of an unencumbered self, but in the name of the intrinsic value or social importance of the practice in which people participate.

Rawls assumes that the right is prior to the good. However, the difference principle 'treats talents as common assets'. According to Sandel, it implicitly relies on a conception of community, a prior moral tie, which it then undercuts. We could only reasonably expect the talented and wealthy to agree to have their advantages treated as common assets if they saw themselves as, morally speaking, already tied to the disadvantaged members of a community. 'Otherwise, it is simply a formula for using some as means to others' ends...' (1984a, p. 22). Of course, that is just the charge that Nozick makes against Rawls. However, *pace* Nozick, Sandel does not reject the types of demand arising from Rawls's difference principle, but rather the argument that right is prior to the good (ibid., p. 23). So, if we are to justify claims of justice, we must first set out just what happens to be our common goods. However, claims of justice may be *secondary* to claims of communal allegiances, claims arising as 'members of this family or community or nation or people, as bearers of that history, citizens of this republic' (ibid.). These allegiances 'allow that to some I owe more than justice requires or even permits' (ibid.). For instance, I owe companionship, commitment, sympathy, and so on, even though no one may claim these things from me as his or her 'right'. However, I also owe more than justice 'permits'. For instance, I may owe clemency when justice would instead demand punishment.

A number of points can be made with respect to Sandel's critique. He has argued that Rawls presupposes an untenable conception of agency, the 'unencumbered self'. However, according to his supporters, Rawls does not defend one single metaphysical account of agency. He offers a theory of justice suitable to a diversity of moral and philosophical doctrines (Gutmann, 1985, p. 126). I return to this on pp. 132–7. Sandel also argues that, in the Rawslian scheme, the good life is arbitrary and subjective. However, first, Rawls's position can allow distinctions between 'better' and 'worse' conceptions of the good, in the sense that they are more or less 'well planned'. Secondly, substantive conceptions of the good are 'arbitrary' for Rawls only in the sense that they are not themselves sufficient to determine the *just* distribution of benefits and burdens. It does not mean that (for any given person) there are no good reasons to adopt one path in life.

Sandel argues that some social conceptions of the good are integral to a person's identity. He must be able to distinguish a social conception of the good that is imposed from one that is not. However, Sandel rejects the idea that moral agents can analyse their reasons for maintaining commitments in a way that does not presuppose just those commitments. For the liberal, none of our ends are exempt from re-examination (Kymlicka, 1989, p. 52). Finally, Sandel is surely right that justice is not the only relevant moral principle. Feminists would concur, as we shall see on pp. 125–32. However, it does not follow that individuals can be free, morally speaking, to do *less* than justice requires. We are not free to neglect the rightful claims of someone simply because some other moral value directs our attention to the needs and interests of someone else.

The feminist critique of Rawls

Feminists criticize Rawls with respect to the same three issues raised by Sandel: Rawls's account of the self, the right, and moral deliberation. According to feminists, Rawls cannot account for women's experiences of subjugation. This is the case as Rawls presupposes an egoistic conception of the self; the rights that his theory justifies are abstract and formal; and his 'rational choice' approach ignores the emotions and caring.

The self: Family and gender

The term 'patriarchy' initially was used to refer to a society based on the power of fathers within the family. However, feminists employ the term to refer to inequalities resulting from gender differences in all areas of social life. In 'modern fraternal patriarchy', men's freedom in the public sphere comes at the expense of women's subjugation (Pateman, 1988, p. 4). The welfare state also perpetuates patriarchy. There are 'two tiers' of welfare provision.

> First, there are the benefits available to individuals as "public" persons by virtue of their participation, and accidents of fortune, in the capitalist market. Second, benefits are available to the "dependents" of individuals in the first category, or to "private" persons, usually women. In the United States....men are the majority of "deserving" workers who receive benefits through the insurance system...[T]he majority of claimants in means-tested programmes are...women who are usually making their claims as wives or mothers.
>
> (ibid., p. 188)

Women usually receive welfare as undeserving dependents. But the welfare state also relies on women to provide certain 'welfare functions' in the home, while simultaneously stigmatizing that role and denying that it is 'work' (ibid., p. 192).

How can feminists respond to the patriarchal experiences of women? They cannot appeal to Rawls's social contract approach, according to Carole Pateman, for the idea (and practice) of a contract is closely associated with patriarchy. Social contract theory is concerned with the division between civil society and the state. It ignores, and implicitly justifies, women's experience of subjugation in the private sphere of the family: 'The social contract is a modern patriarchal pact that establishes men's sex right over women' (ibid., p. 52). The social contract approach guarantees freedom from assault in civil society and at the same time it condones women's subjugation in the family. Also, it has excluded women in its theoretical construction of the individual: the 'civil individual has been constructed in opposition to women and all that our bodies symbolize' (ibid.). Men are constructed as rational and autonomous; women as irrational, dependent, and consumed by 'natural' impulses. Therefore, the Rawlsian approach can only incorporate women to the extent that women adopt 'male' characteristics: an emotionally detached rationality and individualistic outlook. But women are caught in a bind: 'since we are never regarded as other than women, we must simultaneously continue to affirm the patriarchal conception of femininity, or patriarchal subjection' (ibid.).

Ethic of care

This brings us to the second line of feminist critique. Feminists identify two separate moral projects. One deals with rights and justice. Lawrence Kohlberg (1984) provides a 'Rawlsian' vision of moral development. At a pre-conventional level, one is to please parental authority-figures; at a conventional level, one tries to fit in with some larger social group; and at a post-conventional level, the Kantian ideal of mutual respect is used to assess these primary ties. In contrast, Carol Gilligan outlines a morality of caring and emotion: the ethic of care. She identifies three stages of 'women's moral development': caring for one's self; caring for others; and mutual care (1982, pp. 72–4). In the second stage there may be disequilibrium if women are excluded from the receipt of their own care. The third stage involves a positive concern for the welfare of others. It also offers a universal condemnation of all 'exploitation and hurt' (ibid., p. 74).

Gilligan does not assume that all family relations, in fact, are based on an ethic of care. Rather, her point is that when women are excluded from their own care, there will be asymmetry; and when women have no privacy and cannot turn down demands for care, they will lack autonomy. Asymmetry and dominance are the characteristic features of traditional families. Although ethic of care feminism is concerned with the morality suited to a communal environment (the family), as it takes such a critical line with traditional family groups, feminism cannot be equated with communitarianism.

A theory of right is appropriate to voluntary and equal relations, those of civil society, but many relations are neither equal nor freely chosen. 'Vulnerable future generations do not choose their dependence on earlier generations' (Baier, 1987, p. 54). For instance, 'justice as fairness' does not show us how we ought to treat our dependent children. Feminists call for a type of deliberation that employs the emotions, as well as reason. They also suggest there is an observable overlap between women's experiences and the

■ 'Sexual contract'	Women: Private, 'dependent', means-tested benefits.
	Men: Public, 'independent', contribution-based benefits.
■ Two moral projects	Men: Kantian ideal of mutual respect.
	Women: Ethic of care, ideal of mutual care
	(autonomy & reciprocity).

Figure 6.2 Feminism and Rawlsian (social contract) theory

presence of an ethic of care. 'It might be important to father figures to have rational control over their violent urges to beat to death the children whose screams enrage them', but also 'the mother or primary parent, or parent-substitute, . . . [needs] to love their children, not just control their irritation' (ibid., p. 55). Feminists do not claim it is an *a priori* truth that women develop the virtues of a caring person. But feminists must be careful to avoid the kind of essentialism they have denounced as implicit in social contract theory (Figure 6.2). If it is disreputable to ascribe to women the essential characteristics of irrationality and dependency, it is equally disreputable to characterize men as, essentially, aggressive, egoistic, and unsympathetic.

Further, ethic of care feminism highlights the importance of what might be called 'subjective feelings of hurt'. Rawls is concerned with 'objective unfairness'. If gender asymmetry and dominance do not deny primary social goods to those affected, then, for Rawls, they are not 'unfair'. According to feminists, because Rawls's egalitarianism is only formal and abstract, it cannot judge patriarchy to be unjust. Any egalitarian commitments must attend to differences in power. They must also be made concrete within different circumstances (Nussbaum, 2000b, p. 59).

Four feminist proposals

If mainstream political theory has ignored the experiences and needs of women, what does feminist political theory suggest as the best type of welfare entitlements?

(i) *Equal opportunity* – It could be argued that social justice involves 'formal equal opportunity' and that women's marginality and deprivation have been caused by unjust obstacles to equal opportunity. This approach would guarantee basic liberties and also it would guarantee women's right to apply for academic and technical training and employment. It may even guarantee that women should receive the same pay as men for carrying out the same roles. This is indicative of 'first wave', liberal feminism, which emerged at the end of the nineteenth century (Mill, 1869), and also the extension of the franchise to women and the growing number of women in full-time education and formal employment. However, such an approach has been challenged on at least three grounds. First, without social spending to reduce social inequality, this liberal approach may well benefit middle-class women but not women from the working class or ethnic minorities. A Rawlsian feminist would call for measures to ensure 'fair' equal opportunity for all women (see below). However, secondly, the Rawlsian position may fail to remedy the discrimination experienced by women, and so 'affirmative action' may be called for (see below). Finally, even such an approach may simply perpetuate the value judgement that ascribes to women and women's roles an inferior status, and so an ethic of care may be needed (see below).

   (ii) *Affirmative action* – This has been advocated not only for women but also for minority groups, in particular African-Americans. A 'backward-looking approach' concludes that members of minority groups, both men and women, may receive 'preferential treatment' as *'compensation* for past wrongful harms'. A 'forward-looking approach' justifies preferential treatment on 'the grounds that it may secure greater equality or increase total social utility' (Boxill, 1991, p. 270). The backward-looking approach is open to the criticism that those who receive benefits now are not those who were discriminated against in the past, and also, as applicants for university places for instance, they are in a far better position than other members of their race or gender who have fewer qualifications or less ability. Feminists have extended the forward-looking approach to call for 'equal pay for comparable worth' (Sorensen, 1988, p. 293). Due to occupational segregation in the labour market, some jobs are labelled as 'women's work', and for that reason, those who perform these jobs are paid 'less than they would if these jobs employed white men' (ibid., p. 294). Sorensen calls for equal pay for jobs that are equivalent in respect of required knowledge, 'mental demands, accountability, and working conditions' (ibid.).

   (iii) *Ethic of care* – Both equal opportunity and affirmative action extend to women benefits that, in the past, have been enjoyed by men. The ethic of care approach wants to reverse the value judgement that assigns to women's caring work a secondary and peripheral role. Women's work within the family should be recognized as being of equal value to market employment. Such an approach would ensure that if a woman does give priority to caring work, then this is a genuine, free choice, and it is not 'forced' on her by economic necessity or social convention. Further, equal opportunity and laws against discrimination based on differences in gender are not sufficient. A case can be made for 'non-discriminatory differential treatment' as well. Women may require 'different' entitlements: maternity health care, maternity leave, income guarantees when caring for dependents, and so on. The state's services should be differentiated so as to recognize and accept women's differences from men (George and Wilding, 1994, p. 150).

Mary Wollstonecraft [1759–1797] had argued that citizenship must be extended so as to include women, and also society must aid women in their work (Wollstonecraft, 1792). This seems to combine elements of equal opportunity and the ethic of care. Can these two ideals be combined? One possibility is to argue that women can gain employment within the so-called 'caring professions' in the welfare state (in particular, health and education). In that way, women can exercise greater influence over the design and delivery of welfare entitlements that bear directly on women's experiences (Holmwood and Siltanen, 1995, pp. 56–7). This is what is called the 'feminization of the welfare state' (ibid.).

(iv) *Basic Income* – Nancy Fraser offers a second possible solution to the Wollstonecraft dilemma. According to what she calls 'the universal breadwinner model', all have rights to participate in the public sphere. This represents a liberal approach. In contrast, the ideal of 'care-giver parity' ensures the equal value of domestic work is recognized, and this represents the ethic of care approach. Neither is satisfactory, however. The first does nothing to challenge the pervasiveness of male norms; but the latter also does not remedy the marginalization of women who remain in the private sphere. Instead, Fraser defends 'the universal caregiver model'. She calls for 'a universal basic income scheme' (1994, p. 615). This would offer recognition to women for the 'work' they perform in the private sphere. It should therefore reduce the marginality of women in the private sphere. Moreover, it is based on the idea that all adults in the family are care-givers. It could therefore help ensure that both men and women share the responsibilities that come from the private *and* the public sphere (Figure 6.3).

■ **Equal opportunity**	Right of all (men and women) to participate in the public sphere.
■ **Affirmative action**	Backward-looking: Compensation for past discrimination. Forward-looking: Comparable worth.
■ **Ethic of care**	Recognize equal value of domestic caring work ('care-giver parity'). Feminization of the welfare state (clients and professionals).
■ **Basic income**	Basic income guarantee to women in caring roles. Share responsibilities in public and private ('universal care-giver model').
■ **Welfare liberalism**	Fair distribution of benefits & burdens within the family. Could the least well-off representative women accept?

Figure 6.3 Feminism and welfare

Rawlsian feminism

As we saw, ethic of care feminists argue that women's subjective feelings of hurt may provide the basis for a critique of patriarchy. This is a problematic position, however. Feminists insist that communities must be reformed for the sake of reciprocity and autonomy. Can feminists criticize liberalism for the reason that it gives priority to individual rights, and yet, at the same time, give priority to autonomy? Or, if feminists object to asymmetry and dominance, should they not also have to say that such relations are 'unjust', that they infringe the basic rights of the individuals concerned? At the same time, Rawlsian feminists have reformulated Rawls's theory, and their intention is to adequately conceptualize women's experiences in terms of liberal justice.

Rawls failed to address unjustified gender inequality in the family, Susan Moller Okin acknowledges. While Rawls assumes the 'the sense of justice' is learnt in the family (Rawls, 1971, p. 494), he does not investigate whether the family itself is just. Okin accepts the liberal view that principles of justice cannot regulate conduct within freely formed associations (such as the family, clubs, churches, etc.), except in so far as to ensure their conformity with the demands of justice. However, she argues that a distribution of primary social goods *can* satisfy the feminist demand for reciprocity and autonomy in the family. The Rawlsian approach can 'apply the principles of justice to the realm of human nurturance' (Okin, 1989, p. 249). Gender relations are just if they could be agreed to in the original position where we put knowledge of gender (along with the features mentioned by Rawls) to one side. It can even give emotion a central role in moral deliberation. Empathy does not displace a theoretical analysis of justice, but rather provides the motivation to think and act 'fairly'. In fact, empathy is needed so as to 'consider the interests of all possible selves' (ibid., p. 244), something Rawls himself expects from us. Empathy is required as 'the "least advantaged representative woman", who is likely to be considerably *worse* off, has to be considered equally' (ibid., p. 245).

Rawls's political liberalism

Rawls's later work is an effort to respond to both these lines of critique. He argues that not only can liberalism guarantee the rights, liberties, and opportunities of women, but also it will not enforce an equal division of labour within the family. Moreover, in answering the communitarian critique, Rawls concedes that the argument in *A Theory of Justice* did rely on a liberal *moral* doctrine.

A *Political* conception of justice

Only 'political' conceptions of justice are suitable to a situation of 'pluralism', according to Rawls. The 'social and historical conditions of modern democratic regimes' (1987, p. 424) include 'the fact of pluralism' and 'the fact of the permanence of pluralism given democratic institutions' (ibid., p. 425, n. 7). That is, pluralism is the 'normal' outcome when basic liberties are protected, allowing people to exercise their reason (1997, p. 573). Indeed, 'agreement on a single comprehensive doctrine presupposes the oppressive use of state power' (1987, p. 425, n. 7). Rawls proposes a *political* conception of justice.

> A workable conception of justice . . . must allow for a diversity of conflicting, and indeed incommensurable, conceptions of the meaning, value, and purpose of human life (or . . . "conceptions of the good").
>
> (ibid., pp. 424–5)

In contrast, the case made for 'justice as fairness' in *A Theory of Justice* was part of the social contract tradition, he now concedes (1993, p. xv). It was based on a comprehensive moral doctrine. Perhaps Sandel was right to argue that Rawls relied on a controversial moral philosophy, but Rawls claims to have remedied that defect.

A political conception of justice is defended on the basis of 'public reason' (Figure 6.4). Public reason replaces comprehensive doctrines of truth or right with 'an idea of the politically reasonable addressed to citizens as citizens' (Rawls, 1997, p. 574). So, justice as fairness will not be defended as a moral truth. Nonetheless, a political conception of justice cannot be equated with a *modus vivendi* (ibid., p. 589). In a *modus vivendi*, we adhere to principles of justice only because it happens to be in our self-interest and only for so long as it remains in our self-interest. Rather, 'reasonableness' is morally demanding. It requires the virtues suited to democratic politics. First, a 'reasonable' person 'neither criticizes nor attacks any comprehensive doctrine . . . except insofar as that doctrine is incompatible with the essentials of public reason and a democratic polity' (ibid., p. 574). Secondly, reasonable citizens view one another as free and equal, and offer each other fair terms of social cooperation. Thirdly, reasonable people 'agree to act on those terms, even at the cost of their own interests in particular situations, provided the other citizens also accept those terms' (ibid., p. 578). And fourth, in defending a political conception, the reasons given to others are 'reasons we might reasonably expect that they, as free and equal citizens, might also accept' (ibid., p. 579). With these four requirements in place, an 'overlapping consensus' can be attained, which is 'affirmed by the opposing religious, philosophical, and moral doctrines' (1987, p. 421).

■ **Public reason and reasonableness**

1. The politically reasonable addressed to citizens as citizens.
2. Do not criticize a comprehensive doctrine except in so far as it is incompatible with the essentials of public reason and a democratic polity.
3. View one another as free and equal, offer each other fair terms of social cooperation.
4. Agree to act on those terms, even at expense to one's own interests in particular situation.
5. Give reasons we might reasonably expect others, as free and equal citizens, might also accept.

■ **Overlapping consensus**
■ **Toleration**

6. Affirmed by opposing doctrines.
7. Recognize and accept consequences of the 'burdens of judgement'.

■ **Two principles**

8. Eliminate conflicts arising from social/economic inequality.

Figure 6.4 Public reason and reasonableness

People who profess conflicting doctrines can still think and act as 'reasonable' people. They must accept disagreement about 'the meaning, value, and purpose of human life'. For instance, Rawls does not insist on 'the whole truth' of Kant's account of autonomy, although evidently it influences his position. What principles of justice can reasonable people agree to as a political conception? First, reasonable persons are tolerant, as they 'recognize and accept the consequences of the burdens of judgement…' (1997, p. 612, p. 613, n. 95). This refers to the difficulty of '…balancing the weight of different kinds of evidence and values…' (ibid.). Secondly, an overlapping consensus can eliminate conflicts that arise from other sources, from 'differences in status, class position, or occupation, or from differences in ethnicity, gender, or race' (ibid., p. 612). Reasonable people are tolerant of differences that cannot be overcome due to the burdens of judgement. However, reasonable people could agree to 'justice as fairness', which eliminates (or lessens) conflicts between citizens' fundamental interests.

Justice as fairness

Although Rawls changes its moral standing, he still defends 'justice as fairness'. He hopes that, through the use of public reason, an overlapping consensus can be attained in support of it.

I have already discussed Rawls's first formulation of his theory of justice [see pp. 46–51]. His two principles of justice guarantee equal liberty (1), fair equal opportunity (2b), and a distribution of income and wealth that is to the benefit of the least advantaged (2a) (the 'difference principle'). The principles are in an order of priority as well. In his later work, Rawls still defends his two principles, but does so as 'the most reasonable political conception of justice' (1997, p. 581). This is done as part of a debate among 'many liberalisms and related views' (ibid.). All political (liberal) conceptions offer a list of certain basic rights, establish an order of priority, and guarantee 'adequate all-purpose means to make effective use of their freedoms' (ibid., pp. 581–2). Rawls contends that 'Habermas's discourse conception of legitimacy…as well as Catholic views of the common good and solidarity' are both 'liberal' views to the extent 'they are expressed in terms of political values' (ibid., pp. 582–3). (I discuss Habermas's 'radicalism' in Chapter 8, and MacIntyre's Thomist 'communitarianism' in Chapter 7.) Such positions are not always expressed politically. However, Rawls (and everyone else) can only engage with them to the extent they are presented (simply) as the most reasonable terms of cooperation for free and equal individuals.

Rawls defends justice as fairness as the best political conception of justice. He judges a political conception on the following basis. The better conception fixes, 'once and for all, the content of basic rights and liberties', and assigns them 'special priority' (1987, p. 442). The form of public reasoning that it specifies, also, 'can publicly be seen to be, correct and reasonable' (ibid.). Finally, both of these elements, working over time, 'encourage the cooperative virtues of public life' (ibid., pp. 443–4). In *A Theory of Justice*, Rawls assumed that 'justice as fairness' was morally right and true. His second argument is that it is the best political conception of justice. It ensures stability because if fixes rights, employs the correct conception of public reason, and fosters political virtues. The content of welfare entitlements has not changed. Each person should receive a fair distribution of primary social goods. Rawls still does not guarantee a basic level of income as a right. Many different levels of inequalities *can* be justified *if* they are to the benefit of the least advantaged. And his position does not justify compensation for natural disability.

Religion and the family

Rawls defends 'justice as fairness' on the basis of public reason and an overlapping consensus. His argument is that communitarians and feminists can be given good (moral) reasons to accept justice as fairness as a *political* conception of justice.

Rawls claims that religiously motivated communitarians can be given good reasons to accept 'justice as fairness'. We can argue from what we 'conjecture' are other people's basic doctrines, and show that, 'despite what they might think, they can still endorse a reasonable political conception that can provide a basis for public reasons' (1997, p. 594). As a fellow political liberal has claimed, even 'theocrats', who prioritize a 'religious conception of the good that is strict and comprehensive' and believe in the importance of other worldly ends, and the possibility of choosing false ends, are 'rationally committed' to liberty of conscience (Swaine, 2006, pp. 9, 49). They can freely pursue their own conception of the good only in a society that guarantees freedom of conscience (to them and others). Rawls allows us to reason from a comprehensive doctrine, religious or non-religious. He insists on the following *proviso*, however: 'that, in due course, we give properly public reasons to support the principles and policies our comprehensive doctrine is said to support' (1997, p. 584). That is, liberals must offer 'public' reasons to communitarians (and vice versa). And they alone are decisive. Liberals must show that 'justice as fairness' is the most 'stable' conception, and communitarians should accept it for that reason.

Rawls assumes that feminists can be given good reasons to accept 'justice as fairness' as well. Rawls does not equate practical reasoning with the calculations of the self-interested utility maximizer. He rejects the *modus vivendi* approach, and his is a very demanding list of the virtues required for 'reasonableness'. At the same time, he claims that 'principles of political justice are to apply directly to this [basic] structure, but are not to apply directly to the internal life of the many associations within it, the family among them' (ibid., p. 596). Individuals who form a voluntary association are free to do so on whatever grounds they see fit, so long as they do not infringe individual rights. Liberalism guarantees the rights, liberties, and opportunities of women, but it cannot enforce an equal division of labour within the family.

> [A] liberal conception of justice may have to allow for some traditional gendered division of labour within families – assume, say, that this division is based on religion – provided it is fully voluntary and does not result from or lead to injustice.
>
> (ibid., p. 599)

Rawls does assume that 'the worst aspects of this division (of labour) can be surmounted', and 'no one need be servilely dependent on others and made to choose between monotonous and routine occupations which are deadening to human thought and sensibility' (1971, p. 529). However, for Rawls, if primary goods have been distributed to all, and if the traditional division of labour does not deny anyone's primary goods, then there are no *moral* grounds (i.e. political morality) on which to find it objectionable. In contrast, feminists argue that, all things being equal, the traditional division of labour is objectionable in itself.

A critic of Rawls's recent work can take one of a number of lines. First, Martha Nussbaum argues that political liberalism must be developed further so as to adequately conceptualize the experiences of women, and also so as to be appropriate to any and all communities. A theory of justice concerned with 'capabilities' is more promising in this respect, she argues. I turn to her argument next [see p. 137ff]. Secondly, in the next chapter, I return to communitarianism in greater depth. I discuss the communitarian argument that political liberalism simply does not offer morally compelling reasons for non-liberals, despite the best efforts of Rawls and Nussbaum.

Martha Nussbaum's political liberalism

Martha Nussbaum wants to reformulate Rawls's political liberalism, and also show that feminists need not reject liberal theory. Nussbaum makes three crucial arguments. First, she contends, Rawls does not do enough to provide a liberal theory of justice that can adequately conceptualize the experiences of women. Secondly, feminists are mistaken who argue that, due to the importance of emotion, a theory of justice has only a limited relevance. Finally, political liberalism can be a universalizable, cosmopolitan, theory of justice: it can be acceptable in the non-Western and developing world.

Political liberalism revised

'Primary social goods' are resources that would be needed to pursue any system of ends, Rawls assumes. He does not question the use made of these resources. For Nussbaum, 'the Rawlsian model neglects a salient fact of life: that individuals vary greatly in their need for resources and in their ability to convert resources into valuable functionings' (2000a, p. 68). As Rawls hopes not to 'neglect any person's separate and distinct life', he fails on his own terms (ibid., p. 69). Nussbaum focuses on the end that resources can bring about: 'quality of life' (1993) and 'capability to function' (2000a). Welfare entitlements refer directly to those ends. I have already outlined in more detail Nussbaum's 'list of capabilities' [see pp. 62–5]. They include life; bodily health; bodily integrity; senses, imagination, and thought; emotions; practical reason; affiliation; other species; play; and control over one's environment (2000a, pp. 78–80).

The quality of life/capabilities approach relies on a substantive account of well-being. Initially, Nussbaum referred to her position as 'Aristotelian Social Democracy' (1990). Like Aristotle, she is concerned with 'The condition of virtuous character', which 'finds its natural fulfillment and flourishing in activity' (Nussbaum, 1986, p. 324). Nussbaum also accepts Aristotle's argument that even a virtuous person is vulnerable to misfortune, as he or she needs 'goods of the body and external goods and goods of luck, in addition' (Aristotle, NE, VII. 13, 1153b16-22). Nussbaum's 'list of capabilities' has some similarities with what Singer [see pp. 35–9] calls 'important human interests' ('avoiding pain', 'developing ability', 'satisfying basic needs for food and shelter', and being 'free to pursue projects without unnecessary interference'). Both are concerned with ends rather than resources as such. However, as a utilitarian, Singer would not offer an 'objective' account of value. In contrast, Nussbaum provides an account of what *is* the human good, even though individuals, often, do not prefer some or all of its elements. For instance, due to experiences that, Nussbaum contends, 'brutalize' or 'corrupt' perception (1996, p. 32), not all people value and pursue 'critical reflection'.

Nussbaum's second critique of Rawls concerns the emotions. Rawls asks us to view each other as free and equal and choose fair terms of social cooperation. However, we are to put our feelings for specific people to one side. Instead, for Nussbaum, emotions play a decisive role in moral deliberation. Compassion enables us to acknowledge human 'neediness and incompleteness' (1995a, p. 376). Emotion is even a central human capability: the ability 'to have attachments to things and people outside ourselves.... Not having one's emotional development blighted by overwhelming fear and anxiety, or by traumatic events of abuse or neglect' (2000a, p. 79). Emotion plays an important role in a revised political liberalism. By acknowledging human neediness and incompleteness, we can also appreciate that people vary in their need for resources and their ability to convert resources into valuable functionings. Through compassion we can justify welfare entitlements that guarantee not primary goods, but capabilities.

Finally, Nussbaum defends a cosmopolitan theory. She feels that Rawls does not realize just how promising political liberalism is as a basis for 'future thought about quality of life in the international arena' (ibid., p. 67). Rawls would only apply 'justice as fairness' to a culture already thoroughly imbued with Enlightenment moral philosophy (Rawls, 1993, pp. 4–11). In contrast, according to Nussbaum, the 'idea of the dignity and independence of the individual, her control over her material and social environment' (2000a, p. 67), is as relevant in the West as it is among women in Indian squatter settlements (ibid., p. xvii). 'Universal norms of human capability' can be used both for comparisons of cultures and also as the 'underpinning for a set of constitutional guarantees in all countries' (ibid., p. 35). Therefore, citizens of one state may have obligations to make good the welfare entitlements of citizens in another. Nussbaum accepts that 'People are the best judges of what is good for them' (ibid., p. 51). However, this does not rule out universal norms. 'Indeed, it appears to endorse explicitly at least one universal value, the value of having the opportunity to think and choose for oneself' (ibid.). Although liberals should accept obligations concerning the welfare entitlements of the citizens of other countries, they must also insist that welfare resources are used to develop capabilities.

Nussbaum's account of capabilities is universalistic, she argues. It is an account of 'human' capabilities. Nonetheless, Nussbaum argues, it is an empirically established fact that women suffer more from neglect of capability. This is the case with women's work.

> [T]o be a truly human mode of functioning, [work]... must involve being able to behave as a thinking thing...; and it must be capable of being done with and toward others in a way that involves mutual recognition of humanity. Women's work lacks this feature even more often than does men's work.
>
> (ibid., p. 82)

Further, while Rawls's prioritization of resources is in general unsound, it is particularly disadvantageous for women.

> If we operate only with an index of resources, we will frequently reinforce inequalities that are highly relevant to well-being. This is an especially grave defect when it is women's quality of life we want to consider; for women who begin from a position of traditional deprivation and powerlessness will frequently require special attention and aid to arrive at a level of capability that the more powerful can more easily attain.
>
> (ibid., p. 69)

Response to feminist and communitarian critiques of liberalism

Nussbaum proposes a version of political liberalism concerned with capabilities rather than primary goods (Figure 6.5). Now I want to

■ **Capabilities**	People vary in their need for resources and their ability to convert resources into valuable functionings.
■ **Human good**	Not a comprehensive moral doctrine. Suited to pluralism (capabilities are necessary for pursuit of any and all conceptions of the good).
■ **Empathy**	Acknowledge human neediness and incompleteness.
■ **Women**	Empirical fact, women (in developing world in particular) suffer greater deprivation with respect to capability.

Figure 6.5 Nussbaum's political liberalism

look at her defence of liberalism against feminist and communitarian critiques.

First, she argues, liberalism need not employ a conception of the self that is egoistic (2000b, p. 58). It is true that liberalism guarantees the 'autonomy' of each person. It 'should preserve liberties and opportunities for each and every person, taken one by one, respecting each of them as an end, rather than simply as the agent or supporter of the ends of others' (2000a, p. 55). This is 'the principle of each person's *capability*' (ibid., p. 74). However, this does not involve a male or a Western bias towards individual self-sufficiency. Although women often choose to make sacrifices for others, in particular other family members, it does not follow that such a woman ceases to be a 'separate' person. She is still able to distinguish her 'own body and its health from someone else's body and its health' (ibid., p. 57). We should not only acknowledge women's caring role, but also respect their separateness. It is Nussbaum's contention that only liberalism safeguards this feminist commitment to (women's) autonomy (2000b, p. 63).

Nussbaum also defends the liberal conception of the right. To secure a person's rights is to put that person 'in a position of combined capability to function' in a relevant area (2000a, p. 98). This is 'the basis for determining a decent social minimum...' (ibid., p. 75). Rights need not be formal and abstract, therefore. Such liberal rights are an adequate response to gender inequality. Welfare entitlements ought to overcome women's traditional deprivation and powerlessness, and the fact that women's work tends to lack room for practical reason and affiliation. Moreover, Nussbaum agrees with Rawls that a political-liberal approach is suited to a situation of pluralism. However, Nussbaum also claims that capabilities 'have value in themselves' and also 'have a particularly pervasive and central role in everything else people plan and do' (ibid., pp. 74–5). For that reason, 'they have a special importance in making any choice of a way of life possible, and so they have a special claim to be supported for political purposes in a pluralistic society' (ibid., p. 75). It is reasonable to ask even illiberal citizens to commit to the list of capabilities. This is the case even though she brands some traditional ways of life as 'beyond the pale'. Nussbaum's examples include 'female genital mutilation', which she characterizes as a permanent surrender of capability (ibid., p. 94).

In the final element of her defence of political liberalism, Nussbaum argues that liberal theory need not be rationalistic. Emotions are 'not brutish irrational forces, but intelligent and discriminating elements of the personality, closely related to perception and judgement' (1995a, p. 365). For instance, if I feel grief at the death of a loved one, I accept the 'fact that (say) the most important person in my life is dead' (ibid., p. 375). But the emotion is felt only because we 'ascribe high worth or importance to things and persons outside the self' (ibid., p. 376). This acknowledgement of neediness and lack of self-sufficiency is at the centre of compassion as well, an emotion that gives us good reasons to care about social justice.

> Compassion requires...the belief that another person is suffering through no fault of his or her own. The suffering must be thought to be of serious importance. And finally, the person who has compassion must believe that his or her own possibilities are similar to those of the person who suffers.
>
> (ibid., p. 378)

The feeling of compassion is based on the belief that all humans are vulnerable and the belief that some specific human is suffering. Further, this emotive response to concrete situations gives good reasons to care about a political conception of justice.

Impartiality and the capabilities approach

Nussbaum revises Rawls's political liberalism. Her account is deeper (concerned as it is with capabilities, not primary goods) and broader (applying to women and men, and members of all cultures). In this way, she argues, political liberalism can be defended against feminist and communitarian critics. However, Nussbaum defends a substantive account of the moral agent. Is it compatible with a liberal commitment to impartiality? Rawls's 'justice as fairness' guarantees the rights of each individual irrespective of the consequences of doing so. Individuals are free to do what they want with primary social goods. Nussbaum argues that 'to secure rights to citizens in these areas is to put them in a position of combined capability to function in that area' (2000a, p. 98). Nussbaum insists that she supplies a list of capabilities, not of functions, 'precisely because the conception is designed to leave room for choice' (1995b, p. 94). However, she conceives of choice and separateness in substantive terms. Hers is a 'comprehensive concern with flourishing across all areas of life... If one cares about autonomy, then one must care about the rest of the form of life that supports it, and the material conditions that enable one to live that form of life' (ibid., p. 95).

Joseph Raz (1986) is a perfectionist liberal (Cf. Galston, 1991). According to Raz, anyone committed to a perfectionist view of well-being cannot also defend liberalism as a *political* conception of justice (Mulhall and Swift, 1992, p. 250). His 'autonomy principle' 'permits and even requires governments to create morally valuable opportunities, and to eliminate repugnant ones' (Raz, 1986, p. 253). Nussbaum is interested in 'human flourishing', a life 'worthy of a human being' (2000a, p. 73). However, Nussbaum claims she provides, 'emphatically, a partial and not a comprehensive conception of the good' (ibid., p. 96). Therefore, she rejects perfectionism. She feels that perfectionism would lead to citizens being obliged to pursue a set list of functionings (or ways of life). Perfectionism is incompatible with Kantianism as well. The Kantian approach to justice 'is a certain attitude to *justification*, which is not to be derived either from actual preferences or from determinate ideals of human flourishing' (O'Neill, 1995, p. 149). Nussbaum is a Kantian (in the Rawlsian sense of developing Kantian modes of justification to defend welfare liberalism), and for that reason she is not a perfectionist. She is committed to flourishing, but not to any 'determinate ideals of flourishing'. She is of course committed to a substantive view of well-being. For that reason, let us refer to her approach as substantive non-perfectionist liberalism.

Finally, Nussbaum derives her position from Aristotle's ethics. Given Aristotle accepted gender inequalities as expressions of natural differences (Pol, I. 12, 1259b6), is Nussbaum's account of capability compatible with feminism? For Nussbaum, 'an Aristotelian who is both internally consistent and honest about the evidence cannot avoid the egalitarian normative conclusion that women, as much as men, should receive a higher education' (1995b, p. 97). More broadly speaking,

> the presence in a creature of basic (untrained, lower-level) capability to perform the functions in question, given suitable support and education, exerts a claim on society that those capabilities should be developed to the point at which the person is fully capable of choosing the functions in question.

> (ibid.)

Conclusion

The communitarian argues that Rawls's difference principle must presuppose a prior moral tie, which his impartiality then undercuts. In the next chapter, I look in greater depth at the communitarian approach to welfare. The basic contention of communitarians is that Rawls's political liberalism fails to deliver what it has promised, namely fair terms of social cooperation that are impartial. Feminists had argued that Rawls ignores the experiences of women, and for that reason an ethic of care is needed alongside a theory of justice. However, Nussbaum has successfully rebutted this charge. She has shown that a theory of justice need not be rationalistic and also it can address women's experiences and subjugation.

Perhaps, an Aristotelian conception of capability can be deployed so as to adequately conceptualize women's experience. However, serious doubt remains as to whether Aristotelian *perfectionism* can be the basis for a *political* conception of justice. Perhaps an Aristotelian account of the human good may be the best conceptual foundation for welfare entitlements, but it does not follow that, as Nussbaum assumes, in justifying welfare entitlements we can afford to be impartial about different conceptions of the good. This issue is at the centre of the argument for communitarianism.

CHAPTER 7

Communitarianism

I have already discussed Michael Sandel's communitarian critique of Rawls. I turn now to look in more depth at a number of political philosophers who have all been described as 'communitarians' (Mulhall and Swift, 1992).[1] Like conservatives, communitarians assume that considerations of merit are central to justice and welfare. Moreover, they do not reject the idea of rewards in proportion to contribution, which is so central to the conservative idea of the market. Nonetheless, communitarians do not simply repeat the conservative argument. Communitarians are concerned that the market, even the 'social' market defended by conservatives, is undermining two important goods: distributions to the needy that ensure their full membership within the community; and genuine examples of merit (virtue), which are needed to contribute to 'the good'. In fact, communitarianism can provide a critical standpoint from which to analyse the market, that is, in terms of the market's potentially negative impact on communities.

Communitarians also reject Rawls's argument that the right is both prior to the good and independently derived. For instance, Charles Taylor claims that distributive principles are always 'related to some notion of the good which is sustained or realized or sought in the association concerned' (Taylor, 1985, p. 292). As people pursue many different goods within many different communities, there is a plurality of distributive principles. Some communitarians contend that this plurality is irreducible, that there is no order of priority between principles. This reverses the precedence given (by Rawls and others) to justice or, more precisely, to a conception of justice that is independent of the good in any given community. Communitarians do believe that they can resolve conflicts over resources and conflicts between principles, however. They appeal to higher values, which justice is to serve. While the principle of merit, on its own, may justify deep inequalities, inequalities can be legitimately limited on the grounds that they undermine membership of a community and/or the pursuit of genuine goods. Communitarians also assess 'material' goods, in particular, welfare goods, in terms of their contribution to these higher goods. In Alasdair MacIntyre's work, the enjoyment of such material goods is understood with respect to their contribution to the attainment of a life of virtue. Moreover, MacIntyre's argument points towards a conception of human need that, potentially, could be applicable to all humans (1999, p. 124).

The communitarian position is not acceptable to liberals. From Rawls's perspective, communitarianism is not a 'reasonable' response to pluralism. Reasonable people accept that different conceptions of the good life are incommensurable, and therefore, they do not insist on the whole truth of *their* comprehensive doctrines (Rawls, 1997, p. 574). Further, Rawls does agree that distributive principles are plural, but he also argues that arbitrariness results unless an order of priority is placed on different principles (1971, p. 35). Finally, Rawls assumes that individual liberty will not be protected unless basic rights and duties provide a 'framework' for each individual's pursuit of his or her good (ibid., p. 31). This means that people can rightly claim certain entitlements (liberties, opportunities, and a distribution of income and wealth determined by the difference principle) irrespective of whether enjoying those entitlements will bring about communal membership or genuine goods.

Can the liberal critique be answered? Alasdair MacIntyre provides a compelling account of the Aristotelian idea of human flourishing and also our moral obligations to the needy (just-generosity), but he does so in a way that seems to confirm the liberal critique. In contrast, communitarian political theory could be based on a non-relative, universal account of human flourishing. I also look at Charles Taylor's attempt to reconcile communitarianism with some elements of liberalism, as well as Michael Walzer's pluralism.

Alasdair MacIntyre: Tradition-dependent communitarianism

Following Aristotle, MacIntyre contends that justice is a virtue, and he defends a merit-based conception of justice. He offers a needs-based account of 'just-generosity' as well. However, MacIntyre assumes that tradition constitutes political theory, the moral consensus of community shapes practical reasoning, and he equates merit with practical excellence. As a result, MacIntyre leaves himself open to the charge of relativism.

MacIntyre's critique of modern morality

MacIntyre begins with a critique of liberal political philosophy. The 'language of morality', now, is in a 'state of grave disorder' (MacIntyre, 1985, p. 2). One example is the dispute between Nozick's libertarianism and Rawls's welfare liberalism. The claims of each are logically 'incompatible' and are made on the basis of principles that are 'incommensurable', MacIntyre contends (ibid., p. 248). That is, the Rawlsian and Nozickian claims cannot be satisfied simultaneously, and Rawls's position does not impugn the premises of Nozick's (and vice versa). A rational agent in the 'original position' would choose Rawls's two principles, but it is only a rational agent in such a position that would do so. Rawls does not have the conceptual resources to establish that moral deliberation must begin from the original position, and not from (Nozick's) inherent property rights. Rawls engages in political theory but he cannot provide an objective grounding, or foundation, for his arguments. MacIntyre uses the term 'emotivist' to describe the culture in which such an approach to moral debate as Rawls's can be prevalent. For the emotivist, only factual disagreements can be resolved rationally. A 'disagreement in attitude', in contrast, is settled when the 'stronger and psychologically more adroit will' prevails (ibid., p. 17). That is, if there is no rational justification for the starting point of one's approach (such as the original position), then only the force of one's will can be used to secure agreement.

Disagreements in modern (liberal) discourse are interminable, MacIntyre argues, because we rely upon 'moral fictions'. We use a concept as if its meaning were clear, when it is not (ibid., p. 68). This is the case as concepts are available now only as 'fragments' of older traditions. Indeed, the use of 'right' by liberals has the same status now as the use of 'taboo' by nineteenth century Polynesians. The Polynesians no longer understood the concept of taboo, MacIntyre contends, because it derived its intelligibility from certain traditional contexts that had by then been lost. 'Deprive the taboo rules of their original context and they at once are apt to appear as a set of arbitrary prohibitions . . .' (ibid., p. 112).

What is the context that modern moral utterances lack, which once made them intelligible? According to MacIntyre, it is Aristotelian ideas about virtue and Christian (Thomist) ideas about divinely ordained law. They provide the following teleological (purpose-based) view: 'Within that teleological scheme there is a fundamental contrast between man-as-he-happens-to-be and man-as-he-could-be-if-he-realised-his-essential-nature' (ibid., p. 52). Moral theory shows us that it is by exercising virtues that we, as rational animals, move from the first to the second of these stages and so attain the human *telos*. Political theory must retrieve this lost context, MacIntyre assumes. That is, it must show that entitlements are justified if they contribute to the human good and are in accordance with divine law. I focus here on MacIntyre's Aristotelian account of virtue. MacIntyre supplements this with a Thomist understanding of divine law (1988).

Virtue and the *polis*

For the Aristotelian, rules of justice should forbid 'certain types of action' that involve 'harm of such an order that they destroy the bonds of community...' (1985, p. 151). They forbid 'the taking of innocent life, theft and perjury and betrayal' (ibid.). However, the members of a community should also praise virtues, 'qualities of mind and character which would contribute to the realization of their common good or goods' (ibid.). Virtues are praiseworthy character traits; for instance, moderation, courage, wisdom, justice, and just-generosity. Note, a character trait is good, it is a virtue and not a vice, if it contributes to the realization of the common good(s) of a community. However, MacIntyre does not reduce virtue to the character traits needed to pursue what is taken to be a common good, whatever that is.

First, an apprentice in a practice must learn to distinguish 'what is good relative to us here and now' from 'what is good or best unqualifiedly' (1988, p. 30). Some judgements of goodness are relative to a time and place, but we can also judge what is good as such. Secondly, riches, power, status, and prestige are 'external goods', and to achieve them one requires qualities of effectiveness alone (ibid., p. 32). However, external goods should be pursued for the sake of 'goods of excellence' (ibid., pp. 107–8). And to pursue 'goods of excellence' we require the qualities needed 'to perform and to judge well' in regard to 'what is good or best unqualifiedly' (ibid., p. 30). That is, we require the virtues. Finally, the good of a practice is distinguished from the good of the *polis* [community]. The *polis* should provide 'an integrated form of life', a life in which

▪ Good relative to us here and now.	Good and best unqualifiedly.
▪ External goods (riches, power, status, prestige).	Goods of excellence (must exercise virtues: perform and judge well vis-à-vis what is good and best unqualifiedly).
▪ Goods internal to practices.	Good as such. The community provides an integrated form of life.

Figure 7.1 Three distinctions in the analysis of 'good'

each practice and its goods has its proper place (ibid., p. 90) (Figure 7.1). And the goal of the *polis* is what is good as such, not what we take to be good, and not external goods, and not the good of some one practice.

No genuine community takes 'external goods' – riches, power, status, and prestige – as its common good(s). If we do think of society simply as a means to attain external goods, then we will think of justice as the outcome of a social contract between self-interested utility maximizers (ibid., p. 36). The (Rawlsian) social contract may be appropriate for a society that wishes merely to survive, but it is not suited to a society that wishes to pursue goods of excellence. At the same time, MacIntyre rejects Aristotle's theory of 'aristocracy', rule by a virtuous elite (Aristotle, Pol, VIII), which justified slavery and the exclusion of women and manual workers from citizenship. For MacIntyre, although hierarchy is needed to foster the virtues through education, this 'is independent of any thesis about what kinds of persons are or are not capable of excellence' (1988, p. 105).

MacIntyre insists that the concern of the *polis* 'was not with this or that particular good, but with *human good as such*' (ibid., pp. 33–4; emphasis added). However, there is a tension here as MacIntyre assumes that his own political theory is 'context-dependent':

> For all reasoning takes place within the context of some traditional mode of thought, transcending through criticism and invention the limitations of what had hitherto been reasoned in that tradition.
>
> (1985, p. 222)

Moreover, theory cannot provide general rules that will show what is just and unjust in any and every circumstance: 'what it is to fall into vice cannot be adequately specified independently of circumstances' (ibid., p. 154). Perception of salient facts will differ in each circumstance, and it will determine what is just and unjust. Finally, this Aristotelian account gives an important role to the principle of merit, and a person is judged meritorious to the extent that he or she contributes to the common good or goods. The *polis* should provide 'a shared view' of how to judge contributions to this 'common enterprise' (1988, pp. 106–7). It seems that MacIntyre is forced to equate what is just with whatever happens to be the established standards of a given *polis*.

However, MacIntyre's account of virtue does not end here. He conceptualizes need in terms of an individual's potential for flourishing as the member of a specific species. For instance, when 'we identify the harms and dangers to which dolphins are exposed... we presuppose a certain notion of dolphin flourishing' (1999, p. 63). A human flourishes *qua* human by exercising virtues, and a human is in need to the extent that he or she is unable to flourish. And from this account of human flourishing, MacIntyre derives the following moral requirement (Figure 7.2). We should give 'to another in significant need ungrudgingly, from a regard for the other as a human being in need, because it is the minimum owed to that other, and because in relieving the other's distress I relieve my distress at her distress' (ibid., p. 121). This is the virtue of 'just-generosity'. It does not justify a discretionary duty of charity. Also the duties of just-generosity are not conditional, and benefits are not in proportion to the past contributions of the recipient. For instance, we should give to the disabled in direct proportion to

---

What does 'justice' require?	What does 'just-generosity' require?
Reward in proportion to merit.	Give to the needy in proportion to need.
Merit is determined by contributions to the realization of common good(s).	Give to the stranger in proportion to need. A basic requirement of any community.

How are these entitlements justified?
1. As members of the Aristotelian community, our common goods require justice and just-generosity.
OR
2. As humans, we need to live in communities where justice (and just-generosity) is a pervasive virtue.

Figure 7.2 MacIntyre on justice, just-generosity, and rational justification

their need, not their past contributions to the community (ibid., p. 126). And many needy people are also 'strangers' to a community (ibid., p. 123).

For MacIntyre, 'a capacity for *miscercordia* [compassion] that extends beyond communal obligations is itself crucial for communal life'; and also, 'what each of us needs to know in our communal relations is that the attention given to our urgent and extreme needs...will be proportional to the need and not to the relationship' (ibid., p. 124). There are two possible interpretations of this final statement. Either, *as members of an Aristotelian community*, our basic principles and purposes call for just-generosity; or, *as humans*, we need to live in communities where just-generosity is a pervasive virtue and a widely accepted principle. This second position could be called 'universalist', or 'non-relative', communitarianism.

There is some evidence to suggest that MacIntyre wants to give an account of flourishing that is independent of the goods of various contexts:

> in every context it is as someone exercises in a relevant way the capacities of an independent practical reasoner that her or his potentialities for flourishing in a specifically human way are developed.
>
> (ibid., p. 77)

However, MacIntyre still employs a contextualist view of rationality and goodness:

> For we cannot have a practically adequate understanding of our own good, of our own flourishing, apart from and independently of the flourishing of that whole set of social relationships in which we have found our place.
>
> (ibid., pp. 107–8)

MacIntyre is concerned with one's good *qua* human being, but that good turns out to be conceptually inseparable from one's good *qua* participant in various practices. In the final analysis, to flourish is to do what is required to help realize common goods. Therefore, MacIntyre's position entails that the 'just-generous' person is guided by what is required to attain his or her good *qua* member of the community. And the needs of the vulnerable are conceptualized in terms of obstacles preventing flourishing as a member of a community.

Non-relative communitarianism

In response to MacIntyre's position, I want to explore the possibility of a non-relative communitarian political theory. I want to adapt his Aristotelian idea of flourishing so as to place it on a context-independent footing. This is an account of what is good as such for a person *as a human*. Just-generosity, then, requires that we respond to the neediness of another in virtue of our common humanity.

Against pessimism and relativism

MacIntyre defines virtues, in the first place, as character traits needed so as to attain the 'internal goods' of 'practices' (1985, p. 191). The virtues required are justice, courage, honesty, and respect for authority (ibid., p. 191). Any reason can suffice to receive 'external goods', that is, material success (1988, p. 32); but in order to attain the internal goods of a practice one must 'conform' to its 'standards of excellence' (ibid., p. 141). MacIntyre notes that many areas of modern social life are *not* suited to practices. Aristotle assumed the 'political community not only requires the exercise of the virtues for its own sustenance', but also it is to educate citizens in the life of virtue (MacIntyre, 1985, p. 195). However, MacIntyre accepts the liberal (anti-perfectionist) description of modern society: as a bureaucratic entity, it may be able to distribute 'external goods', but 'the modern state is totally unfitted to act as a moral educator of any community' (ibid.).

MacIntyre assumes the life of virtues is led within a restricted sphere. It is possible among 'traditional' groups close to, or on, the 'margins' of American society: Irish Catholics, Orthodox Greeks and Jews, and Protestants from the Southern states (ibid., p. 252). Communitarian politics is not possible at the level of the nation state, as 'modern systematic politics' is a 'systematic rejection' of 'the tradition of the virtues' (ibid., p. 255). The state must perform many tasks: 'the rule of law ... has to be vindicated, injustice and unwarranted suffering have to be dealt with, generosity has to be exercised, and liberty has to be defended ...' (ibid.). Nonetheless, 'each particular task, each particular responsibility has to be evaluated on its own merits' (ibid., pp. 254–5). Although some interpret MacIntyre as a revolutionary who rejects the modern state and market and its prioritization of external goods (Knight, 2007, p. 173), I believe his is a thoroughly 'pessimistic' account of the possibilities for Aristotelian politics. MacIntyre assumes that we are living through the new 'dark ages'. Like St Benedict, during the decline of the 'Roman imperium', we should try to construct 'new forms of community within which the moral life could be sustained so that both morality and civility might survive the coming age of barbarism and darkness' (1985, p. 263).

The second problem is relativism. The goods of a practice are 'internal', according to MacIntyre. They 'can only be identified and recognized by the experience of participating in the practice in question. Those who lack the relevant experience are incompetent thereby as judges of internal goods' (ibid., pp. 188–9). However, if a community (such as Classical Athens) is based on slavery, and the exclusion of women and manual labourers from citizenship, can the person who 'lacks the relevant experience' nonetheless criticize these activities? MacIntyre tries to provide a basis for judgement that extends beyond practices. First, he argues, a moral agent is someone that can give 'an intelligible account' of his or her actions, an agent that can be, therefore, 'held to account'; and the 'unity of a human life is the unity of a *narrative* quest' (ibid., p. 129). That is, an individual's actions must be judged against the background of his or her life narrative. Secondly, moral *traditions* provide the historical contexts for both practices and narratives; and tradition is not antithetical to reason. Although reason is 'tradition-constituted', reason in turn constitutes tradition (1988, p. 10). But if the 'tradition' or 'traditions' of Classical Athenian society also justify slavery, can those of us who do not belong to those traditions still criticize the practice?

MacIntyre explicitly rejects the 'relativist' thesis that a claim 'can be rational relative to the standards of some particular tradition, but not rational as such' (ibid., p. 352). However, MacIntyre assumes that all enquiry is constituted by tradition. He does argue that one can engage in an inter-traditional dialogue to discover new ways in which to conceptualize and respond to challenges that cannot be solved within one's own tradition. His supporters claim that MacIntyre adequately attends to the historical specificity of rationality, and yet provides a way to account for a tradition that 'offers the possibility of a more adequate grasp of reality...' (Porter, 1993, p. 521; see also Herdt, 1998, p. 538; Breen, 2002, p. 190; Kuna, 2005, p. 253). Nonetheless, for MacIntyre, when traditions confront one another 'there is no neutral way of characterizing either the subject matter about which they give rival accounts or the standards by which their claims are to be evaluated' (1988, pp. 166–7). We can reason from our own tradition (whatever it is) or from shared traditions. However, there is no traditional-neutral viewpoint from which to assess the perspective offered by each tradition, by shared traditions, or even by failed traditions. That is, as relativists assume, a claim can be rational 'relative to' some tradition but not 'rational as such'.

Finally, as Russell Keat has noted, MacIntyre is guilty of 'a normatively questionable endorsement of certain aspects of pre-modern society as against their modern counterparts' (2000, p. 123). First, he rejects individualism because rights can be justified only within the Aristotelian tradition, which provides a conception of human nature and also man's purpose (*telos*). In mainstream society and philosophy, the concept of 'right' is a mere 'fiction' (MacIntyre, 1985, p. 68). There 'are no such rights, and belief in them is one with belief in witches and in unicorns' (ibid., p. 67). Humans can enjoy rights within an Aristotelian community; they are not owed rights as persons: 'Separated from the *polis*, what would have been a human being becomes instead a wild animal' (1988, pp. 97–8). Secondly, MacIntyre believes that modern pluralism and value differentiation prevent the pursuit and attainment of the human good. The *polis* should provide 'a shared view' of how to judge contributions to this 'common enterprise' (ibid., 106–7). He objects to incommensurable values *within* a community. While he assumes that traditional points of view are incommensurable, he also assumes that each community/ tradition is based on moral consensus (1985, p. 254). The above-mentioned points are summarized in Figure 7.3.

Pessimism
Aristotelian community possible only at the margins of mainstream society. This is the same conclusion as liberal anti-perfectionism.

Relativism
Practices are based in traditions, and inter-traditional dialogue is possible. Forced to accept that claims can be rational 'relative to' a tradition and not 'rational as such'.

Normatively questionable
Traditions are incommensurable, and individual rights may be justified within *polis*. Hostile to individualism and pluralism.

Figure 7.3 Three critiques of MacIntyre

Communitarianism within mainstream political philosophy

I have charged MacIntyre with pessimism, relativism, and hostility to modern individualism and pluralism. Communitarian political theory can escape these charges, I think. Communitarians can try to play a central part in mainstream theory and offer solutions to the problems of mainstream society.

(i) *Perfectionism* – In contrast to the liberal 'unencumbered self', for communitarians, the individual is not a self-sufficient moral agent. We rely on others for a sense of what is right and good, and also for a sense of who we are. The nature and quality of social participation, and the goods pursued, are vitally important aspects of the human condition (Selznick, 1992, p. 183). And instrumental participation is different from various kinds of 'core' participation where a person sustains connections that are essential to his or her life experience and identity (Selznick, 2001, p. 174). Communitarians must also show that such core participation helps realize what is 'good as such' (in MacIntyre's terms), not just what we take to be good, or what is the good of one specific practice or community. The role of welfare is crucial as well. Welfare can be distributed so as to sustain core participation or to remedy problems such as poverty and atomism caused by the market. That is, the state can help sustain the shared pursuit of goods, and also respond to the serious needs of individuals.

(ii) *Universalism* – Communitarians do not simply reject individual rights as mere 'fictions'. However, they do argue that liberal individualism leads to a socially destructive proliferation of rights (Etzioni, 1995a, p. 6), and the 'cultivation of social responsibilities is the only way to ensure the societal conditions that rights require' (Etzioni, 1995b, p. 20). Communitarians accept that there is a tension here between universalism and particularism (Selznick, 1992, p. 194). Communitarians judge the rights and rules of a society with respect to their contribution to the substantive justice of the community (ibid., pp. 197–8). However, universalism, or 'inclusive altruism', is central to a community that looks outward rather than inward (ibid., p. 196). Communitarians should judge the substantive justice of the community against some higher standard. MacIntyre's idea of just-generosity could provide such a universal standard, if we can set it free from its contextual moorings.

(iii) *Critique* – Finally, it is argued that a 'democratic society needs some commonly recognized definition of the good life' (Taylor, 1989b, p. 182). Communitarians seek to discover and then outline the goods that we do, or ought to, pursue. However, it does not follow that a character trait is a virtue *because* it contributes to the realization of common goods. Virtue involves concern for others and willingness to make sacrifices for others (those in great need and those who are near and dear). But, as MacIntyre insists as well, virtue involves a willingness to put to the question what we take to be our ethical standards, and also virtue involves engagement in democratic debate about the content of our shared goods (1999, p. 157). However, there is no reason, *a priori*, why this democratic engagement cannot be pursued at the level of the state. Also, an analysis of ethics can appeal to universal principles if it begins from a concern with the flourishing of individuals *qua* human beings (Foot, 2001, p. 16).

Non-relative communitarianism

As I said, I want to explore the possibility of non-relative communitarian political philosophy, a position based on the Aristotelian idea of flourishing (Figure 7.4). MacIntyre has been charged with relativism. To avoid that charge, we must provide a rationale for

Against relativism	Practical reason	To deliberate well about the end in the unqualified sense, flourishing (as well as qualified ends).
Against pessimism and normatively questionable commitments	Pluralism	A way of life is valuable *if* it is compatible with a life of virtue.
	Welfare policy	1. Final good (flourishing). 2. Good as such and useful (capabilities, trust, opportunity). 3. Expedient goods (income, security).
	Principles	Criterion of need: just-generosity. Criterion of merit: justice. Moral equality: flourishing of persons. Rights of individuals to the goods needed to flourish.

Figure 7.4 Non-relative communitarianism

debate that does not presuppose just what is in fact in question, namely the truth of the beliefs that are associated with our perspective. We can start with what Aristotle has to say about practical reason and goods.

For Aristotle, the person exercising virtue does not simply 'conform' to practical standards of excellence: '...those who act win, and rightly win, the noble and good things in life' (NE, I. 8, 1099a5). That same point can be put in another way. While 'excellence in deliberation in a particular sense' 'succeeds relatively to a particular end', 'excellence in deliberation in the unqualified sense...is that which succeeds with reference to what is the end in the unqualified sense' (VI. 9, 1142b29ff). Excellence *qua* farmer, for instance, is what is required to excel in this specific practice. However, one's excellences *qua* human being are virtues, qualities required to win the noble and good things in life. The goals of practices, or a community, or a tradition are all qualified goods, and we can ask of each, do they contribute to a virtuous life? Virtue contributes to the human good, but the human good, the 'end in the unqualified sense', turns out to be a life of virtue. We must define virtues in terms of *human* flourishing. In turn, justice is a concern with human merit; just-generosity a concern with human need.

Our second objective is to show that non-relative communitarians can avoid pessimism and also the normatively questionable endorsement of pre-modern community. According to Rawls, liberal rights (and duties) provide a framework within which communities will flourish. Non-relative communitarianism makes a different claim. Rights of justice are justified by a perfectionist conception of the human good, flourishing, but the Aristotelian concept of flourishing is universalistic. This provides a way to account for pluralism (Fives, 2005). It must be recognized that the human good is pursued in ways that differ greatly. However, while there are many different kinds of life, it does not follow that all of them are good, or that they are justified by values that are incommensurable. Some standards of evaluation are required, standards that are not context-dependent, with which to judge what happens in that context. We should ask the following questions: Does the community foster and reward true merit? Does it meet the needs of the most needy without attaching conditions to that aid?

As Aristotle (NE, I.7) and MacIntyre (1988, p. 108) argue, some 'goods' are merely expedient and/or pleasurable (e.g. external goods); some are 'good as such' as they are valued for their own sake *and* because they constitute flourishing [*eudaimonia*]; and flourishing is the 'final good', it is good as such and good *qua* human being. This distinction is crucial for a discussion of welfare. I have argued for just-generosity as a context-independent standard. Just-generosity requires as well that we respond to neediness with goods that are expedient and/or goods that contribute to flourishing.

First, *expedient goods* could include income and security distributed by the state to the vulnerable and dependent. They would be expedient in meeting basic needs of human flourishing, and just-generosity requires that we give to the needy in direct proportion to their needs. On this argument, welfare rights that guarantee income are justified because of their use to persons. Secondly, a number of other goods are good as such and *also* useful in attaining flourishing. They could include the following: the full development of human capabilities, human capital (training and education), and social capital (trust and shared beliefs). This list of goods combines Nussbaum's [see pp. 137–43] capabilities, Rawls's [see pp. 46–57] fair equal opportunity, and what Fukuyama [see pp. 76–81] presented as goods relating to trust. Thirdly, however, communitarianism conceptualizes capabilities and opportunities as means to flourishing, and therefore, *pace* Nussbaum and Rawls, it does not claim to offer an impartial view of these goods. Also, *pace* Fukuyama, non-relative communitarianism provides universal standards against which to frame and conceptualize the social virtues and social aims of any given community.

MacIntyre was criticized for his views on individualism and pluralism. Also, I have argued that income and security are expedient goods, and capabilities, opportunities, and trust are good as such and *also* means to flourishing. Should we accept the duty to guarantee individual rights to such goods? To give an affirmative answer to this question we must also accept (and MacIntyre does not) the ideal of moral equality and also the validity of individual rights. If we do accept that human flourishing is a good, then we must also accept the duties to both respect and promote flourishing. I want to stress that while we should be duty-bound to promote flourishing, we must do so in a way that does not violate the flourishing of others. As it is flourishing itself that is important (not the good condition of a community where flourishing occurs), it must be the flourishing of individuals that we value. And if this is the case, then my duty to respect and promote flourishing can correlate with other individuals' rights to flourish.

This position gives priority to criteria of need and merit, and from these principles it derives a conception of moral equality and individual rights. As humans can attain an excellent life, we can define the requirements of anyone's flourishing as basic or fundamental needs. While justice requires rewards in accordance with merit, just-generosity requires that we give to the needy in direct proportion to their needs. Finally, the moral commitment to the equality of persons follows on from the importance attached to flourishing, and this in turn justifies the rights of the needy. Now, two further questions need to be addressed. What rights should persons have as citizens? And in what way should citizens be given equal treatment?

Charles Taylor: Liberal communitarianism

It could be said that Charles Taylor already offers a version of communitarianism that embraces modern pluralism and individualism, and justifies rights to equal treatment. However, what Taylor defends is best described as a liberal theory hospitable to communal difference. At the same time, he assumes principles of distributive justice are irreducibly plural. This returns us to something like MacIntyre's view that perspectives are incommensurable.

Distributive justice *within* communities

As we saw, MacIntyre assumes that Aristotelian ethics is incompatible with modern individualism and pluralism. However, Taylor argues, there has been confusion in the debate between liberals and communitarians. Despite assuming that humans are socially embedded, Taylor prizes liberty and difference highly. This is the position of Mill as well, Taylor argues, which he calls 'holist individualism' (Taylor, 1989b, p. 185). This Aristotelian position states that 'what man derives from society is not some aid in realizing his good, but the very possibility of being an agent seeking that good' (1985, p. 293). In contrast, 'atomists' assume that the aim of society is simply an aggregate of the aims of its individual members, which can be framed outside that society. For Taylor, 'a certain kind of structure of society . . . [is] an essential condition of human potentiality' (ibid., p. 294). For that reason, 'the structure itself cannot be called into question in the name of distributive justice' (ibid.). Social structures and social goods provide boundaries within which questions of distributive justice can be raised. Distributive principles only 'tell us how to resolve questions of distribution which can be considered as open and allowable in the light of the framework' (ibid., pp. 300–1).

So, what is the framework of modern society? Western societies are not only 'republican societies sustaining the sense of individual liberty and common deliberation', but also 'collaborative enterprises for the furtherance of individual prosperity' (ibid., p. 313). As individual prosperity is a good, the 'contribution principle' is here to stay; that is, some people deserve more than others if their 'contribution to this common good is more marked' (ibid., p. 298). Rawls treats the natural assets of each as a common asset, but, Taylor argues, the 'difference principle is defined for a quite different world' (ibid., p. 309). In a more recent work, Taylor in fact appeals to Rawls to justify a second principle of justice. Like MacIntyre, Taylor believes we should distribute benefits within practices on the basis of merit, where merit is determined by success in pursuit of the goods of the practice. But in contrast to MacIntyre, Taylor has also accepted a 'transcendent' (Rawlsian) standard of justice, which insists 'that we ought to eschew any claim to special treatment over others on any other basis but benefit to those others' (Taylor, 1994, p. 39). In other words, the contribution principle is mitigated in its effects by commitments associated with republicanism (Figure 7.5). A certain measure of equality is required 'if people are to be *citizens* of the same state' (Taylor, 1985, p. 311).

Holist individualism	Aristotelianism combined with individualism and pluralism. A certain kind of society is an essential precondition of human potentiality. Distributive principles answer questions considered as open in the light of the social framework.
Modern goods	■ Individual prosperity: the contribution principle. ■ Republican self-government: equal shares (& the difference principle). ■ Affirmation of ordinary life: family and production. ■ Protection against needless suffering: welfare services to the needy.

Figure 7.5 Liberal communitarianism (1): shared goods

How can a communitarian justify both equal shares and the contribution principle? Taylor discusses what he calls the 'background picture' underlying our moral intuitions in modern society. There are three 'axes of moral thinking', flourishing, status, and respect, the latter being the most significant in modern societies (1989a, p. 15). The idea of respect for other persons is connected to respect for the autonomy of such persons. However, modern respect has two other features as well: 'the importance we put on avoiding suffering' (ibid., p. 12) and also 'the affirmation of ordinary life' (ibid., p. 13). There ought to be protection offered against needless and senseless suffering, and we also value highly 'the life of production and the family' (ibid.). The former commitment can justify aid to the most needy through welfare services. The latter could justify not only demands for contribution-based rewards from work, but also claims for more autonomy and discretion for workers in work.

However, Taylor goes on to make the problematic claim that modern society 'can be seen under different, mutually irreducible perspectives, and consequently can be judged by independent, mutually irreducible principles of distributive justice' (Taylor, 1985, p. 312). For instance, because of the contribution principle, we must accept inequalities of power, responsibility, and rewards, but Taylor also offers a republican justification for the principle of equal shares. Contemporary US society does not adequately balance these two goods, he has argued. 'And perhaps this has something to do with the underdeveloped nature of the welfare state in the United States, in particular, the lack of a public universal health scheme' (1992/1993, p. 213). It is also the case that there is 'no single answer to the question of the unit within which men owe each other distributive justice' (1985, p. 312). We have duties as citizens, which include paying for unconditional universalistic services. Yet, 'the more intense or culturally vital relations of local community give rise to more far-reaching obligations of distributive justice' (ibid.). There is, he claims, an irreducible plurality of distributive principles and communal allegiances. Taylor suggests resolving these disputes by a 'politics of recognition'.

Politics of recognition

Recognition comes on the agenda once discontent emerges with approaches exclusively concerned with the distribution of resources. Recognition focuses attention on the distinctive perspectives (and experiences) of ethnicity, race, sexuality, gender, ability, etc. Should we approach recognition from a universalist (Kantian or liberal) position, which emphasizes 'the equal dignity of all citizens, and . . . the equalization of rights and entitlements' (1992, p. 37); or should we accept a post-modern 'politics of difference'? According to the latter, what we 'are asked to recognize is the unique identity of this individual or group, their distinctness from everyone else' (ibid., p. 38). And the latter position arises out of the (perceived) faults of the former. Post-modernists claim that liberalism offers recognition on terms that reflect the particular abilities and situations and dispositions of some, and not others. It is an 'assimilationist ideal' (Young, 1993, p. 162). In particular, it reflects a Western, 'white', male, and middle class perspective and experience [see pp.176–82].

Taylor rejects the 'stronger' (post-modernist) version of the politics of difference, which insists 'that one accord equal respect to actually evolved cultures' (1992, p. 42). It is, he argues, 'condescending' to accept the worth of a culture without consideration of its value. Post-modernists also assume that all perceived injustices can be re-conceptualized as instances of mis-recognition. In contrast, Taylor retains both concepts of mis-recognition and mal-distribution. Taylor also rejects a 'restrictive view' of the 'liberalism of equal rights'. In contrast to the restrictive view, Taylor assumes that rights *can* 'apply differently in one cultural context than they do in another' and that their application *can* 'take account of different collective goals' (ibid., p. 52).

For Taylor, community membership raises two issues for liberalism. First, we should 'weigh the importance of certain uniform forms of treatment against the importance of cultural survival, and *opt sometimes in favor of the latter*' (ibid., p. 61; emphasis added). Taylor's example is the attempt to ensure the survival of Quebec's Francophone culture. It does not simply make 'the French language available for those who might choose it', for 'it also involves making sure there is a community of people here in the future that will want to avail itself of the opportunity to use the French language' (ibid., p. 58). Taylor contrasts these linguistic 'privileges' with what he assumes are 'fundamental and crucial' rights, and liberties 'that should never be infringed' (ibid., p. 59): 'rights to life, liberty, due process, free speech, free practice of religion, and so on' (ibid.). His approach is 'liberal' because of the rights it guarantees to the individual members of minority groups. At the same time, as 'the more hospitable variant' of 'the politics of equal respect' (ibid., p. 61), it does not homogenize difference. However, it follows that Taylor's politics of recognition may favour cultural survival at the expense of *non-fundamental* rights. But such non-fundamental rights are brought about by (among others) the principle of equal shares. So, it would seem, departure from a commitment to equal shares is justified for the sake of cultural survival.

The second issue raised for liberalism is whether to '*recognize* the equal value of different cultures' (ibid., p. 64). Calls for recognition of a culture seem to involve the following presumption: 'that absent . . . distorting factors, true judgements of value of different works would place all cultures more or less on the same footing' (ibid., p. 66). It is only 'a starting hypothesis', according to Taylor. 'The validity of the claim has to be demonstrated concretely in the actual study of the culture' (ibid., pp. 66–7). For Taylor, however, there is no culture-neutral point of view from which to judge another culture. To ensure the judgement will not be a presumptuous imposition, a shared cultural perspective must be created. This is very similar to MacIntyre's account of inter-traditional dialogue [see pp. 151–3]. Taylor is explicitly following Hans-Georg Gadamer (1975, p. 306), and proposes a 'hermeneutic' dialogue, the search for a 'fusion of horizons' (Figure 7.6).

Mis-recognition	Plus injustice. OR Injustice can be reduced to mis-recognition.	Taylor's 'recognition'	Against condescending post-modernism. Against restrictive liberalism.
Recognition	Politics of difference: liberalism is assimilationist. OR Universalism: equal respect & equal rights.	Taylor's 'liberalism'	Ensure cultural survival *and* respect fundamental rights. After 'fusion of horizons', can recognize equal value of different cultures.

Figure 7.6 Liberal communitarianism (2): the politics of recognition

We learn to move within a broader horizon, within which what we have formerly taken for granted as the background to valuation can be situated as one possibility alongside the different background of the formerly unfamiliar culture... [I]f and when we do find substantive support for our initial presumption [of equal worth], it is on the basis of an understanding of what constitutes worth that we couldn't possibly have had at the beginning.

(Taylor, 1992, p. 67)

Taylor's work seems, at first, to overcome both pessimism and relativism. He defends a modified version of liberal equal respect, and he assumes that we can attain shared understandings of the good and of distributive justice. However, as I hope to show below, Taylor's position is problematic to the extent that he does not endorse certain universal values and rules.

Some problems with hermeneutics

Taylor seems to offer a universalistic account of the human good. He identifies a 'crucial feature of human agency, that we cannot do without some orientation to the good' (1989a, p. 33). We cannot do without 'strong evaluations', standards by which we judge our desires, inclinations, and choices (ibid., p. 20). However, following Gadamer, Taylor also adopts a 'hermeneutic' approach to identity and morality. He not only accepts 'the fundamental dependence of our thought on language' (ibid., p. 38), but also claims that a 'language exists and is maintained within a language community' (ibid., p. 35). Rationality is 'maintained' in different language communities, or horizons. Through dialogue we can attain a fusion of horizons. However, this provides us with an understanding of what constitutes worth *that we couldn't possibly have had at the beginning*. It follows that, while communities provide irreducibly plural languages of evaluation, dialogue creates new languages of evaluation that are, again, irreducibly plural. Of course, the point of entering into a dialogue, and seeking a fusion of horizons, is to attain a better understanding (not just a different one). Yet, Gadamer himself assumed that

the experienced person proves to be... radically undogmatic... The dialectic of experience has its proper fulfillment not in definitive knowledge but in the openness to experience that is made possible by experience itself.

(1975, p. 355)

We can agree with Gadamer that the fulfilment of dialogue is not 'definitive knowledge' (knowledge that is complete and final), but it does not follow that dialogue has its fulfilment in 'openness to experience'. It may be the case that we ought to be open in the sense that we ought to respect other persons and protect their right to express their opinions. But what justification can Gadamer give for *that* requirement? The other person's rights have significance not because of the otherness of his or her views, as Gadamer must assume, but because of what he or she is, namely a person. Gadamer also contends that Kantian morality requires 'that the other should never be used as a means but always as an end in himself' (ibid., p. 358). But Kant said something quite different: 'never treat *humanity* simply as a means'. Whatever the faults of Kant's actual moral philosophy, unlike hermeneutics, it sets out to provide standards with which to understand and assess each experience and perspective. As hermeneutics places value in otherness itself, it cannot step back from and assess each experience and perspective (Fives, 2006).

Like some other communitarians, Taylor accepts that basic human rights (that protect civil and political freedoms) cannot be infringed for the sake of a community's shared good (Cf. Etzioni, 2004, p. 219). However, he argues that a community's structures and goods can be safeguarded *against* claims for distributive justice that are based on inalienable or human rights. To implement the rights that would end global inequality, we would have to 'smash the present matrices in which existing standards of distributive justice have grown' (Taylor, 1985, p. 303). Moreover, at the level of each community, Taylor gives priority to the contextual good. His position entails that we may have to choose to opt for cultural survival *over* distributive justice. This would seem to lead us back in the direction of MacIntyre's pessimism and relativism: political guarantees of welfare are conditional on their compatibility with cultural survival; and standards of evaluation are dependent on each horizon (and each fusion of horizons).

Michael Walzer: Pluralist communitarianism

Taylor has argued that distributive principles and forms of communal allegiance are 'irreducibly plural'. Is pluralism a tenable position? I want to look at pluralism in more detail now, in particular, the work of Michael Walzer (Figure 7.7). He starts from the plurality of 'social goods'.

'Complex equality'	Internal standards of justice (any appeal to external standards is tyrannous). No one dominant good to be (re-)distributed. Criteria of distribution: need, free exchange, merit. Welfare: to sustain membership, and meet (socially defined) needs.

Figure 7.7 Walzer's pluralism

The distribution of goods is, he argues, 'patterned in accordance with shared conceptions of what the goods are and what they are for' (1983, p. 7).

> [D]ifferent social goods ought to be distributed for different reasons, in accordance with different procedures, by different agents; and...all these differences derive from different understandings of the social goods themselves – the inevitable product of historical and cultural particularism.
>
> (ibid., p. 6)

Walzer describes the 'just society' as one lived 'in a way faithful to the shared understandings of the members' (ibid., p. 313). He takes the caste system in a rural Indian village as his example. The just distribution in such a village is unequal. A visitor may try to convince the members of the community that all people are in fact created equal. If 'he succeeded, a variety of new distributive principles would come into view', according to Walzer (ibid., p. 314). And if those principles are violated, 'we may begin, because they will begin, to talk about injustice' (ibid.). That is, one can only describe the caste system in terms of '(internal) standards of justice' (ibid., p. 315). A system can be described as unjust only by employing the terms that its members accept.

Furthermore, there is no single set of primary social goods, *pace* Rawls (ibid., p. 8). Indeed, when 'meanings are distinct, distributions must be autonomous' (ibid., p. 10). What Walzer is opposed to is 'dominance'. One example of dominance is money determining the distribution of goods in other spheres, like welfare or education or health. Walzer defends a theory of 'complex equality' against Rawls's 'simple equality'. The difference principle states that the talented can demand unequal rewards, but they must be to the benefit of the least advantaged. This assumes that 'the dominant good . . . should be redistributed so that it can be equally or at least more widely shared' (ibid., p. 13). However, according to Walzer, this 'would require continual state intervention to break up or constrain incipient monopolies and to repress new forms of dominance' (ibid., p. 15). In any case, Rawls is wrong to assume justice is concerned with one dominant good. Walzer identifies three main criteria of distribution: free exchange, desert, and need (ibid., p. 20). Welfare is one social good among others. Distributive justice in this sphere 'has a two-fold meaning: it refers, first, to the recognition of need and, second, to the recognition of membership' (ibid., p. 78). The 'communal provision of security and welfare' is the first thing we owe to other members (ibid., p. 64). We should provide goods so as to sustain membership (ibid., p. 78), and the 'culture, character, and common understandings' of the community determines what 'wants' to provide for (ibid., p. 79).

Walzer rightly points out that 'dominance' is a serious problem. It is indeed unjust if the possession of money determines access to welfare. However, perhaps this shows how Walzer underestimates the extent to which different goods *are* commensurable. For, if it is wrong for wealth or talent to lead to the dominance of welfare, it is equally wrong for the lack of welfare to lead to lack of money (poverty) and education (ignorance). The wrongness of the situation seems to lie in the fact that humans need a variety of goods so as to lead a life that can then be called 'good'. Goods are plural, yes, but we can judge goods by a single, community-independent, standard: 'do they contribute to the human good (of this person, in this community)?' This suggests that, *pace* pluralism, the meaning of goods and distributive principles are not irreducibly plural. Secondly, Walzer assumes that the purpose of welfare is to bring about membership of the given community. However, if the community is unjust (according to community-independent standards), and if membership entails socialization, then welfare will perpetuate (and seemingly validate) injustice. That is, in particular, the caste system can be judged to be unjust without limiting ourselves to 'internal' standards of justice.

Conclusion

I have looked at four different communitarian political theories. First, I have argued that MacIntyre is pessimistic about the possibilities of exercising virtue and sustaining a genuine community in a modern emotivist culture and bureaucratic institutions. Relativism follows as he assumes that political theory and practical reason are constituted by tradition and that character traits are virtues if they contribute to the realization of common goods. MacIntyre is also guilty of a normatively questionable endorsement of pre-modern community, a hostility to modern pluralism and individualism.

Secondly, in response to the shortcomings in MacIntyre's work, I investigated the idea of a universalistic Aristotelian conception of human flourishing. Justice requires distribution according to merit, and just-generosity requires distribution according to need, as MacIntyre outlined. Receipt of resources to meet need should be conditional only on demonstrating neediness, while receipt of what one is due is conditional on having contributed in a meritorious (virtuous) way to what is 'good'. Unlike liberal impartiality, this position understands basic needs and capabilities from a controversial ethic. Unlike MacIntyre, however, this position would judge the norms and institutions of any community against a higher (context-independent) standard of human flourishing. It gives priority to need and merit (both defined with respect to flourishing), and from there derives a conception of the equal worth of persons and the welfare rights of each.

Thirdly, Taylor defends a liberal politics of equal respect that is hospitable to the recognition of difference. However, Taylor concludes that principles of justice and forms of allegiance are irreducibly plural. Difference is overcome through a fusion of horizon, but this itself creates yet further irreducibly plural principles and conceptions of the good. Finally, for Walzer, principles of justice are plural because there are a plurality of societies and a plurality of goods. In fact, it seems possible to make goods commensurable, and formulate a political philosophy that is community-independent.

I have defended the principles of justice and just-generosity in a specific way. First, they are context-independent standards, and so they can call into question any given social framework and its goods. Our obligations to others because of their neediness or their merit are fundamental moral requirements, and therefore have priority over projects for cultural survival. Secondly, so as to ensure a lack of dominance, we must be able to compare and judge the worth of different goods. Moreover, this is the case as moral equality requires us to show respect for each person, a creature with the capacity to be virtuous and a creature who may be unable to flourish. Finally, what kind of equal treatment is justified? We could accept Rawls's idea of making the situation of the worst off as good as possible, but we must judge neediness with respect to human flourishing.

These conclusions can only be accepted if we first address two important lines of critique. First, *radicalism* suggests that power relations and strategic thinking have already deeply influenced political theory, never mind political institutions. As a result, a communitarian political philosophy and communitarian politics will (unwittingly) perpetuate domination, even while attempting to be just and just-generous. The second line of critique comes from the *New Right*. They have argued that any extensive provision of unconditional welfare by the state will have a number of short-comings: it will be inefficient, unjust, and perpetuate a dysfunctional culture of poverty.

CHAPTER 8

Radicalism

As the last two chapters have shown, political theories now raise serious questions for assumptions central to modernity itself. Communitarianism and political liberalism problematize the claim that political philosophy can resolve disputes about values and principles and that the political community can implement morally justified welfare policies. For Rawls, the political community can act only on the basis of a *political* conception of justice, and communitarians give priority to virtue and the pursuit of 'goods'. This chapter takes the problematization of modernity one step further. I already discussed the Marxist argument that ideas and consciousness are the effects of class relations and forces of production [see pp. 96–103]. This is an attitude of 'suspicion', in the sense that it looks behind ideas and thoughts and feelings to their hidden causes. 'Radicals', both post-modernists and critical theorists, also take an attitude of suspicion. They set out to discover the hidden, unacknowledged relations of power and instrumental rationality that can be found in political society and also political philosophy. These relations are evident even in political liberalism and communitarianism, they contend.

For post-modernism, modernism was based on ideals of freedom, truth, and justice, but these aspirations were only apparently benign or noble. The legacy of modernism can be seen in the totalitarian concentration camp, as well as liberal and communitarian welfare states. Post-modernists do not focus on the state and its 'prohibitive' (coercive) power. Michel Foucault instead looks at the 'productive' power evident in practices like psychiatry. For instance, although the stated goal of psychiatry is self-knowledge and emancipation (for the patient), the practice is based on technologies of subordination (using knowledge to control patients as if they were objects) and strategic rationality (selecting the most efficient means to further one's aims). In making this claim, post-modernism owes a great debt to Friedrich Nietzsche's critique of charity and pity:

that clumsy deceitfulness which first adjusts and adapts him who is to be helped: as if, for example, he "deserved" help, desired precisely their help, and would prove profoundly grateful, faithful and submissive to them in return for all the help he had received – with these imaginings they dispose of those in need as if they were possessions, and are charitable and helpful at all only from a desire for possessions.

(Nietzsche, 1886, p. 117)

Jurgen Habermas's 'critical theory' represents an alternative radical approach. It arose, initially, as a response to the perceived shortcomings of Marxism (Adorno and Horkheimer, 1944). Classical Marxism assumed that humans attain their true nature through work, 'productive life'. Habermas points out that this is a one-sided view of social life and human nature, and it is a view already prevalent in the capitalist society that Marxism was to challenge. This one-sidedness tends to prioritize 'instrumental rationality' at the expense of 'communicative action'. Instrumental rationality is concerned with selecting the most effective means to administer power or seek profits; in contrast, communicative action involves dialogue whose goal is mutual understanding. The ideals of modern society (freedom, truth, and justice) *can* be realized, *pace* post-modernism, but only if neither instrumental rationality nor communicative action is given undue precedence. However, bureaucratic welfare state measures, through 'colonization', tend to impose instrumental rationality upon social interaction and, as a result, eliminate genuine communication and democracy (Habermas, 1987, p. 356).

Michel Foucault and post-modernism

Michel Foucault is concerned with what he calls 'discourses' like psychiatry, criminology, education, and social welfare. Three 'axes' characterize discourses. In discourses, we are constituted as subjects of *knowledge*, and as subjects who exercise or submit to *power* relations, but also as *ethical* subjects of our own actions. In this way, knowledge is mobilized, bodies are disciplined, persons are subjugated, *and* resistance is mobilized.

Genealogy

All types of knowledge are implicated in power relations, according to Foucault. However, he focuses on 'humanism'. It best typifies the spirit of modernity and, by extension, the modern welfare state. Humanists assume that we can, through politics, strive to overcome ignorance and injustice. However, these need not be benign or even noble aspirations, according to Foucault, as even Nazism and Stalinism strove for these ideals (1984a, p. 44). Moreover, 'humanism has been obliged to lean on certain conceptions of man borrowed from religion, science, or politics' (ibid.). This is contrary to what Foucault calls the 'philosophical ethos' of Kant's enlightenment, which Foucault differentiates from a faithfulness to the 'doctrinal elements' of Kant's philosophy (ibid., p. 42) (Figure 8.1). According to Kant, the 'mature' person does not rely on others for his or her rational and moral standards. Moreover, Foucault's 'ethos' is 'the principle of a critique and a permanent creation of ourselves in our autonomy' (ibid.). This ethos is incompatible with humanism (whether or not it takes the form of totalitarianism) precisely because humanism is hostile to critical reflection and to personal autonomy.

What does Foucault mean by 'critique' and 'autonomy'? These terms do *not* refer to the absence, or regulation, of prohibitive power. For instance, Foucault does not believe that the availability of birth control, because it limits the prohibitive power exercised over women, enhances women's well-being (1976, pp. 145, 147). Power is also productive: it 'produces' subjects of power, knowledge, and ethics. In modern medical discourse, women are subjected to medical technologies, they are made the subject matter of medical expertise, and they are encouraged to think that they realize their true identity and well-being primarily through sexuality, that is, sexuality regulated by medical expertise and techniques. More generally speaking, liberal society itself is pervaded by productive power. Liberal law is *not* the antithesis of a state of war, *pace* Locke. 'On the contrary, the law...permits the perpetual instigation of new dominations and the staging of meticulously repeated scenes of violence' (Foucault, 1971, p. 85). So, Foucault

---

1. The principle of a critique and a permanent creation of ourselves in our autonomy.
2. No foundations can be discovered for truth (and freedom and justice).
3. Productive power cannot be avoided (even in political philosophy).
4. Genealogy must be seized and turned against its birth.
Critique of 'limits': e.g. sanity, health. Experiment in going beyond limits.

Figure 8.1 Foucault's 'enlightenment' philosophical ethos

directly rejects the social contract approach of Rawls and others, because that approach is ignorant of, and will not limit or diminish the pervasiveness of, productive power.

Following Nietzsche, Foucault claims, 'there is no right, not even in the act of knowing, to truth or a foundation for truth' (ibid., p. 95). He rejects foundationalism: when we unmask power relations we do not then discover the 'real' foundations of knowledge. Foucault also rejects universalistic theory, and replaces it with many local rhetorics of critique (Fraser, 1989, p. 59). Foucault's approach, 'genealogy', is itself the product of discourses like psychiatry. There is no standpoint for critique that is not implicated in what it criticizes. Therefore, genealogy must be 'seized, dominated, and turned against its birth' (1971, p. 92). This is a 'critical ontology of ourselves' (1984a, p. 50). Its goal is not only a 'critique of what we are', a critique of limits like 'sanity' or 'illness', but also 'an experiment with the possibility of going beyond them' (ibid. p. 50). He asks, 'in what is given to us as universal, necessary, obligatory, what place is occupied by whatever is singular, contingent, and the product of arbitrary constraints?' (ibid., p. 45).

Critique works to undermine our misplaced confidence in so-called 'universal' values and norms, and in that way open up the possibilities for autonomy. Like existentialism, choice rests on will, on the determination to choose: 'in choosing his ethics he makes himself' (Sartre, 1947, p. 56). To rely on external standards (taken from religion, history, class, reason, etc.) is to be guilty of 'bad faith'.

Dissociation of identity

Foucault rejects humanist theory. He also rejects the humanist conception of the self. For humanists, each self has equal moral worth because of human rationality and autonomy; each person's autonomy must be respected; and therefore, each person, one by one, must be granted rights that protect them from coercion, that is, intentional constraints on their free choice and action. However, according to Foucault, humanism is blind to the role of productive power. Foucault is concerned with discipline (not coercion), with the body (not the mind), and with plurality (not identity) (Figure 8.2).

The notion of human identity, and in particular the equation of identity with the mind, is an illusion. 'The body is the inscribed surface of events', and it is 'the locus of a dissociated

Self (and the body)	Ethics
■ The body is the inscribed surface of events: it is disciplined in discourses.	1. Re-inscribe the body.
■ It is the locus of a dissociated self: there is a plurality of constructions & resistances.	2. Modes of relation to oneself.
■ It creates the illusion of a substantial unity: this gives way to parody.	3. Strategic and technological rationality.

Figure 8.2 Self and ethics in Foucault

self' although it adopts 'the illusion of a substantial unity' (1971, p. 83). The self is constituted by the ways in which the body is disciplined, but this constitution is never complete and the self is never a unity. Foucault rejects the Aristotelian conception of the human good. He ascribes the historical 'emergence' of the term 'goodness' to 'the various systems of subjugation: not the anticipatory power of meaning, but the hazardous play of dominations' (ibid.). He also assumes the terms used to denote liberty indicate the way in which the self has been constituted in a bourgeois society (ibid., 78–9). We cannot discover one true identity based on rationality and autonomy, therefore. At the same time, the 'body' is

> molded by a great many distinct regimes; it is broken down by the rhythms of work, rest, and holidays; it is poisoned by food or values, through eating habits and moral laws; it constructs resistances.

> (ibid., p. 87)

The body is constructed in many different ways, but it remains the site of critique and autonomy: 'it constructs resistances'.

Foucault calls for the 'systematic dissociation of identity' (ibid., p. 94). He notes (with apparent approval) that Nietzsche would 'push the masquerade to its limit and prepare the great carnival of time where masks are constantly reappearing' (ibid.). Foucault calls for parody and resistance: there is no 'real' identity to discover, but autonomy requires our resisting such identities that are imposed. How is this to come about? The body is 'the inscribed surface of events', and Foucault suggests a re-inscription of the body. This involves 'the axis of ethics' (1984a, p. 48) and 'modes of relation to oneself' (ibid., p, 49). He refers here to the Greek notion of 'cultivation of the self' (1984b, p. 43; Barker, 1993, p. 43). What Foucault suggests is a kind of self-discipline, or self-formation, through ethical practices. Such practices have a 'technological side', 'the forms of rationality that organize their ways of doing things', and a 'strategic side', 'the freedom with which they act within these practical systems, reacting to others, modifying the rules of the game, up to a certain point' (1984a, p. 48).

We are not only constituted as subjects of knowledge and subjects who exercise or submit to power. We are also 'constituted as moral subjects of our own actions' (ibid., p. 49). However, Foucault does not distinguish ethics from technological and strategic rationality.

Critique and resistance

Why do post-modernists resist the humanist goal of trying to help others and improve their lot? Foucault's 'ethos' has been described as a 'recoiling movement' that keeps ethics itself 'in question' (Scott, 1990, p. 58). He owes a great debt here to Nietzsche's account of the 'will to power'. The will to power is what is vital and strong, and therefore 'good', but it is smothered by mainstream morality, and in particular the Christian virtue of pity. 'Pity stands opposed to the tonic emotions which heighten our vitality' (Nietzsche, 1888, pp. 572–3). Pity serves only to subordinate the sufferer, prolong his or her suffering, and weaken those who feel pity. What type of post-modern politics can Foucault offer? At times, he is loath to make political proposals. Determinate projects close off possibilities, whereas Foucault prefers 'a scene where forces are risked in the chance of confrontations' (1971, p. 93). Nonetheless, in particular in later work, a political orientation can be discerned. He asks, 'How can the growth of capabilities be disconnected from the intensification of power relations?' (1984a, p. 49). His solution, ethical practices, are described 'as strategic games of liberties' (ibid., p. 43) (Figure 8.3).

The later works of Foucault seem to herald a change in direction, a change from political nihilism to political commitment, from discourse-bound relativism to ethical critical analysis. However, Foucault equates 'games of liberties' with 'strategic' and 'technological' rationality (ibid.). It is not clear that Foucault has introduced a distinctively normative element here. While moral conclusions require right actions or good character traits or beneficial consequences

An ethical stance.	Or is this a strategic use of concepts?
No longer context-bound.	Or do discourses constitute only determined historical figures?
Reject all meta-narratives.	Or is this a commitment to the 'meta-narrative' of resistance?

Figure 8.3 Critique and resistance (strategic games of liberty)

because they are right or good or beneficial, the conclusions of strategic reasoning require us to adopt a certain means simply because it best furthers our ends, whatever they may be. Moreover, moral reasoning provides us with a viewpoint that cannot be collapsed back into conventional norms and institutions. Foucault argues that the problems analysed by genealogy have their 'generality', as they recur throughout Western history (sanity and insanity, sickness and health, crime and the law). However, genealogy is always context-bound:

> what we know of it, the forms of power that are exercised in it, and the experience that we have in it of ourselves, *constitute nothing but determined historical figures*, through a certain form of problematization that defines objects, rules of action, modes of relation to oneself.
>
> (ibid., 49; emphasis added)

For post-modernists, we cannot challenge our culture in terms that transcend our self-understanding (Benhabib, 1995, p. 242). Post-modernists do appeal to mainstream values (toleration, democratic participation, and satisfaction of basic needs). Foucault himself makes a 'strategic' appeal to ideas of truth, identity, and justice (Fraser, 1989, pp. 30–1). However, the use of such values is based on a strategic interest in maintaining 'openness' to 'otherness'. Post-modern politics will not be justified with universal norms: the good, autonomy, utility, or productive life. Post-modernists assume that political projects based on what they call 'grand narratives' will lead to heteronomy (domination), because they are hostile to the plurality of identities and rationalities (Lyotard, 1984). Foucault rejects 'the programmes for a new man that the worst political systems have perpetuated throughout the twentieth century' (1984a, p. 47). However, he concludes as follows:

> I prefer the very specific transformations that have proved to be possible in the last twenty years in a certain number of areas that concern our ways

of being and thinking, relations to authority, relations between the sexes, the way in which we perceive insanity or illness.

(ibid., pp. 46–7)

Foucault is offering support for local rhetorics of critique and resistance. How can his support be justified, and what reasons can be given to accept that such resistances are beneficial or just? For instance, in the treatment of the disabled, we may praise programmes that show a genuine appreciation for human vulnerability (MacIntyre [see pp. 145–50]) or those that justly compensate for natural disadvantage (Dworkin [see pp. 59–61]). But giving this praise must be based on something more than strategic efforts to resist domination. Surely they must be based on some (genuine, true) 'grand narrative'?

The post-modern welfare state

Foucault's genealogical analysis not only focuses on the disciplinary practices of the body, but also investigates the contemporary limits of subjugation (productive power) and the spaces available for strategic games of liberty (autonomy). A 'Foucauldian' approach to welfare starts from these commitments.

Genealogy of 'dependency'

Nancy Fraser and Linda Gordon employ 'genealogy' as a tool of feminist analysis. Like Foucault, they 'aim to defamiliarise taken-for-granted beliefs in order to render them susceptible to critique and to illuminate present-day conflicts' (Fraser and Gordon, 1994, pp. 310–11). Their concern is with 'dependency'. They analyse the ways in which 'dependency' has been constructed in pre-industrial, industrial, and post-industrial society. It was only with industrial society that dependency came to be a morally or psychologically deviant trait of individuals, they argue. In particular, women's economic dependence came to signify moral and psychological dependence as well. This genealogy of dependency is to show that 'independence' is a socially constituted identity. 'Fear of dependency, both explicit and implicit, posits an ideal, independent personality in contrast to which those considered dependent are deviant' (ibid., p. 332). Further, the opposition between independent and dependent 'maps onto a whole series of hierarchical oppositions and dichotomies': 'masculine/feminine, public/private, work/care, success/love, individual/community, economy/family, and competitive/self-sacrificing' (ibid.). Therefore, independence is a socially constructed identity, but also it helps perpetuate hierarchy and asymmetrical relations, in particular, patriarchal domination.

What does this approach offer? 'A genealogy cannot tell us how to respond to today's discourse about welfare dependency' (ibid.). However, it does 'suggest' that an 'adequate response would need to question our received valuations and definitions of dependency in order to allow new, emancipatory social visions to emerge' (ibid.). Indeed, a number of 'oppositional discourses' have been generated among welfare recipients to challenge the prevailing view of dependency. They 'reject the dominant emphasis on dependency as an individual trait. They seek to shift the focus back to the social relations of subordination' (ibid., p. 330). They also call for more substantial allowances and an end to 'infantilization due to supervision, loss of privacy, and a maze of bureaucratic rules...' (ibid.). For example, the National Welfare Rights Organization, established in the United States in the 1960s, sought to cast welfare as an active relationship of claiming rights rather than receiving charity; and they 'insisted that their [women's] domestic labour was socially necessary and praiseworthy' (ibid., p. 329).

A post-modern approach to welfare will do the following, therefore: (i) it will stress the social construction of the situation of dependency, as well as the category 'dependency'; (ii) it will call for welfare 'rights' so as to limit surveillance and discipline; and (iii) it will try to open up spaces of ethical practice, for instance the freedom to remain outside the formal economy.

Hegemony and welfare

Post-modernism is described as an exercise in 'clearing the ground', in 'undermining accepted narrative accounts so that the disadvantaged are able to make new claims against those with whom they are in perpetual struggle' (Fitzpatrick, 2001, p. 180). Nonetheless, Foucauldian genealogy 'allows new, emancipatory social visions to emerge'. What is the justificatory basis of post-modern emancipation? Some post-modernists make a 'strategic' use of values and principles. For Iris Marion Young, post-modern critique not only 'exposes the meaning of categories as *contextual*, but also reveals their differentiation from others as *undecideable*' (1993, p. 159; emphasis added). That is, the categories we use are always context-bound (within situations, or discourses). Moreover, these categories can never demarcate clear boundaries between things (e.g. the able and the disabled person) or between concepts (e.g. 'ability' and 'disability'). Nonetheless, Young also claims to have identified 'the primary moral ground' of a 'heterogeneous unity': individual civil and political rights, a guaranteed basic minimum of social goods, and group-related rights (ibid., pp. 165–6) (Figure 8.4). What are the *contextual-strategic* reasons for accepting this political vision? In a 'heterogeneous' public, she claims, 'the social groups of the society have a differentiated place in that public, with mutual recognition of the *specificity* of the groups in the public' (ibid., p. 165; emphasis added). That is, the reason for adopting these norms is the attainment of public recognition of what one takes to be one's specificity (Cf. Leonard, 1997, p. xiv).

For Chantal Mouffe, a heterogeneous public sphere requires what she calls 'hegemony'.[1] 'Hegemony' is the political construction of a shared identity, 'we' (Mouffe, 1992a, p. 234). It is always an expression of power, although one that is challengeable; and as it presupposes an excluded other, a fully inclusive community is never realized (ibid., p. 235). Mouffe defends liberal-democratic values 'in a contextualist manner', as 'constitutive of our form of life' (1996, p. 5). However, this defence is also a critique. Mouffe defends a social democratic conception of citizenship, but she argues that social democrats have not given due consideration to differences of identity (1992b, p. 4). She does accept the need to limit openness. A pluralist society needs allegiance to the political principles of modern democracy (ibid., p. 11). However, room is left

---

Demands made by post-modernists:	Incoherence?
▪ Individual civil & political rights.	Recognize specificity of identity and contextual meaning of categories **BUT**
▪ Basic social minimum.	Differentiation of categories undecideable (i.e. cannot
▪ Group rights.	demarcate clear boundaries between things and concepts)

Figure 8.4 Post-modernist argument made for heterogeneous unity

for resistance. An 'unresolveable tension' between liberty and equality preserves 'undecideability' (ibid.).

Mouffe's point is that if we accept that political issues are undecideable then we will see the reason for vibrant democratic participation (Cf. Bauman, 1991, p. 234.). However, there is a strong suspicion that Mouffe empties democratic participation of any rational or reasonable grounds by insisting, at the outset, that the questions it deals with are undecideable. In MacIntyre's terms, if there is no rational basis for the decision to adopt one principle rather than another (liberty rather than equality, say), then such a decision will be compelling only in so far as 'the stronger and more adroit will prevails' (MacIntyre, 1985, p. 17). This is an odd move for Mouffe, as she wishes to defend democracy against those who would use force rather than argument when faced with 'otherness'. Moreover, it shows little interest in the efforts that are being made (by almost all the theorists discussed in this book so far) to reconcile values like liberty and equality. Further, if categories are undecideable, how can the post-modernist ensure the recognition of the 'specificity' of groups, and how can it be claimed that meanings are 'contextual'? To recognize specificity, or to identify a context, presupposes the ability to delineate one thing from another.

Modes of relation to oneself

Foucault is not just concerned with knowledge and power. He calls for greater possibilities for strategic games of liberties (or 'ethics'). In a similar vein, Mitchel Dean discusses the provision of welfare in terms of 'governmentality'. It refers to the 'calculated means' taken to 'direct human conduct' (1995, p. 561). He also argues that there is a close link between 'practices of government' and 'practices of the self'. State agencies seek to shape the conduct, aspirations, and capacities of specified political and social categories, and 'enlist' them in particular 'strategies of ethical self-formation' (ibid., p. 563). Therefore, ethical practice can arise from resistance, but also it can be enlisted by disciplinary practices. Dean also contends that no particular political project is more suited to enlisting ethical practices (1991, p. 14). Policies designed to encourage economic self-reliance and those that, in contrast, extend the scope of state provision both involve 'discursive constitution' and moral and political 'governance'. They create ways of theorizing, knowing, and classifying; and they implement governance in different forms of treatment, relief, discipline, deterrence, and administration (ibid., p. 9).

Can we conceptualize welfare entitlements in terms of governance? Post-modernism represents 'deteriorating confidence in universalizing approaches...and...increasing fragmentation and uncertainty of social life' (Taylor-Gooby, 1994, pp. 398–9). It rejects a 'traditional' approach to 'human betterment based on a logic of universalism and substitutes its own account based on particular interests' (ibid., p. 399). This limits the role of a central organizing agency in welfare, the state, and extends the role of informal social groups along with consumerism. It also reflects growing skepticism of professional authority. Post-modernism also directs focus away from issues of redistribution onto those of 'recognition'. Claims to welfare are justified now by 'age, gender, ethnicity, sexuality and disability' (ibid.). Difference is given priority over equality. Finally, rather than challenging current practices, it could be argued that it simply reflects the principle recent changes in social policy: 'decentralization, consumerism, the use of new technology to transform management, stress on the non-state sector, the decline in status of professionals...and the growth of privatization' (ibid.).

Some problems with post-modernism

If post-modernists have one aspiration, or basic commitment, it is openness to otherness. For post-modernists, this involves a necessary awareness of undecideability. However, I think they have denied themselves the conceptual resources needed to rebut the charge that post-modernism involves a willing capitulation to relativism and immoralism.

First, for post-modernism, *welfare is an area of strategic games of liberty that must be reclaimed within (or at the margins of) disciplinary practices, and resistance can be carried out within practices that deliver welfare* (Cf. O'Brien and Penna, 1998, p. 9). However, as Dean's work makes apparent, disciplinary practices also enlist ethical self-formation for their ends. Post-modernists call for greater ethical self-determination, yet also refuse to demarcate 'games of liberty' from subjugation. This is a form of immoralism to the extent that they refuse to distinguish right and wrong, good and bad. Similar ambiguity is evident when post-modernists address the market. They call for parody, and it is as consumers chiefly that we can pursue such frivolous identity construction. However, for post-modernism, consumerism is also a disciplinary practice in which subjects are constituted. Just as self-worth is decided by what one consumes (Schram, 1995, p. 35), the 'underclass' is defined as those who are deficient as consumers (ibid., pp. 64–5).

Secondly, post-modernists claim, *grand narratives must be replaced by local rhetorics of critique*. They seem to accept the relativist contention that claims can be rational 'relative to' a discourse or set of interests, but never 'rational as such'. However, post-modernists also make strategic use of transcendent, non-insular values so as to keep political horizons open to otherness. They seem to rely on values for which they cannot (are unwilling to) provide a justification. At the same time, post-modernists may be impotent when faced with unjust, or harmful, political movements, that is, movements antithetical to post-modern values of autonomy and critique. This is the case because they deny the significance of *any* such grand narratives. For instance, 'economic liberalism' involves '. . . financial constraint, the privatization of services, . . . increased inequality' (Taylor-Gooby, 1994, p. 388). Economic liberalism is a 'grand narrative' with (it is claimed) harmful effects on the autonomy of the marginal and vulnerable, but post-modernism can oppose it only with local rhetorics and ethical practices.

Post-modernism is open to two serious objections. It calls for greater ethical practice, and yet, due to immoralism, it cannot distinguish games of liberty from subjugation; and due to relativism, it cannot oppose unjust and harmful developments, even those that are directly opposed to post-modernist goals of autonomy and critique. However, Habermas offers an alterative 'radical' approach. To introduce Habermas's critical theory, I will recap on the main themes of radicalism.

(i) *Theory* – Radicals 'unmask' the power relations and instrumental rationality that are evident even in political theory itself. However, Foucault assumes that knowledge is context-dependent and also inseparable from power. His genealogical approach offers an 'affirmation of knowledge as perspective', and a 'rancorous will to knowledge' (1971, pp. 90, 95). Habermas argues that not only is post-modernism unacceptable on moral and epistemological grounds, as it involves relativism and immoralism. It is incoherent as well, as post-modernists must implicitly assume that their argument will be accepted on the basis of its rationality (1990, p. 80).

(ii) *Self* – Radical positions focus on inter-subjective relations rather than subjectivity because social forces constitute knowledge and morality. Post-modernists conceptualize the self as the creation of specific discourses. Within discourses, there is a plurality of positions to occupy and a 'proliferation of struggles' (Laclau, 1988, p. 252). However, Habermas offers a universalizable account of the human capacity to speak and act. In all efforts to reach understanding, humans assume certain universal rules of argumentation, namely that a morally right proposal is in everyone's interests and would be approved by the participants in a practical discourse (1990, pp. 65, 67).

(iii) *Politics* – For radicals, power is productive, as well as prohibitive. While Foucault claims that power is capillary, for Habermas it has 'capillary effects' (Habermas, 1994a, p. 290). However, post-modernists make 'strategic' use of mainstream principles and they defend democracy 'in a contextualist manner' as 'constitutive of our form of life' (Mouffe, 1996, p. 5). In contrast, for Habermas, in 'communicative action' we are motivated by rationality alone, by the 'force of the better argument' (1990, p. 89). We *can* employ universal principles in defending principles of social justice.

Jurgen Habermas and critical theory

Habermas rejects what he sees as post-modernist relativism, immoralism, and incoherence. He also claims to have identified the universal pragmatic presuppositions of all communication, and offers a radical-democratic interpretation of political liberalism.

Communicative action and universal pragmatic rules of argumentation

Habermas describes Foucault's post-modernism as a relativistic will to power. Foucault claims there is no way to validate statements by 'standards of truth claims that would transcend local agreements', and Foucault also assumes 'the meaning of validity claims consists in their power effects' (Habermas, 1994a, p. 279). However, Habermas contends, the attempt to state the relativist position involves a 'performative contradiction' (1990, p. 80) (Figure 8.5). The post-modernist 'concludes that attempts to ground the universal validity of principles are meaningless' (ibid., p. 80), but he or she

1. Performative contradiction: the claim made is that reason is context-bound and
                                    strategic. Yet, this implicitly appeals to universal
                                    standards of rationality.
2. Reject immoralism: distinguish 'communicative action' from 'instrumental
   rationality'.
3. Reject relativism: universal pragmatic presuppositions of communication; the
   ideal speech situation.

Figure 8.5 Habermas's rejection of post-modernism

'necessarily assumes the validity of at least those logical rules that
are irreplaceable if we are to understand his argument as a refutation' (ibid., p. 81). The act of stating the relativist position contradicts the content of that statement. To defend relativism is to
presuppose just that which relativism denies: that this claim
could be justified by context-independent standards of rational
justification.

Foucault also offers an immoralist position. He equates ethical
modes of relation to oneself with 'strategic' rationality. Habermas
instead argues that whereas strategic rationality is an attempt 'to
influence the behaviour of another by means of the threat of sanc-
tions or the prospect of gratification', in communicative action we
seek '*rationally* to *motivate*' another by the offer contained in the
speech act (ibid., p. 58). Foucault's is an immoralist position, as he
praises Nietzschean qualities of 'vitality', and also refuses to distinguish right from wrong. However, although Foucault assumes
resistance is preferable to submission, he cannot say why resistance
is ever the *morally* right response (Habermas, 1994a, pp. 283–4).
How can he show that resistance is justified if his own intervention is
nothing more than a context-dependent rancorous will to
knowledge?

Moral issues in the political realm should be debated through
communicative action, according to Habermas. It is the pursuit of
mutual understanding, that is, 'the intersubjective recognition of
validity claims' (1990, p. 58). Why should we restrict ourselves to
communicative action? Habermas identifies certain universal pragmatic rules of moral argumentation. A proposed norm must satisfy
the 'principle of universalization': 'All concerned can accept the
consequences and the side effects its *general* observance can be
anticipated to have for the satisfaction of *everyone's* interests...'
(ibid., p. 65). However, we cannot justify norms by theoretical

analysis alone, *pace* Rawls. Moral argumentation is 'to settle conflicts of action by consensual means' (ibid., p. 67), whereas a purely theoretical approach, due to the unnoticed prejudices of the theorist, could unwittingly perpetuate the subordination of marginal and powerless groups. Therefore, Habermas proposes 'the principle of discourse ethics' in addition: 'Only those norms can claim to be valid that meet (or could meet) with the approval of all affected in their capacity *as participants in a practical discourse*' (ibid., p. 66).

What does Habermas mean by 'practical discourse'? All argumentation presupposes the following rules of the 'ideal speech situation' (ibid., p. 89):

(3.1) Every subject with the competence to speak and act is allowed to take part in a discourse.

(3.2) a. Everyone is allowed to question any assertion whatever.

b. Everyone is allowed to introduce any assertion whatever into the discourse.

c. Everyone is allowed to express his attitudes, desires, and needs.

(3.3) No speaker may be prevented, by internal or external coercion, from exercising his rights as laid down in (3.1) and (3.2).

These are 'ideal', improbable, conditions of communication. However, they are the conditions presupposed by every claim to validity. Even the post-modernist must presuppose them, and, for this reason, the post-modernist is guilty of the performative contradiction. The structure of communication 'rules out all external or internal coercion other than *the force of the better argument* and thereby also neutralizes all motives other than that of *the cooperative search for truth*' (pp. 88–9; emphasis added). Habermas's point is that we cannot understand the post-modernist to be making a validity claim if he or she also insists that every such claim is a merely context-dependent, strategic move in ongoing relations of subjugation.

A radical-democratic interpretation of political liberalism

Habermas identifies a distinctively moral perspective. In communicative action, we can, and should, relate to ourselves from the perspective of 'the other'. Society, in part at least, is reproduced through communicative action. However, people are not only

Moral perspective: take the perspective of the other in communicative action.
Observer: from external standpoint, see through illusions (one by one).
Private autonomy: necessary (*pace* republicans).
Public autonomy: necessary (*pace* Rawls's liberalism).

Figure 8.6 Radical-democratic interpretation of political liberalism

'participants' in the process of social reproduction. In modernity in particular, through communicative action we can also adopt the standpoint of the 'observer' (Benhabib, 1995, p. 238) (Figure 8.6). We can rationally analyse the features of any given context as if we were outside that context. Habermas conceives of the self in terms of 'linguistically generated intersubjectivity' (1994a, p. 297). Like post-modernists, he rejects a subject-centred approach. However, Foucault uses the term 'individualization' to describe the ways in which persons are 'constituted' through disciplinary practices. He never accepts that modernity brings greater scope for self-determination. According to Habermas, through reflection we can 'dissolve' 'self-engendered objective illusions' (1994a, p. 300). 'But its liberating force is directed towards *single* illusions: It cannot make transparent the *totality* of a course of life . . .' (ibid.).

Habermas accepts Rousseau's republican belief that 'equal rights to communication and participation are not just important for the elaboration of subjective private rights' (Habermas, 2005, p. 2). Rather, they make possible 'a practice carried out by citizens jointly and valued as an end in itself' (ibid.). However, Rousseau's republicanism grants equal rights 'only within the restrictions of a particular ethos' (ibid., p. 3). Habermas agrees with Rawls's 'political' liberalism that a clear distinction should be made between the 'right' and the 'good' (Habermas, 2005, p. 10). A society should guarantee 'equal respect for and consideration of everyone', along with each person's 'right to conduct her life according to her own preferences and convictions' (ibid., p. 1). At the same time, Rawls is wrong to think that political norms are justified by theoretical analysis, independent of political participation. Citizens 'in their roles as democratic co-legislators are bound to procedures of *reciprocal* perspective-taking' (Habermas, 2005, p. 12). For this reason, private and public autonomy are mutually necessary. *Pace* Rousseau, we can exercise political rights only if we are in a position to 'judge and act independently'; and *pace* Rawls, we can enjoy private autonomy only if we also exercise political rights for the sake of 'the common good' (ibid.).

Critical theory and the welfare state

The distinction Habermas makes between communicative action and strategic rationality is crucial for his theory of welfare. Welfare entitlements are acceptable only if they can be justified in the 'ideal speech situation'. They not only must overcome both mal-distribution of goods and the mis-recognition of identities, but also welfare entitlements must not lead to a damaging spread of strategic rationality.

Politics of recognition and basic income

Habermas wants to give due consideration to the issues of distribution *and* recognition. A system of rights must not be blind to unequal social conditions *or* to cultural differences. A theory of rights 'requires a politics of recognition that protects the integrity of the individual in the life contexts in which his or her identity is formed' (1994b, p. 113). Habermas assumes that political struggles have been necessary for the consistent actualization of rights. The feminist movement is taken as illustrative. Some welfare programmes have led to 'overrepresentation of women in the lower wage brackets, the problematic notion of "child welfare", the increasing "feminization" of poverty' (ibid., p. 115). This mal-distribution of goods is caused by mis-recognition of the women concerned. For instance, single mothers in poverty suffer from the presumption that they should be playing a traditional role within a family that has a male breadwinner. Due to 'normalizing' (ibid.) interventions made on the basis of a controversial conception of the good, women are mis-recognized and suffer from mal-distribution.

Habermas defends the following basic welfare guarantees: 'a roughly equal minimum wage' and 'the creation of identical conditions for forging individual life plans' (1999, p. 57). The latter could represent what Philippe van Parijs defines as a 'basic income'. It is paid '1. to individuals rather than households; 2. irrespective of any income from other sources; 3. without requiring any present or past work performance, or the willingness to accept a job if offered' (Van Parijs, 1992, p. 3). At the same time, Habermas's call for a 'roughly equal minimum wage', in contrast, is obviously conditional on employment. This could be brought about by a 'negative income tax', which makes payments based on how far the recipient's income falls below the tax threshold. This policy is associated with the pro-market, anti-statist thinking of Milton Friedman (1962), US president Richard Nixon in the 1970s, and New Labour's use of 'tax credits' in Britain [see pp. 200–203]. Habermas shares a suspicion of statism and a belief that welfare entitlements can be illegitimate when they extend bureaucracy [see pp. 189–92].

Habermas defends a basic income on the basis of both autonomy and impartiality. A basic income is received without conditions attached. It is generous enough to ensure that recipients can make career and family decisions that are not determined by economic necessity. Also, it should help ensure each has an independent standing within a community of participants in democratic debate. Moreover, the distribution of a basic income is impartial: it does not involve value judgements of a person's work performance or family structure. In contrast, Charles Taylor's principle of 'equal shares' involves a communitarian commitment to controversial values [see pp. 158–64]. Like Habermas, John Rawls is concerned to ensure impartiality and protect autonomy. Rawls also believes that socio-economic deprivation may lessen the 'worth of liberty' of those affected. Finally, although 'the government guarantees a social minimum' in Rawls's scheme, he believes that this can be attained either by 'family allowances and special payments for sickness and unemployment' or by a negative income tax (1971, p. 275).

Habermas agrees with the 'radical feminist' Nancy Fraser that the relevance of different experiences of 'need' must be publicly debated (Habermas, 1994b, p.115). Fraser and Gordon's position [see pp. 176–7] does depart from Foucault's approach. While Foucault claims to avoid moral judgement, they 'welcome normative-political reflection' (Fraser and Gordon, 1994, p. 311). However, in a manner reminiscent of Foucault, Fraser and Gordon 'seek to dispel the *doxa* surrounding current US discussions of dependency by reconsidering that term's genealogy' (ibid., p. 310). Habermas explicitly rejected post-modernism for its incoherence, immoralism, and relativism. Habermas and Foucault do share a generalized suspicion of power. Habermas noted the 'importance of his [Foucault's] fascinating unmasking of the capillary effects of power' (1994a, p. 290). However, Fraser and Habermas agree that issues of recognition and reward are irreducible. Therefore, they reject the post-modernist approach that reconceptualizes questions of distribution as struggles for identity recognition (Fraser, 1999, p. 30).

As we saw, Habermas rejects communitarianism. According to Habermas, Taylor's approach to recognition gives 'collective rights' priority over 'respect for the unique identities of each individual, regardless of gender, race, or ethnicity' (Habermas, 1994b, p. 110). Habermas assumes we cannot attain consensus on 'ethical' issues. Ethical judgement

> is based on strong evaluations and determined by the self-understanding and perspectival life-projects of particular groups, that is, *by what is from their point of view "good for us," all things considered*.
>
> (pp. 122–3; emphasis added)

Habermas rejected Foucault's position as it involves the following contradiction: the claim that all reasoning is context-bound and merely strategic conflicts with the implicit appeal made to universal rational standards. However, Habermas also believes that when we reason about what is 'good' we do so in a way that is context-bound and presupposes our interests. Habermas avoids contradiction, however, if it is the case that his own theory and 'moral' deliberation about justice are context-independent. We could call such a two-tier approach 'benign relativism' (Scanlon, 1995, p. 230). He is offering a non-relativistic account of how 'ethical' reflection is relativistic.

We cannot attain consensus about what is 'good', he claims. However, we also cannot attain consensus with those who refuse to enter communication or to respect the rights of others to engage in communication. Habermas agrees with Rawls that we need only try to accommodate 'non-fundamentalist worldviews', those 'not unreasonable comprehensive doctrines' (Habermas, 1994b, p. 133). Political integration of 'citizens ensures loyalty to the common political culture' (ibid., p. 134). However, the system is neutral 'vis-à-vis communities that are ethically integrated at a sub-political level' (ibid.). Can Habermas really maintain that democratic participation is necessary for the justification of political norms, and yet agree with Rawls that recognition cannot be extended to 'fundamentalists'? Rawls justifies this exclusion through a theoretical analysis of moral equality, but Habermas had argued that political norms can be justified only through practical discourse. Moreover, Habermas had stated that all those capable of speech and action have a right to engage in the ideal speech situation [see pp. 182–4].

If Habermas wants to avoid falling back on a Rawlsian liberalism
to justify this restriction of political inclusion, then, I would argue,
he should turn to ethics. One could legitimately exclude fundamentalists to the extent that their position is inimical to certain virtues or
goods deemed essential in a just society (Cf. Habermas, 1996).
However, Habermas had hoped to base the just society on universal
pragmatic rules of argumentation, and he hoped that norms would
be justified by the (non-ethical) moral consideration of rightness
and the general interest.

Colonization of the life-world and environmentalism

Both public and private autonomy are required for communicative
action, according to Habermas. Also, through communicative action
we attain 'life-world' integration. Habermas distinguishes integration
in the life-world from integration in 'systems' (1987, p. 309). He also
argues that social crises may result if integration is prevented. First,
'cultural impoverishment' occurs as a result of the elitist splitting off
of expert cultures from everyday life: this can lead to 'fragmented
consciousness', the inability to engage in communicative action
(White, 1988, p. 117). Consciousness is fragmented in this way
when life-world integration is compromised. Secondly, 'colonization
of the life-world' occurs when the imperatives of independent sub-
systems press in from the outside on the life-world, that is, when
communicative action is displaced by concerns with profitability and
administration. Moreover, according to Habermas, colonization is
caused not only by an unregulated capitalism (colonization by the
medium of money), but also by a welfare state (colonization by
administrative power) (Figure 8.7).

Social crises	Colonization of life-world and displacement of democratic will-formation. Cultural impoverishment and fragmented consciousness.
Constitutive juridification	Freedom-reducing. This critique is not applicable to guaranteed basic income.
Post-productivism/ environmentalism	1. Autonomous production: convivial tools. 2. Consume less and equitable distribution. 3. Work less: job-sharing.

Figure 8.7 Anti-statism and environmentalism

The welfare state threatens colonization of the life-world, but only to the extent that it extends freedom-reducing 'juridification' (Habermas, 1987, p. 362). Juridification can be freedom-guaranteeing when it gives state-sanction to already informally constituted action. Examples include basic constitutional rights and criminal law. In contrast, juridification is freedom-reducing when its rules are 'constitutive' (White, 1988, pp. 114–15). For instance, welfare state regulation comes in the name of expanding social rights. However, it also creates a new sort of dependency between clients and bureaucratic administrators (ibid., p. 112). Social policy may guarantee legal entitlements to income in cases of illness or old age, but this is a 'juridification of life risks' that exacts a 'noteworthy price' (Habermas, 1987, p. 362). The price paid includes the 'bureaucratic implementation' and 'monetary redemption' of welfare entitlements (ibid.). Habermas's discussion of juridification is evidence once again of a considerable affinity with Foucault's approach. Both claim that even ameliorative measures can involve 'productive' power. However, Habermas, unlike Foucault, distinguishes legitimate from illegitimate power. Juridification is illegitimate only when it is 'constitutive'.

Habermas is a critic of welfare programmes that lead to constitutive juridification. However, this suspicion of statism, according to his critics, simply supports the already dominant New Right [see pp. 196–203] position (Holmwood, 1993, p. 99). At the same time, Habermas defends substantial welfare guarantees, as we saw. Negative income tax and guaranteed basic income are defended on the basis that they require less (rather than more) 'normalizing' intrusion. He also argues that politics must 'catch up' with globalized markets. Starting with the European Union, we should build towards cosmopolitan democracy. He is 'not challenging the primacy of market led integration per se' (1999, p. 54). Nonetheless, 'every step towards market deregulation entails a simultaneous disqualification or self-restriction of political authority *qua* medium for enacting binding decisions' (ibid., pp. 54–5). Habermas does not want to move communicative action into the realm of systems integration; for instance, he does not call for workers' democratic control of the process of production. However, Habermas is calling for a strengthening of democracy. This in turn depends 'on the existence of a political culture shared by all citizens' (ibid., p. 58). Only then will people be willing to 'stand by one another' with respect to basic welfare guarantees.

Although Habermas supports rights to an unconditional basic minimum, he remains hostile to bureaucratic or juridified welfare state structures. He calls for the 'democratization of decision-making structures' in both the family and education (1987, p. 371). Conflicts over child custody, for instance, should be settled by a 'discursive process of will formation' (ibid.). For Habermas, in both a state-centred and a market-centred approach, legal subjects encounter one another in an 'objectivizing, success-oriented way' (ibid., p. 369). However, it is not clear how Habermas can maintain the boundary between areas of social life that must be based on a discursive process of will formation, and those that must be based on instrumental rationality. It would seem that Habermas's state-guaranteed basic minimum will be enjoyed in the life-world, and therefore, it would be, on his own terms, an example of unacceptable constitutive jur-idification. Even if it were possible to apply such a distinction, how-ever, Habermas's approach seems unduly pessimistic about the possible benefits of legal regulation and bureaucratic organization. He states that, in principle, such modes of existence will be antitheti-cal to communicative action. It could be argued instead that it is a matter of empirical investigation to determine whether and in what ways different state mechanisms have the negative effects that Habermas fears.

Habermas maintains a distinction between life-world and sys-temic integration. 'Environmentalist' approaches to welfare main-tain an analogous distinction: between the productivist sphere of industrial work and the state and a post-productivist sphere where production is 'autonomous' [see pp. 39–42 and pp. 196–200].

Productivists assume that a society is efficient if it produces more goods, and it is a just society if more and more people get to enjoy these goods. However, productivism is not sustainable. Because it treats all aspects of life as a means to attain growth, it has depleted ecological resources and undermined valuable cultural practices outside the market. We must appreciate that human life depends on an 'environment', which includes not only diversity of species but also cultural diversity. Post-productivists call for three basic policies (Gorz, 1980, pp. 1–13, 85ff): (i) we should reduce the amount of goods we consume, and the rate of growth, while also ensuring an equitable distribution of its products; (ii) we should reduce the amount of time and effort we spend in the production of material goods so as to ensure that all have an equal chance to participate in formal employment; and (iii) we should have greater freedom to engage in 'autonomous production' outside the formal productivist sphere of work.

In a productivist welfare state, only market-based work has value. In that context, welfare programmes will tend to be selective, conditional, and repressive, as they must compel those who are 'able-bodied' and of 'working age' into paid employment. Productivists undervalue unpaid work in the family, and also the women who usually perform it. Post-productivists, in contrast, start from the assumption that women can liberate men (ibid., p. 85). Domestic labour provides the model for what Andre Gorz calls 'autonomous production'. Autonomous production is possible in any activities that are not sold as labour on the market, nor distributed as a benefit by the state, nor controlled as a monopoly by a profession (what, with our productivist mindset, we call 'hobbies'). Autonomous production requires the use of 'convivial tools': they allow one to make or do anything whose aesthetic or use-value is enhanced by doing it oneself (ibid., p. 87; Illich, 1973). These are 'own sake activities' [see pp. 208–14]. Further, a basic income will remove the need to 'police' welfare recipients, and job-sharing would limit the power of employers, and expand the numbers taking part in the formal economy.

The environmentalist approach to welfare has some obvious similarities with Habermas's theory. Both call for an unconditional basic income. Both divide the world into two spheres: one is bureaucratic and profit-seeking, the other is informal and motivated by moral or ethical values. Both positions arise from dissatisfaction with classical Marxism: Gorz bases his approach on an appeal to 'the non-class of non-workers' (1980, p. 10). However, Habermas ascribes to humans a very specific nature: we are rational, language-using creatures whose most significant attainments occur through dialogue and debate. In contrast, Gorz believes that autonomy is attained through production (although outside the sphere of formal work). Habermas also seeks impartiality with respect to conceptions of the good life. Gorz, however, praises and promotes the values of a given way of life, the non-economic rationality of the household: the values of reciprocity, tenderness, spontaneity, and love of life in all its forms (ibid., p. 85).

Conclusion

Habermas identified three shortcomings of post-modernism. First, Foucault puts forward the thesis that we can assess the validity of knowledge claims only from within specific discourses. However, this entails the relativist contention that a claim can be rational 'relative to' a discourse, and so on, but not 'rational as such'. Secondly, Foucault assumes power should be resisted, but also, as an immoralist, he does not give a normative justification for resistance. Indeed, Foucault's own statement of his own thesis is itself an exercise of strategic rationality. Finally, Foucault's statement of his own position entails a performative contradiction. The act of stating the relativistic immoralist position implies commitment to universal rational standards, and therefore contradicts the content of the statement.

I want to make a further criticism of post-modernism. Foucault calls for three goals to be pursued: parody and dissociation of identity, resistance, and a sacrifice of the subject of knowledge (1971, p. 95). However, the character traits corresponding to these goals are the antitheses of widely accepted virtues (wisdom, moderation, *sophia*). First, parody runs counter to the virtue of practical wisdom. As a wise person I accept that I may be held accountable for my own emotions, conclusions, and actions. Secondly, the post-modern subject is encouraged to be strategic in the promotion of his or her own interests. However, even when a person has the strength (or the right) to seize more than he or she needs, we praise the person for moderately refraining from doing so. Finally, *sophia* (or philosophical wisdom) is antithetical to the genealogical spirit. *Sophia* requires, at the very least, showing respect for facts, logic, experience, and basic principles. I think Habermas is right when he argues that genealogy is incoherent and a relativistic immoralism. However, Habermas cannot justify his exclusion of ethics, that is goods and virtues, from the realm of rational debate.

For Habermas, power relations are legitimate when there is reciprocity and symmetry. In the ideal speech situation, conclusions are justified only if they can be accepted by all using universalizable criteria of validity. This removes all power to 'influence' the behaviour of others by a claim to 'authority'. It is not a legitimate move to say, 'if you had my wisdom, then you would appreciate why my approach is a valid one'. In practical reasoning and debate we must be able to justify our conclusions with considerations or principles that are generally applicable. However, I do not think it follows that, as Habermas claims, consensus is a necessary feature of valid claims. Even Habermas agrees with Rawls that some people (fundamentalists) simply cannot be included in dialogue. Habermas therefore must accept that the non-participation of some in dialogue need not make the conclusion reached any less rationally binding on those who did not participate but will be affected. If that is the case, then Habermas has not shown that consensus is always necessary to justify norms.

Secondly, Habermas, I think rightly, argues that a claim is valid only if it is also 'generalizable'. However, I think he is wrong to argue that social norms are valid only if they are impartial. Impartiality is not the only criterion for moral justification that is generalizable. For instance, it is a generalizable claim that those who have contributed in the past should be rewarded for doing so. However, rewarding according to merit presupposes a controversial (but perhaps true) conception of value. Similarly, a controversial (but perhaps true) conception of flourishing can justify use of the criterion of need.

Finally, Habermas's cosmopolitanism is problematic. Despite the formation of supranational bodies (e.g. the European Union), our primary political communities are still the national communities that we make contributions to and receive rewards from. This is evident in tax and welfare, and social insurance systems. It is as citizens of a nation state that we have *primary political* duties towards needy strangers: our duties to needy strangers of other nation states lie outside the first circle of political obligation.

CHAPTER 9

In Defence of State Welfare

Neo-liberals are perhaps the most vehement opponents of state-provided unconditional welfare benefits. However, neo-liberalism (or the New Right) may also be described as the new orthodoxy in welfare thought. It first emerged in response to Democratic Party 'liberalism' in the United States, and also Labour Party 'socialism' in the United Kingdom. However, Anthony Giddens's Third Way [see pp. 200–3] is based on the assumption that, although the British *New* Labour party is not simply 'warmed up neo-liberalism' (1998, p. 25), social democracy must be reformed in the light of the neo-liberal critique. The New Right is a combination of liberal and conservative elements (Gamble, 1988). Some aspects are similar to Nozick's libertarianism [see pp. 65–7], while others recall the conservatism of Fukuyama and Nisbet [see pp. 69–81]. It not only restricts the state and promotes market conditions (like libertarianism), but also (like conservatism) encourages certain values such as enterprise and philanthropy.

Neo-liberals are concerned that excessive state welfare in fact perpetuates welfare dependency among its recipients. This is a development of the 'radical' argument that state welfare can undermine autonomy. However, unlike critical theory, neo-liberals have no such problem with the market as a system, or the bureaucratic nature of market firms. Neo-liberals also agree with a number of widely accepted findings about 'globalization' (Pierson, 1998; Mishra, 1999; George and Wilding, 2002). While it had been assumed that the state, economy, and society are co-extensive within the same national boundaries, the nation state, now, does not have the power to regulate the market so as to directly enhance well-being. In any case, for the New Right, the state is less efficient than the market as a mechanism to distribute benefits and burdens. The New Right also raises the problem of 'moral pluralism', like political liberals. They concur that there is no way to agree about what, or who, is more or less deserving of reward. However, neo-liberals go on to argue that, because of the incommensurability of moral doctrines, *any* extensive collective provision of unconditional welfare entitlements will be objectionable.

What, if anything, can answer these neo-liberal arguments? First, the theorists discussed in this chapter try to provide a renewed defence of the state's welfare function and also of humanist ideals. They challenge the widespread assumption that, because of globalization, the state no longer has the *power* to intervene in the market so as to promote welfare and that, in the context of post-modernity, the state simply does not have the moral *authority* to do so. Secondly, pluralism need not be an obstacle to quite ambitious collective provision of unconditional welfare entitlements. Raymond Plant defends a positive conception of freedom; Russell Keat offers a perfectionist justification for greater equality of income and of challenging and discretionary work; and G.A. Cohen argues that when Rawls's difference principle is adhered to by individuals, it will require from us 'virtually unqualified equality itself'. Finally, they address the widespread belief that state welfare is antithetical to market efficiency. Each theorist will attempt to show that certain commitments that are usually seen to be uncontroversial elements of a capitalist market (individual rights, consumer choice, and Rawls's difference principle) can in fact be used to defend state welfare.

The New Right critique of state welfare

The New Right is a 'liberal' position to the extent that it restricts the state's role in the provision of welfare. However, as a 'conservative' position, it also sees the economy as an arena in which morally valuable traits are fostered.

Efficiency

Neo-liberals reject state welfare as a highly inefficient system of production and distribution (Figure 9.1). For Friedrich Hayek, 'where effective competition can be created, it is a better way of guiding individual efforts than any other' (1944, p. 27). And market

| (1) Antithesis of market competitiveness: | removes monetary costs the market places on the satisfaction of preferences. |
| (2) Macro-economic inefficiency caused by: | poor targeting of entitlements; high replacement rates. |

Figure 9.1 The 'inefficiency' of unconditional welfare entitlements

competition is 'in most circumstances the most efficient method known' (ibid.). It is sometimes argued that a system of distribution or production is 'efficient' if it meets the requirements of 'Pareto optimality' (Cf. Rawls, 1971, p. 67). When a system is efficient, it is impossible to change it so as to make at least one person better off without making others (at least one) worse off. The market is 'efficient' in this way because it is based on reciprocal relations. Like is exchanged for like as monetary costs are imposed on the satisfaction of my preferences. And those monetary costs are determined simply by other people's preferences for the things I hope to receive or the things I have to offer. For instance, I may prefer to drink a glass of vintage wine every evening, and wine sellers may want €100 for such a bottle. I can only satisfy my preference, therefore, if I can also provide some service or goods that others want and for which they are willing to pay me sufficient money to finance my wine-drinking habits (unless I am lucky enough to have other sources of income: an inheritance, a lottery win, etc.). I am made better off (by receiving the wine) without making any one else worse off (no one is forced to subsidize my taste for wine without compensation).

A state distribution of welfare will be inefficient, it is argued. It will attempt to make some people (for instance, the least advantaged) better off, and in doing so it will make others (the advantaged) worse off. It also removes the monetary costs that the market places on the satisfaction of people's preferences. When the state distributes goods without imposing a monetary cost, there is no obstacle preventing citizens from demanding more of those goods, and indeed there is an incentive to demand more. Moreover, when the state is distributing goods to individuals simply because they are citizens, citizens tend to think that they have a moral right to such goods (Plant, 1991, p. 85). This may also lead to 'government overload' and 'ungovernability' because there is no objective way to determine what each person deserves or needs. The role of justice will become a matter of 'a competition between interest groups to get their own subjective views about deserts or needs as the politically accepted ones' (ibid.). As the state's decisions about justice are 'arbitrary', they lead to 'resentment' and, as part of a vicious circle, an escalation of demands.

According to the New Right, unconditional rights to ever-more extensive state-provided welfare is inefficient. It also produces both low economic growth and low per-capita income (Goodin et al., 1999, p. 127). First, 'social programmes with high replacement rates pay people about the same as they would have earned from paid labour, and that constitutes a powerful disincentive for them to bother working' (ibid., p. 126). The second claim is that 'poorly targeted benefits being paid to needy and non-needy people alike are ... dead weight losses associated with the "fiscal churning" involved in collecting tax revenues and distributing them back to the very same people' (ibid., p. 127). So, if the levels of welfare benefits are close to or equal to previous levels of income received through employment, those benefits create a strong motivation to stay out of work and remain dependent on state welfare as a source of income. And if welfare receipt is universal and non-selective (or at least if it benefits many who are not poor), then this creates extra running costs. Both lead to low employment rates and high rates of welfare dependency, 'which in turn constitute a drag on economic growth, thus reducing per-capita income' (ibid.).

Justice

Neo-liberals assume that an outcome is *just* if it simply is what has resulted from the freely made and freely implemented decisions of each person. Competition is not only efficient, according to Hayek, but also 'the only method by which our activities can be adjusted to each other without coercive or arbitrary intervention of authority' (1944, p. 27). Why is a 'competitive' market also 'just'? The New Right is concerned with negative liberty. Coercion is 'deliberate interference of other human beings within the area in which I could otherwise act' (Berlin, 1958, p. 142). An extensive welfare state would (among other things) distribute resources from the advantaged to the disadvantaged. Such a re-distribution will infringe the negative liberty of the advantaged *unless* they are free to refrain from taking part in these exchanges. However, welfare state policies (by and large) do not respect negative liberty, and this is the case because they are often justified by a commitment to so-called 'positive freedom'. A conception of positive freedom

presupposes some notion of what persons 'ought' to be free to do or
to be. Because of the plurality of moral doctrines, however, such a
conception of freedom will be controversial and no rational justification could be offered for it.

Positive freedom conflates 'freedom and goodness'. For Isaiah
Berlin, the idea of positive freedom posits a 'real', 'higher' self. It
entails an assumption 'that whatever is the true goal of man (happiness, fulfilment of duty, wisdom, a just society, self-fulfilment) must
be identical with his freedom' (ibid., p. 151). The community can
also impose its will upon 'recalcitrant members' so as to achieve
its own, and therefore their, higher freedom (ibid., p. 150).
Individuals can be forced to be free! (Rousseau, 1762, I. 7.).
Positive freedom also conflates 'freedom and ability'. It is assumed
that I am free only if I have the resources needed to exercise my
agency and pursue my goals. However, as it is always possible to
develop one's abilities further, then everyone is, in some sense,
heteronomous or unfree. For neo-liberals, if I lack the resources
needed to do everything that I want to do, I am still free so long as
my lack was not caused by coercion. As Hayek argues,

> the manner in which the benefits and burdens are apportioned by the
> market mechanism in many instances have to be regarded as very unjust
> *if* it were the result of a deliberate allocation to particular people. But this
> is not the case. Those shares are the outcome of a process the effect of
> which on particular people was neither intended nor foreseen by anyone
> when the institutions first appeared – institutions which were then per-
> mitted to continue because it was found that they improve for all or most
> the prospects of having their needs satisfied.
>
> (1976, p. 64)

Culture of dependency

The New Right is a 'liberal' position to the extent that it would
safeguard economic competition and protect negative liberty.
However, neo-liberals also make a 'conservative' critique of a 'culture of dependency'. The welfare state is permissive, according to
the New Right. People are not held responsible for their actions, as
they receive benefits for the reason that they occupy a specific social
category, irrespective of their choices and actions in the past. This
permissive atmosphere also fosters dependency. This is the case
because a permissive culture does not impose 'stigmas'. Charles

Murray believes that the weakening of stigmas against single-motherhood, welfare receipt, and the black market all help perpetuate a culture of poverty (1986 p. 28). Gertrude Himmelfarb also notes, 'If work, independence, responsibility, respectability are valued, then their converse must be devalued, seen as disrespectable' (1995, p. 142; Fukuyama [see pp. 78–80].). Lawrence Mead accepts that social welfare has been received in a 'passive' manner (1993, p. 181). However, while Murray calls for restriction of state welfare, Mead argues that state welfare can be defended if it is *duty-based*. Welfare can be distributed as part of a social contract, where rights must be matched by duties (1997, p. 221). His objective is 'neither to expand aid as it is nor to deny it, but to change its nature so that support is coupled to employment' (ibid., p. 222).

At the same time, the New Right wants to foster a 'culture of enterprise' to replace the culture of dependency (Cf. Keat, 1991, p. 1). The market demands self-help. It is 'character forming' (Whelan, 1996, p. 48). In contrast, the welfare state removes the costs of failure and the rewards for success. The New Right assumes that 'the "new" world of enterprise is populated by people whose self-understanding and psychological functioning is of the right kind' (Healas, 1991, p. 72). Some critics have responded by arguing that New Right policies simply perpetuate the existence of an underclass (Gans, 1995; Katz, 1999; Moore, 1985). As they seek to isolate and stigmatize the 'undeserving poor', they will perpetuate institutional and cultural barriers between included and excluded. However, the New Right imposes duties on all citizens, not just the disadvantaged. The able, the lucky, the successful are duty-bound to provide charitable aid. This is an ideal of 'philanthropy'. The philanthropist does not simply give money; he or she gives time and commitment as well (Himmelfarb, 1995, p. 149). Moreover, the philanthropist must not be indiscriminate. He or she should strive 'to do good' to others (ibid., p. 148). It is right to distinguish those who are worthy of help from the 'unworthy poor' (Whelan, 1996, p. 82). Neo-liberals, therefore, call for a rejuvenation of charitable work as a way to limit the role of the state and extend that of civil society. The above-mentioned points are summarized in Figure 9.2.

The Third way

Neo-liberals are trying to re-write the history of social policy. Whereas social democrats in the United Kingdom see the post-war

■ Efficiency	Efficiency is equated with market competitiveness.
■ Justice	Justice is equated with respect for rights that protect negative freedoms.
■ Culture of dependency	Stigmatize the underclass. Duty-based welfare **or** privatization of welfare. Values of enterprise **and** philanthropy.

Figure 9.2 The New Right critique

Labour government as the beginning (or empty promise (Miliband, 1969, p. 175ff.)) of a socialist Valhalla, neo-liberals represent it as the period of decline that followed the great Victorian era (Pierson, 1998, p. 2). However, the Third Way, both Anthony Giddens's political theory and the policies of New Labour, is an attempt to bridge the gulf between social democracy and the New Right.

Giddens starts by making the case for post-productivism [see pp. 39–42 and pp. 189–92]. For productivism, men's employment in the formal economy was to be the source of income and of entitlements to welfare. Women's work in the home was the necessary, but undervalued, 'shadow economy' (Giddens, 1994, p. 177). However, the single-minded pursuit of greater productivity is incompatible with 'reflexivity', which is 'the demand to subject motives to open interrogation' (ibid.). What is more, 'women's mass entry into the paid labour market' makes established gender divisions obsolete (ibid.). 'Philosophical Conservatism' is another key component of the Third Way (ibid., p. 174). Work must be 'productive', Giddens readily concedes. However, what he calls 'lean production' takes place 'within a rich social context and as part of long-term processes of investment' (ibid.). It is not surprising that he refers here to Japanese social thought. This is a conservative approach (1998, p. 49) that marries economic prosperity and the promotion of social interests (Fukuyama [see pp. 76–81]).

As a conservative and a post-productivist, Giddens rejects unrestrained capitalism. However, Giddens's argument is that 'progressive' (social democratic) politics must reject extensive statism and unconditional welfare entitlements. He argues that the purpose of state welfare is to 'promote the pursuit of happiness', which he defines as security, self-respect, and the opportunity for self-actualization (1994, p. 180). Tellingly, happiness bears 'no particular relation to either wealth or the possession of power' (ibid.,

1. Purpose of government	Happiness: security, self-respect, self-actualization.
2. Against reliance on 'precautionary aftercare'	Positive welfare. No rights without responsibilities.
3. Wider set of life concerns	Reflexivity. New ethics of individual and collective responsibility.
4. Politics of second chances	Healing damaged identities. Acquiring human capital.
5. New 'settlement'	Not a cross-class agreement.
6. Generative model of equality	Autotelic self. Against centralized control.

Figure 9.3 Giddens's 'positive welfare' model

p. 181). Further, Giddens wishes 'to escape from reliance on "precautionary aftercare" ' (ibid., p. 182). In its place he proposes the notion of 'positive welfare' (Figure 9.3). He insists that, so as to diminish welfare dependency among the 'underclass' (ibid., p. 145), there should be 'no rights without responsibilities' (1998, p. 65). Such welfare policies also must be 'integrated into a wider set of life concerns' (1994, p. 182). What this means is that, in an era with greater reflexivity, an era that is less predictable, 'new ethics of individual and collective responsibility need to be formed' (ibid., p. 184). As conservatives would agree, welfare policies must not destroy 'local ties and modes of life' (ibid., p. 185). At the same time, in an era of reflexivity, greater individual responsibility can be demanded from welfare recipients.

The poor are to be given economic incentives to work. For instance, New Labour introduced tax credits for low-paid workers and childcare for low-paid working families. Also, a 'politics of second chances' would provide training and education (human capital) for those who did not avail of them earlier in life (Giddens, 1994, p. 185). This is not a measure to reduce class inequality. Instead, it is part of a new 'settlement' between old and young, men and women, the employed and unemployed, and parents and children. Moreover, welfare recipients should have the 'desire to work' (ibid., p. 186). This desire can be instilled through counselling so that 'damaged identities can be healed and a strong sense of self-respect developed' (ibid., p. 186). In the same way, New Labour's 'welfare to work' policy made receipt of means-tested income assistance conditional on searching for employment and participation in counselling. This is the 'generative model of equality' (ibid., p. 191). It eschews centralized direction and its concern is with independence (the 'autotelic self') rather than material deprivation.

Giddens's Third Way has a great deal in common with the New Right. It promotes the ethos of a 'lifestyle attuned to the world market' and it sees every citizen as 'an entrepreneur managing his own human capital' (Habermas, 1999, p. 53). This may do a disservice to the efforts made by the New Labour government both to reduce poverty and to increase government spending in health and education. It should also be remembered that conservative ideas have been discerned in Tawney's work, the classic example of English ethical socialism [see pp. 111–15], and he has been appealed to in an effort to justify the Third Way (Jones, 1996, p. 131ff.). Nonetheless, Tawney believed that a great deal of economic equalization was necessary for both community and a just distribution of social functions. The Third Way will not commit to goals like these, and therefore, it cannot claim to be the heir to this tradition.

Raymond Plant: Social rights

Raymond Plant accepts that rights should protect freedoms, but he rejects the New Right critique of social rights. Social rights can be justified as protections of *positive* freedom. Plant also accepts that, due to moral pluralism, it is not possible to agree on what is meritorious. Nonetheless, he claims that well-being and autonomy provide the moral foundations for social rights because they are basic 'needs' of all persons.

Positive freedom and rights

The New Right objects to social rights that protect so-called 'positive freedom'. Plant does not want to link positive freedom to a conception of 'the good', or a comprehensive moral doctrine. However, his argument is that there are reasons to doubt that freedom and 'ability' are categorically distinct. He defends rights that protect 'positive freedom – the freedom to *do* things and thus the associated abilities, capabilities, resources and opportunities which such freedom would entail' (2003, pp. 2–3). Plant makes the following 'strong claim': 'freedom can only be made intelligible in terms of a conception of human agency' which 'cannot be formulated without reference to human abilities, needs, capacities' (ibid., p. 4). It does

---

If rights are to protect freedoms,

if agency is necessary for freedom, and

if income is a generic condition for the exercise of agency,

then, each individual has an inherent human right to income.

Figure 9.4 From positive freedom to social rights

not follow that a person can be said to be free only if he or she has the ability to do *everything* he or she may want, however unrealistic those aims. However [see Figure 9.4], if it can be shown

> that a resource such as income is a generic condition for the exercise of . . . agency, if this agency is a necessary condition for the intelligibility of the ascription of freedom, and if rights are there to protect such freedom, then a right to such a resource could be seen as a genuine right on this view.

> (ibid., pp. 4–5)

Plant, like Charles Taylor, defends a 'qualitative' view of freedom. Taylor notes that although the United Kingdom has a greater number of traffic restrictions, it is still a freer society than communist-era Albania, which had abolished religious practice (Taylor, 1979, p. 150). People in the United Kingdom are 'able to do things like emigrate and criticize the government which are regarded as valuable human capacities (and freedoms)' (Plant, 2003, p. 5). 'What makes these freedoms valuable . . . is that there are certain basic or generic capacities for agency which we regard as being more valuable and these freedoms protect these capacities' (ibid.). Therefore, a negative conception of freedom can be rejected, as freedom cannot be understood in terms of the quantity, or number, of restrictions. In any case, as G.A. Cohen has also argued, a lack of income infringes even the negative variety of freedom (Cohen, 1995, Ch 2). A law preventing air travel for specific groups of people infringes their negative liberty. However, the law also prevents from travelling those who do not have, that is, have not purchased, a valid ticket. In such a case we cannot distinguish clearly 'between a legal restriction on my choice, namely to travel, and a resource restriction which prevents people flying if they do not have a valid ticket' (Plant, 2003, p. 6).

Social human rights

Plant has argued that freedom can be defined 'positively'. He goes on to claim that social rights are genuine human rights, as the United Nations has declared (UN, 1948), because they protect positive freedom. He must contend with the neo-liberal argument that only civil and political rights belong to the list of human rights.

For neo-liberals, human rights are fundamental ways of protecting negative liberty, while welfare provision takes the form of discretionary acts of charity. As a result, 'the recipients [of welfare] have no moral right to what they receive because no individual person can have a right to another person's charity' (Plant, 1980, p. 52). In contrast, civil and political rights are negative and 'the duties that correspond to negative rights are clear and categorical: they are to abstain from interference, for example, from coercion, compulsion, assault, rape, etc' (Plant, 2003, p. 8). These duties do not involve resources, neo-liberals claim. They simply require our *not* doing things. They are also 'perfect duties': they are always capable of being performed, and performed simultaneously. In contrast, so-called 'social rights' cannot generate perfect duties, according to neo-liberals. Because of the need to ration resources, social rights cannot be enjoyed simultaneously. Social rights also suffer from 'indeterminacy' as it is not clear what would be regarded as fulfilling a social right. Dispute and negotiation, rather than rational argument, determine the content of so-called 'social rights'.

Plant does not accept that social rights are invalid. He argues that social rights can pass any test that civil and political rights can pass (Figure 9.5). First, even civil rights involve resource commitments. These include 'the police, the courts, imprisonment, and... street lighting and security measures in at risk areas' (ibid., p. 10). These rights raise questions of distributive justice. Secondly, discretion is

1. Scarce resources are used.	e.g. prison service, income maintenance.
2. Discretion is needed.	In the distribution of resources.
3. Non-arbitrariness of decisions.	Only basic, vital, human interests turned into rights.
4. Market outcomes can be unjust.	Although unintended, they are foreseeable.

Figure 9.5 Any test that civil and political rights can pass, social rights pass as well

necessary in the allocation of resources needed to enforce civil and political rights. Indeterminacy need not ensue, however, as only some of our interests are turned into rights: basic, vital, or human interests. As I discuss on pp. 206–8, welfare rights also meet such vital interests. Therefore, welfare provision 'is a matter of strict obligation for those who hold resources' (1980, p. 52). 'Their [the deprived] needs create a right to welfare and a duty on the part of the better endowed to grant welfare benefits to meet such needs' (ibid.). Finally, the outcomes of the market can be unjust even if they have not been caused by coercion. While 'it is no doubt true that the outcomes of markets are unintended they can, at least in aggregate, be foreseen and it is this degree of foreseeability that grounds the idea of collective responsibility' (2003, p. 14). Contrary to Hayek, even if deprivation is not caused by coercion, it is a foreseeable consequence of unregulated capitalism, and for that reason we can have (as a group) a perfect duty to remove deprivation.

Well-being and autonomy

It has been argued that welfare rights meet vital human interests. Plant argues as well that the adherents of incommensurable doctrines can agree on these interests. He accepts one aspect of political liberalism [see pp. 132–4]. We cannot hope to agree on, and impose, a single conception of the human good. However, while Rawls assumes that we can attain an 'overlapping consensus' only about 'primary goods', Plant wants to base social rights on a positive (substantive) view of freedom [see pp. 141–3].

According to Plant, the adherents of incommensurable conceptions of the human good are logically committed to the following principle: all have rights to resources necessary to satisfy well-being and autonomy.

> Ends (however different) and duties (however varied) can be pursued and performed only by human beings acting autonomously; and therefore any moral view to be coherent must recognize the maintenance of human life and the development of autonomy as basic obligations.
>
> (1980, p. 93)

Agency is essential to an account of freedom, and well-being and autonomy are general or generic conditions of the exercise of agency (Plant, 2003, p. 16). There are certain needs of well-being without which an autonomous character will not be developed: physical integrity, and an appropriate level of education, and income and social security (ibid., p. 17). Finally, 'the capacity for autonomy seems to be what the end result of the exercise of human agency and freedom would be' (ibid., p. 16; Cf. Gerwith, 1978).

Freedom cannot be conceptualized without reference to ability. However, Plant does *not* link this substantive conception of freedom with 'perfectionism'. In contrast, Joseph Raz argues that 'it is the goal of all political action to enable individuals to pursue *valid* conceptions of the good and to discourage *evil* or *empty* ones' (1986, p. 133; emphasis added). Raz defends perfectionist liberalism; Plant, like Nussbaum, leans more towards substantive (but impartial) liberalism. Plant wants to base this theory on Kant's categorical imperative, which insists upon 'the idea of acting under rules equally applicable to all' (Plant, 1980, p. 89). A maxim can only be put forward as a moral rule if it can be 'willed' that all act in accordance with that rule. According to Plant, it is not possible to will that all act in accordance with the rule that individuals are *not* under a strict obligation to give aid to others in need.

> For a will which decided in this way would be in conflict with itself, since many a situation might arise in which a man needed love and sympathy from others and in which, by such a law of nature issuing from his own will, he would rob himself of all hope of the help which he wants for himself.
>
> (ibid.)

Plant's argument here is problematic for three reasons I think. First, Plant begins by stating a fact, that my autonomy and well-being are the necessary conditions of my agency, which is necessary for my (positive) freedom. He then goes on to deduce that I have a 'right' to the goods needed for autonomy and well-being. It is not clear that the latter is entailed by the former, however. Kantian ethics does conceptualize moral issues in terms of duties and rights relating to action, and it does assume morality is as it is because we are rational autonomous creatures (O'Neill, 1991, pp. 181–2). Therefore, *for Kantians* it makes sense to argue both that fundamental moral duties relate to respect for autonomy and that the fundamental moral consideration concerns duties governing action. Not all moral doctrines can be reconciled with Kantianism, however. For instance, virtue ethics assumes that basic moral requirements refer to virtue (not autonomy) and that praise-worthiness is a fundamental consideration along with duty.

Secondly, as Hegel and his followers have argued, Kantian ethics suffers from 'impotence of the "ought"' (Cf. Habermas, 1990, p. 207). Kantian ethics shows us only what can*not* be a moral principle, that is, a norm that cannot be made universal. It could be argued that Kantian ethics is powerless to show what we ought to do, and this is the case in part because it disengages actions and norms 'from the substantive ethics of their lived contexts' (ibid.). For instance, while it is the case that we could not all will the maxim that states that we need not give aid to the needy, it does not follow that the aid given to the needy should be given as a duty of justice. Indeed, we could easily will the universal duty to give charity to the needy.

Finally, Plant defends a substantive conception of freedom, yet he also accepts Rawls's political (impartial) conception of justice. As Hegelians (and Aristotelians) would note, perfectionism offers a better grounding for a substantive conception of freedom, and it may be better defended from within communitarianism. That is, persons require autonomy and well-being so as to pursue what is good and best, but also, they do so (by and large) by contributing in a virtuous way within already-formed communities. For this reason, I turn to Keat's justification, and limitation, of the market, as it draws on perfectionism and some elements of communitarianism.

Russell Keat: Common goods and market limits

Russell Keat's work directly challenges the neo-liberal view that state welfare is inefficient and that it generates dependency. He also disagrees with MacIntyre's claim that modern society, and the market in particular, is incompatible with 'practices'. However, Keat also proposes limits to markets. A democratic politics concerned with common goods can provide good reasons to limit the market so as to enhance well-being.

Practices and the market

Keat agrees with Alasdair MacIntyre that 'practices' are important and also that they have a marginal role in modern societies. However, Keat rejects MacIntyre's 'community requirement for productive practices' (Keat, 2000, p. 127). MacIntyre relies on 'a normatively questionable endorsement of certain aspects of pre-modern society as against their modern counterparts' (ibid., p. 123). First, MacIntyre assumes that modern pluralism is incompatible with a coherent moral discourse and living a good life. It has led to a number of distinct spheres in which social activity is conducted 'without any overall sense of their respective positions either in the shared life of the community or in the individual lives of its members' (Keat, 2000, p. 126). Keat responds that pluralism need not be incompatible with perfectionism. The fact that conceptions of the human good are plural may 'be viewed as reflecting "objectively" the richness, complexity and open-endedness of human existence' (ibid.). Secondly, the modern individual also tends to understand his or her own good as being separate from those of others. As a result, MacIntyre assumes, 'the purpose of [modern] morality is seen as being to deal with egoism' (Keat, 2000, p. 127). Instead, according to Keat, 'one might view separate identities as conditions of individual autonomy and hence...more reflective and critical judgement' (ibid.).

MacIntyre also assumes that the market is inherently incompatible with 'practice-characteristics'. While participants in practices are concerned with 'internal goods', market activities are based exclusively on the use and pursuit of 'external goods' (riches, power, status, and prestige). MacIntyre agrees with neo-liberals that, in the capitalist market, individuals tend to be motivated by 'their single-minded pursuit of their own (material) interests' (Keat, 2000, p. 118). However, as Keat points out, MacIntyre also assumes that no practice can survive without 'institutions', even though institutions are concerned with external goods. Keat suggests that the market is a macro-level institution, and it does not make it 'impossible' for market firms to possess 'an institutional form compatible with their conduct as a practice' (ibid., p. 114). For instance, practice-like 'emulation' is possible in the market. It involves competition with those 'recognised for the excellence of their performance' (ibid., p. 120), and also competitive 'success' must be 'achieved consistently with the standards of the practice concerned and their related virtues' (ibid., p. 121). Emulation is possible in productive market activities where excellence is measured in terms of improving the quality of the products that are then offered for sale.

Keat has argued that we should reject MacIntyre's 'community requirement for productive practices', and also we should accept that the market is not inherently incompatible with practice

1. 'Community requirement' for practices.	Hostile to modern pluralism, individualism, rational critique.
2. *A priori* assumption that market is antithetical to practices.	Market always prioritizes external goods over internal goods.

Figure 9.6 What Keat rejects from MacIntyre's view of practice

characteristics (Figure 9.6). Why does this matter? It matters because of 'the potential contribution of practices to human well-being' (ibid., p. 127). 'Subjective well-being' is primarily a matter of 'people's *life-satisfaction*: how well they consider their lives to be going'. On the other hand, 'human development' includes '*cognitive complexity* (people's ability to engage in abstract, analytical thought, and their intellectual flexibility and objectivity); *self-attribution* (their belief in their ability to shape and control their own lives); and *self-esteem* (their sense of being worthy of respect and decent treatment by others)' (ibid., p. 134). Participating in practices can contribute to well-being in this sense. Although MacIntyre is concerned with a practice's internal goods, David Miller notes that many practices 'exist to serve social ends beyond themselves' (Miller, 1994, p. 250). MacIntyre is also blind to the fact that well-being *can* be promoted by market consumption. If we question MacIntyre's 'view that the market is inherently practice-antithetical', then it is possible that goods consumed in the market can be genuine goods (Keat, 2000, p. 131).

Consumer-friendly practices *and* practice-friendly consumption

Keat argues that well-being can be enhanced through practice-like production. Also, the state can regulate the market to support practice-like production. Finally, as market consumers, we can support the practice-like production of others and also purchase the goods needed for our own practice-like activities.

Keat agrees with Robert Lane (1991) that well-being is not greatly enhanced by undemanding, monotonous, and closely supervised work. However, Keat does not accept Lane's thesis that, in a capitalist society, workers are costs and consumers are the source of profits, and therefore, the market 'necessarily sacrifices the well-being of producers to that of consumers *if* some conflict between the two occurs' (Keat, 2000, p. 136). Rather, the qualities required to excel in a practice, 'co-operation, mutual respect and commitment to its collective goals', are the qualities that many managers would like from their workers (ibid., p. 118). Therefore, by enhancing the well-being of producers one can also better satisfy the needs of consumers. At the same time, Keat does not trust the market to produce such results without state interference. The citizens of a democracy may 'wish to design this institution [the market], and the conditions under which it operates, in such a way that it is also conducive to productive activities conducted in a practice-like manner' (ibid., p. 131). Like 'market socialists', Keat accepts that the market can ensure efficiency and freedom of choice, but also the institutional framework of capitalism can be altered to promote socialist values: an end to exploitation, greater equality, and the satisfaction of basic needs (Miller, 1989; Estrin and Le Grand, 1989).

The state can rightly promote practice-like production. But consumption in the market can bring about the same results. There is a type of consumption that is 'practice friendly'. Both 'performances' and the 'non-performing arts' are 'activities performed for "their own sake"' (Keat, 2000, p. 141), and the goods produced are desirable to consumers *only* if they are produced in own-sake activities. These 'creative products' generate excitement and supply positive gratification and satisfaction. Examples include sport, humour, entertainment, literature, art, and pleasurable intellectual pursuits. In contrast, 'defensive products' are to contribute to personal comfort and also reduce pains, injury, or distress. Keat concludes that creative goods make a *greater* contribution to well-being *once* people have attained an adequate level of defensive goods. Material goods are necessary but hardly sufficient for 'human development'.

Market consumption can support 'own-sake activities' performed in the market. Moreover, consumption itself can generate 'production-like benefits'. Consumers can purchase 'equipment goods' used in 'own-sake activities' (walking, cooking, crafts, gardening, bird watching, etc.). We can thereby attain the benefits available from production 'at its best': cognitive complexity, self-direction, and self-esteem. Keat also argues that this provides a justification for the equalization of income. Lane had claimed that inequality of discretionary, challenging work was of greater significance to well-being than inequality of income. However, there is a close correlation between income and the capacity to purchase

1. Consumer-friendly production	Requires cooperation, mutual respect, collective goals.
2. Practice-friendly consumption	Own-sake activities. Consumption of creative goods.
3. Equalization of income	To enable consumption with 'production-like' benefits.

Figure 9.7 Keat's market socialism

equipment goods. Therefore, equalization of income is justified as a means to reduce inequality in discretionary challenging work (ibid., p. 145) (Figure 9.7).

Politics of common goods

So far Keat has argued that the market and practices *need not* be incompatible. For that reason, he rejects the pessimism of MacIntyre. However, he does not assume that the market is always compatible with practices. Keat accepts what he calls the 'classical' justification of the market (associated with Adam Smith): 'the market is the most effective device, amongst those we know of, for generating the kinds of human goods that contribute to people's material well-being' (ibid., p. 150). In contrast, the 'liberal' defence of the market insists that it has intrinsic value, 'since its defining procedures are seen as essentially consistent with' negative freedom (ibid.). The classical defence of the market leaves room to argue that, *if* the market does not in fact work to enhance well-being, limits should be placed upon it. In contrast, as liberals assume that the market has intrinsic value, there seems to be no situation that would justify state interference in the market. Keat has already called for a redistribution of income necessary to engage in 'own-sake activities' outside the market; and he has argued that the citizens of a democracy can design the institution of the market in such a way as to be conducive to practice-like production. He now argues that, left to themselves, markets are likely to under-produce an important type of good, namely cultural goods.

'Cultural goods' do not refer primarily to theoretical practices of academic philosophy. Keat is concerned with 'the more engaging representations of the various ways in which human life may be conducted', which can be found 'in novels, films, plays, television drama, soap operas...' (ibid., p. 156). They are 'meta-goods',

'goods whose nature resides at least partly in addressing questions about the nature of (other) human goods and their potential contribution to human well-being' (ibid.). They are 'transformative value' goods, goods necessary so as to develop 'complex discriminative capacities' (ibid., p. 155), rather than 'demand value' goods, which satisfy already-existing preferences (ibid., p. 157). He suggests that citizens, if they are aware of this thesis, have good reason to limit the market. This is the case as 'the producers of cultural goods with transformative value need to secure some degree of "free space" in which they can act without immediate threat from their demand-value competitors . . .' (ibid., p. 158). In television, for instance, some programmes have 'transformative value', but many programmes are designed to 'give viewers just what they want', and nothing more (Figure 9.8).

Keat contends that 'the market is a means by which the good of all can be enhanced' (ibid., p. 166). However, can he provide an account of the human good that is not antithetical to market consumption? Keat argues that 'the good' would include consumption, but also this would be 'a shared value'. Therefore, the subjective 'good' of consumers cannot be allowed to triumph at the expense of common goods. Citizens may also agree to limit the operation of the market if, through 'reflective dialogue', they discover that the market has negative effects on the pursuit of non-market goods. Secondly, Keat must address the objection that there are no rational grounds for such value judgements and also that such judgements can only be implemented in an arbitrary, coercive manner. He argues that the 'idea of "common goods" is compatible with recognizing both their objective plurality and the possibility of choice on the part of individuals as to which they may pursue' (ibid., p. 169). This has clear affinities with Raz's perfectionist liberalism as it insists that the pursuit of goods must be compatible with individual autonomy and pluralism [see pp. 206–8]. Finally, Keat acknowledges that 'there is no guarantee that all such conceptions of the good can in fact be co-realized' (ibid.). We cannot avoid making decisions about human goods, the decisions are difficult, and they must be

| ■ Justification | Classical: market is justified *if* it enhances well-being. |
| ■ Limitation | Market is likely to under-produce cultural goods: meta-goods; goods with transformative value. |

Figure 9.8 Justification (and limitation) of the market

made democratically. On what basis can we, as citizens, make rational and objective judgements about the good to be enhanced? First, some guidelines are required to help determine what is or is not a good life. This question has been explored already [see pp. 145–58]. Secondly, Keat calls for the equalization of income. A principle of distribution may at least help resolve the conflict of goods. I turn to this issue next.

G.A. Cohen: Reformulation of Rawls's 'difference principle'

G.A. Cohen's work provides a more detailed justification of egalitarian distribution. Much of Cohen's argument (for our purposes) is outlined as a critique of John Rawls's interpretation of the difference principle.

Who should (unilaterally) help whom?

According to David Hume, justice is an 'artificial virtue', but one made necessary by the unchanging conditions of human existence (1739–1740, III. 2, § ii). As there will always be scarcity of goods and limited generosity, principles of justice continue to be necessary. These are the 'circumstances of justice'. Like Hume, both Cohen and Rawls reject the view that (due to abundance and/or generosity) a good society need not implement decisions about the just distribution of benefits and burdens. However, Cohen rejects Rawls's 'social contract' approach (Figure 9.9). Rawls's social ideal is 'cooperation among equals for mutual advantage' (1971, p. 14), a society in which we can regard 'the distribution of natural talents as a common asset' (ibid., p. 101). That is, when we make this (hypothetical) contract, we do so without knowledge of our natural advantages, and we can agree to principles of justice that re-distribute the products of those natural advantages.

■ Concept of self-ownership.	Natural talents are not simply common assets.
■ Some are radically disabled, and therefore, radically unproductive.	Society is not simply a system of cooperation for mutual advantage.
■ The question of justice.	Who should (unilaterally) help whom?

Figure 9.9 Against the social contract model

Cohen rejects Rawls's idea that natural talents are simply common assets. As we saw, Cohen discovered the concept of 'self-ownership' playing a central role not only in Nozick's libertarianism but also in classical Marxism [see pp. 104–5]. 'If I am the moral owner of myself, and, therefore, of this right arm, ... no one is entitled, without my consent, to press it into their own or anybody else's service ...' (Cohen, 1995, p. 68). Cohen wants to retain the Marxist insight that although workers are right to feel a sense of self-ownership over their person and powers (*pace* Rawls), this does *not* justify 'unlimited original rights in virtually unrestricted unequal amounts of external natural resources' (*pace* Nozick) (ibid., p. 118). Moreover, there will always be some, for instance the 'radically disabled', who are, because of misfortune, 'radically unproductive' (ibid., p. 224). Therefore, the just society is not, *pace* Rawls, a 'system of mutual advantage'. It follows that Rawls is asking the wrong 'question of justice' (ibid.). He asks *how should the fruits of cooperation, a process in which everyone benefits everyone, be distributed?* According to Cohen, as only some need give, and as a sense of self-ownership is reasonable, the question of justice is, *who should (unilaterally) help whom?*

The 'difference principle' revised

Cohen's second line of argument is to revise Rawls's difference principle (Figure 9.10). It states, 'the higher expectations of those better situated are just if and only if they work as part of a scheme which improves the expectations of the least advantaged members of society' (Rawls, 1971, p. 75). Material 'incentives' are necessary only if, in their absence, the 'talented' would neither work productively nor take up vacant positions, but incentives may result in 'deep inequalities' in initial life chances (ibid., p. 7). For Rawls, 'the primary subject of justice is the basic structure of society' (ibid.). At

---

In a just society the members of that society adhere to its principles of justice.

Therefore, the 'talented' must adhere to the difference principle.

If they do they will only demand rewards necessary to improve the condition of the least well-off.

Therefore, the difference principle will not justify deep inequalities in initial life chances.

Figure 9.10 The difference principle revised

the same time, however, Rawls argues, in 'a well-ordered society', which is 'effectively regulated by a public conception of justice' (ibid., p. 5), 'each person understands the first principles that govern the whole scheme . . .; and all have a settled intention to adhere to these principles in their plan of life' (ibid., p. 528). That is, a society is just if and only if its members adhere to the principles of justice instituted in its basic structure.

According to Cohen, Rawls is, therefore, rationally committed to the idea that the 'talented' must adhere to the difference principle if their society is to be just (2000, p. 126). At the same time, if they do, they will only demand rewards necessary to improve the condition of the least well-off. 'High rewards are . . . necessary only because the choices of talented people are not appropriately informed by the difference principle' (ibid., p. 127). A just person would never demand more than others simply out of self-interest. And to *affirm* the difference principle ' . . . implies that justice requires (virtually) unqualified equality itself' (ibid., p. 124). Inequalities may rightly reflect 'differences in the arduousness of different people's labors', but it is unjust for inequalities to reflect the 'lucky circumstance' that one's talents or services can attract a high market price (ibid., p. 130). Therefore, Cohen agrees with 'luck egalitarians' (Dworkin [see pp. 59–61]) that inequalities are just if they arise from freely made choices, rather than luck. However, Cohen believes that one's social and economic environment can count as an (un)lucky circumstance as well, rather than the objective context one must accept as the parameters of one's life choices (Cf. Dworkin, 2000, p. 293). In any case, Cohen assumes that deep inequalities in initial life chances can never be justified by the difference principle.

Virtue and community

Cohen has argued that we should adhere to the difference principle as individuals. That is, we should exercise the *virtue* of justice. And the rules of justice are determined by considering what the just person would willingly do (i.e. he or she would only demand unequal rewards that were to the benefit of the least well-off). However, it is not clear why, for Cohen, we should care about being just: why is being just 'good' for us?

That which the virtuous individual willing does is in fact the standard to be enforced in the rules of the 'basic structure': 'able-bodied people have a duty, which the state should enforce through taxation, to produce a surplus over what they need to support themselves, to sustain disabled people who would otherwise die' (Cohen, 1995, p. 240). Justice is also sustained by 'social sanction'. If citizens 'willingly submit' to the standard of justice, they will sustain an 'ethos' of justice, 'a structure of response lodged in the motivations that inform everyday life' (2000, p. 128). Neo-Aristotelians like MacIntyre also argue that justice is a virtue and that it is sustained by a community's ethos. However, Cohen seems to agree with Marx that community is 'a *means* to the independently specified goal of the development of each person's powers' (1995, p. 123, n. 16). Cohen remains sympathetic to the classical Marxist conception of the human good: with the ending of the division of labour and the private ownership of property, liberated labour will become life's prime want (ibid., p. 122). However, Cohen criticizes the Marxist view that, in a good society, cooperation arises spontaneously without moral exhortation or coercion [see pp. 103–5]. This is the case as the general facts of human existence include not only the sense of self-ownership and unfortunate circumstances, but also (as Rawls and Hume noted) scarcity of goods and limited generosity. So, in the final analysis, Cohen rejects ideas of the human good associated with revolutionary Marxism as well.

Cohen does not provide an account of how exercising virtue, and in particular, adhering to the difference principle, contributes to 'the good' of the advantaged (and anyone else). He does show that exercising virtue is necessary for *his* (Cohen's) sense of identity. To an important extent, Cohen continues to believe in equality *for the reason that* he was induced to do so. He describes how his upbringing in a communist (and secular-Jewish) community instilled in him this belief. This involves the 'paradox of conviction' (2000, p. 13). For Cohen, the facts about a particular social or historical context, which may play 'a significant part in the genesis of our principled commitments', cannot necessarily play 'a role in the assessment of those principles' underlying truth' (Stears, 2005, p. 334). Cohen's discussion of his own upbringing is certainly affective but, by his own standards, it is not sufficient to 'justifiably believe' that his grounds for defending socialism (virtually unqualified equality) are better than another's grounds for rejecting it.

Let us address an alternative approach. First, a perfectionist can offer a theoretical defence of the difference principle. For a virtue-based approach, what justice requires of us is what the just person would willingly do. However, we need not accept MacIntyre's position and its contextualism. Giving priority to virtue in this way does *not* entail that 'the practical cannot be treated with, handled, mastered or managed by means of precepts that are at once general and unrestrictedly correct' (Wiggins, 2004, p. 481). Such a view would lead to arbitrariness if at some point the 'giving of reasons' by the virtuous person comes to an end. A just person would then be able to determine what was indeed the just thing to do in a specific instance, but he or she could not justify that decision with generally applicable considerations. Alternatively, we could say that a person is virtuous to the extent that he or she acknowledges the significance of general rational principles that govern just acts, and these *general* rational principles can be justified through theoretical reflection. This is something Rawls insists on as well. 'Reasonable' people offer 'one another fair terms of cooperation' and 'agree to act on those terms, even at the cost of their own interests in particular situations' (1997, p. 578).

Secondly, we should account for the virtue of justice and the rules of justice in terms of a universal conception of the human good. This is lacking in Cohen's work. However, Philippa Foot argues that 'moral virtues must be connected with human goods and harm, and that it is quite impossible to call anything you like good or harm' (1958, p. 120). Due to the conditions of human existence, we benefit from exercising virtues: we 'want' to be able to resist temptation and to be able to face what is fearful. For these reasons, moderation and courage are 'good' for us as humans. MacIntyre has also argued that virtues like just-generosity, justice, and practical wisdom are necessary for any human if he or she is to flourish as a human. If we live in a society where justice is *not* thought of as a virtue, then we do not live in a just society. Rawls and Cohen both make this point. And they both agree that living in a just society is a benefit to humans. However, it is the perfectionist who can show that justice is *good* for the just person.

Conclusion

In the opening chapter, I categorized theories of welfare with respect to the position they adopt on three basic philosophical considerations: do they offer a perfectionist view of well-being, do they accept that an argument appeals to standards that transcend the given situation, and do they see modernity as an ongoing project? These same issues have arisen again in our discussion of various responses to neo-liberalism. Neo-liberals have tried to re-write the history of social policy. They redefined the humanist aspirations of the welfare state as a social catastrophe. However, each author analysed here goes some way to neutralizing the neo-liberal critique. Plant shows that 'social' rights, which protect positive freedoms, fulfil the same requirements as civil and political rights, and he defends a substantive conception of freedom. However, as I argued already, a *political* conception of justice that appeals to Kantianism may be objectionable to those committed to other moral doctrines. Moreover, *perfectionism* may be a better basis for a substantive conception of freedom, and it may be better defended from within communitarianism.

Keat defends a substantive account of well-being, and a perfectionist account of human goods, yet he rejects MacIntyre's pessimism. Keat shows that practice-like activity is possible within market employment and consumption, and also, if the state places limits on the market, we will better enhance practices and the goods that can be pursued in practices. So genuine goods can be enjoyed through the market, and this can be facilitated by a generous welfare state. Finally, Cohen has shown that markets are not immune to moral criticism: participants in the market 'ought' to accept only those inequalities that are necessary to improve the condition of the least advantaged. He shows that if we do adhere to the difference principle, as just persons, justice would require of us virtually unqualified equality. What Cohen does not provide is an argument showing why we should care about being just. As Mill, Aristotle, and MacIntyre have argued, exercising virtue is a necessary feature of a flourishing life. And as MacIntyre has shown, happiness requires the virtue of just-generosity as well. We can flourish as humans only if we give to the needy in direct proportion to their need.

Notes

Chapter 1   Introduction: Political Philosophy and Welfare

1. Even utilitarians who reject excessive experimentation on animals, and the factory-farm conditions in which many animals live, nonetheless accept that, under certain circumstances, the interests of humans can be given priority over those of non-human sentient creatures (Singer, 1993, p. 67).

Chapter 2   Utilitarianism

1. There is one important difference between Mill and Foot, namely Foot's rejection of consequentialism.

Chapter 3   Liberalism

1. Rawls uses the term 'talented' to refer to those whose abilities, skills, and training just happen to be in demand; this is not a value judgement of the worth, merit, of these people.

Chapter 4   Conservatism

1. *Professional Ethics and Civic Morals* was first published in 1950, and in 1957 it was translated into English. It is based on lectures given by Durkheim in the 1890s, which remained unpublished in his own lifetime. However, Durkheim's 'Preface' to the second edition of *The Division of Labour in Society* (1902) contained many observations similar to those in the lectures.

Chapter 5   Socialism

1. This translation appears in D. McLellan (ed.), *Karl Marx. Selected Writings* (Oxford, Oxford University Press, 2000), p. 611. An alternative

translation reads as follows: 'when labour is no longer just a means of keeping alive but has itself become a vital need' (Marx, 1875, p. 347).
2. Note, Cohen focuses on Marx's account of exploitation, not alienation.
3. Other noted ethical socialists include William Temple (1926) and John Macmurray (1949).

Chapter 7   Communitarianism

1. I should note that Alasdair MacIntyre rejects that description of his work (MacIntyre, 1991, 1995).

Chapter 8   Radicalism

1. She is adapting Antonio Gramsci's use of this term: see her work with Ernesto Laclau (1985); and for a recent qualified defence of her 'agonistic' model of democracy, see Schaap (2006).

Bibliography

Adorno, T. and M. Horkheimer [1944] *Dialectic of Enlightenment* (London: Verso, 1997).

Aristotle, *The Nicomachean Ethics* [NE], trans. D. Ross, revised by J.L. Ackrill and J.O. Urmson (Oxford: Oxford University Press, 1980).

Aristotle, *Politics* [Pol], trans. E. Barker, revised by R.F. Stalley (Oxford: Oxford University Press, 1995).

Baier, A.C. 'The Need for More than Justice', *Canadian Journal of Philosophy*, Supplementary Volume, 13 (1987) 41–56.

Barker, P. *Michel Foucault. Subversions of the Subject* (London: Harvester Wheatsheaf, 1993).

Barry, B. *The Liberal Theory of Justice* (Oxford: Oxford University Press, 1973).

Barry, B. *Theories of Justice* (Berkley: University of California Press, 1989).

Barry, B. *Why Social Justice Matters* (Cambridge: Polity Press, 2005).

Bauman, Z. *Modernity and Ambivalence* (Cambridge: Polity Press, 1991).

Becker, G. [1964] *Human Capital*, third edition (London: University of Chicago Press, 1993).

Benhabib, S. 'Cultural Complexity, Moral Interdependence, and the Global Dialogical Community', pp. 235–255, in M. Nussbaum and J. Glover (eds), *Women, Culture, and Development. A Study of Human Capabilities* (Oxford: Clarendon Press, 1995).

Bentham, J. [1789] *An Introduction to the Principles of Morals and Legislation*, J.H. Burns and H.L.A. Hart (eds) (Oxford: Clarendon Press, 1996).

Berlin, I. [1958] 'Two Concepts of Liberty', pp. 141–152, in A. Quinton (ed.), *Political Philosophy* (Oxford: Oxford University Press, 1967).

Beveridge, W.H. *Social Insurance and Allied Services* (London: George Allen & Unwin, 1942).

Boxill, B. [1991] 'The Case for Affirmative Action', pp. 260–279, in J.P. Sterba (ed.), *Morality in Practice* (Belmont: Wadsworth, 1999).

Brandt, R. *A Theory of the Good and the Right* (Oxford: Clarendon Press, 1979).

Breen, K. 'Alasdair MacIntyre and the Hope for a Politics of Virtuous Acknowledged Dependence', *Contemporary Political Theory*, Vol. 1 (2002) 181–201.

Buchanan, J. *Ethics and Economic Progress* (London: University of Oklahoma, 1994).

Bufacchi, V. 'Motivating Justice', *Contemporary Political Theory*, Vol. 4 (2005) 25–41.

Burke, E. [1790] *Reflections on the Revolution in France* (London: Penguin, 1986).

Castles, F. *The Social Democratic Image of Society* (London: Routledge & Kegan Paul, 1978).

Clarke, J., A. Cochrane, C. Smart, *Ideologies of Welfare: From Dreams to Disillusion* (London: Hutchinson, 1987).

Cohen, G.A. *Karl Marx's Theory of History: A Defence* (Oxford: Clarendon Press, 1978).

Cohen, G.A. *Self-Ownership, freedom, and equality* (Cambridge: Cambridge University Press, 1995).

Cohen, G.A. *If You're an Egalitarian, How Come You're So Rich?* (London: Harvard University Press, 2000).

Crosland, C.A.R. *The Future of Socialism* (London: Jonathan Cape, 1956).

Crosland, C.A.R. *Socialism Now* (London: Jonathan Cape, 1976).

Daniel, C. 'Socialists and Equality', pp. 11–27, in J. Franklin (ed.), *Equality* (London: Institute for Public Policy Research, 1997).

Dean, M. *The Constitution of Poverty* (London: Routledge, 1991).

Dean, M. 'Governing the Unemployed Self in an Active Society', *Economy and Society*, Vol. 24, no. 4 (1995) 559–583.

De Tocqueville, A. [1835–1840] *Democracy in America*, trans H.C. Mansfield and D. Winthrop (Chicago: University of Chicago Press, 2000).

Dickens, C. [1854] *Hard Times* (Oxford: Oxford University Press, 1989).

Dierickx, G. 'Christian Democracy and its Ideological Rivals', pp. 15–31, in D. Hanly (ed.), *Christian Democracy in Europe* (London: Pinter, 1994).

Disraeli, B. [1845] *Sybil, or, The Two Nations*, S.M. Smith (ed.), (Oxford: Oxford University Press, 1981).

Durkheim, E. [1902] *The Division of Labour in Society*, second ed., first published 1893, trans. W.D. Halls (London: Macmillan, 1984).

Durkheim, E. *Professional Ethics and Civic Morals*, published posthumously, trans. C. Brookfield (London: Routledge & Kegan Paul, 1957).

Dworkin, R. [1981] 'What is Equality? Part 1: Equality of Welfare; Part II: Equality of Resources', *Philosophy and Public Affairs*, Vol. 10, no. 3/4 (1981) 185–246, 283–345; reprinted in *Sovereign Virtue* (London: Harvard University Press, 2000).

Dworkin, R. *A Matter of Principle* (Oxford: Clarendon Press, 1985).

Dworkin, R. *Sovereign Virtue* (London: Harvard University Press, 2000).

Elliot, G. [1871–72] *Middlemarch* (Harmondsworth: Penguin, 1994).

Engels, F. [1845] *The Condition of the Working Class in England*, reprinted in Marx/Engels, *Collected Works Vol. IV* (London: Lawrence & Wishart, 1975).

Engels, F. *Socialism: Utopian and Scientific* (London: George Allen & Unwin, 1892).

Esping-Andersen, G. *Politics Against Markets* (Princeton: Princeton University Press, 1985).

Esping-Andersen, G. [1989] 'The Three Political Economies of the Welfare State', pp. 175–201, in Goodin, R.E., and Mitchell, D. (eds), *The Foundations of the Welfare State, vol. II* (Cheltenham: Edward Elgar, 2000).

Esping-Andersen, G. *The Three Worlds of Welfare Capitalism* (Cambridge: Cambridge University Press, 1990).

Esping-Andersen, G. *Social Foundations of Post-Industrial Economies* (Oxford: Oxford University Press, 1999).

Estrin, S. and Le Grand, J. 'Market Socialism', in Le Grand and Estrin (eds), *Market Socialism* (Oxford: Clarendon Press, 1989).

Etzioni, A. *The Spirit of Community* (Glasgow: Harper Collins, 1995a).

Etzioni, A. 'Old Chestnuts and New Spurs', pp. 16–34, in A. Etzioni (ed.), *New Communitarian Thinking* (London: University Press of Virginia, 1995b).

Etzioni, A. 'The Emerging Global Normative Synthesis', *The Journal of Political Philosophy*, Vol. 12, no. 2 (2004) 214–244.

Fitzpatrick, T. *Welfare Theory. An Introduction* (Houndmills: Palgrave, 2001).

Fives, A. 'Virtue, Justice and the Human Good: Non-relative communitarian ethics and the life of religious commitment', *Contemporary Politics*, Vol. 11, no. 2–3 (2005) 117–131.

Fives, A. 'Aristotle's Ethics and Contemporary Political Philosophy: Virtue and the human good', *21st Century Society*, Vol. 1, no. 2 (2006) 201–220.

Foot, P. [1958] 'Moral Beliefs', pp. 110–132, in P. Foot, *Virtues and Vices* (Oxford: Blackwell, 1978).

Foot, P. *Natural Goodness* (Oxford: Clarendon Press, 2001).

Foote, G. *The Labour Party's Political Thought. A History* (London: Croom Helm, 1985).

Foucault, M. [1971] 'Nietzsche, Genealogy, History', pp. 76–100, in P. Rabinow (ed.), *The Foucault Reader* (New York: Pantheon Books, 1984).

Foucault, M. *The History of Sexuality. Volume 1* (London: Billing & Sons, 1976).

Foucault, M. 'What is Enlightenment?' pp. 32–50, in P. Rabinow (ed.), *The Foucault Reader* (New York: Pantheon Books, 1984a).

Foucault, M. *The History of Sexuality. Volume III* (New York: Pantheon Books, 1984b).

Fraser, N. *Unruly Practices* (University of Minnesota: Polity Press, 1989).

Fraser, N. 'After the Family Wage: Gender Equity and the Welfare State', *Political Theory*, Vol. 22, no. 4 (1994) 591–618.

Fraser, N. 'Social Justice in the Age of Identity Politics', pp. 25–52, in L. Ray and A. Sayer (eds), *Culture and Economy after the Cultural Turn* (London: Sage, 1999).

Fraser and L., Gordon, N. [1994] 'A genealogy of dependency', pp. 310–337, in Goodin and Mitchell (eds), *The Foundations of the Welfare State, vol. III* (Cheltenham: Edward Elgar, 2000).

Friedman, M. [1962] *Capitalism and Freedom* (London: University of Chicago, 1982).

Fukuyama, F. *The End of History and the Last Man* (New York: The Free Press, 1992).

Fukuyama, F. *Trust. The social virtues and the creation of prosperity* (London: Hamish Hamilton, 1995).

Gadamer, H.-G. [1975] *Truth and Method*, second edition, first published 1960 (London: Sheed & Ward, 1989).

Galston, W.A. *Liberal Purposes* (Cambridge: Cambridge University Press, 1991).

Gamble, A. *The Free Economy and the Strong State* (London: Macmillan, 1989).

Gans, H.J. *The War against the Poor* (New York: Basic Books, 1995).

George, V. and R. Page (eds), *Modern Thinkers on Welfare* (London: Harvester Wheatsheaf, 1995).

George, V. and P. Wilding, *Welfare and Ideology* (London: Harvester Wheatsheaf, 1994).

George, V. and P. Wilding, *Globalization and Human Welfare* (New York: Palgrave, 2002).

Gerwith, A. *Reason and Morality* (Chicago: University of Chicago Press, 1978).

Giddens, A. *Beyond Left and Right. The Future of Radical Politics* (Cambridge: Polity Press, 1994).

Giddens, A. *The Third Way. The Renewal of Social Democracy* (Cambridge: Polity Press, 1998).

Gilligan, C. *In a Different Voice: Psychological Theory and Women's Development* (Cambridge, MA: Harvard University Press, 1982).

Ginsburg, N. *Divisions of Welfare* (London: Sage, 1992).

Goodin, R.E. *Reasons for Welfare. The Political Theory of the Welfare State* (Chichester: Princeton University Press, 1988).

Goodin, R.E. 'Utility and the Good', pp. 241–249, in P. Singer (ed.), *A Companion to Ethics* (Oxford: Blackwell, 1991).

Goodin, R.E. *Utilitarianism as a Public Philosophy* (Cambridge: Cambridge University Press, 1995).

Goodin, R.E. 'Work and Welfare: Towards a post-productivist welfare regime', *British Journal of Political Science*, Vol. 31, no. 1 (January 2001) 13–39.

Goodin, R.E., B. Headey, R. Muffels, and H-J. Dirven, *The Real Worlds of Welfare Capitalism* (Cambridge: Cambridge University Press, 1999).

Gorz, A. [1980] *Farewell to the Working Class*, trans. M. Sonenscher (London: Pluto Press, 1982).

Gutmann, A. [1985] 'Communitarian Critics of Liberalism', pp. 120–136, in S. Avineri and A. de-Shalit (eds), *Communitarianism and Individualism* (Oxford: Oxford University Press, 1992).

Habermas, J. *The Theory of Communicative Action. Vol. II*, trans. T. McCarthy (Oxford: Polity Press, 1987).

Habermas, J. *Moral Consciousness and Communicative Action*, trans. by C. Lenhardt and S. Weber Nicholsen (Cambridge: Polity Press, 1990).

Habermas, J. *The Philosophical Discourse of Modernity*, trans. F. Lawrence (Cambridge: Polity Press, 1994a).

Habermas, J. 'Struggles for Recognition in the Democratic Constitutional State', pp. 107–148, in A. Gutmann (ed.), *Multiculturalism. Examining the Politics of Recognition* (New Jersey: Princeton University Press, 1994b).

Habermas, J. *Between Facts and Norms. Contributions to a Discourse Theory of Law and Democracy* (Cambridge: Polity Press, 1996).

Habermas, J. 'The European Nation State and the Pressures of Globalization', *New Left Review*, Vol. 235 (1999) 46–59.

Habermas, J. 'Equal Treatment of Cultures and the Limits of Postmodern Liberalism', *The Journal of Political Philosophy*, Vol. 13, no. 1 (2005) 1–28.

Hare, R.M. *Moral Thinking. Its Levels, Method, and Point* (Oxford: Clarendon Press, 1981).

Harsanyi, J.C. [1977] 'Morality and the Theory of Rational Behaviour', in A. Sen and B. Williams (eds), *Utilitarianism and Beyond* (Cambridge: Cambridge University Press, 1982).

Hayek, F.A. [1944] *The Road to Serfdom* (London: Routledge, 1991).

Hayek, F.A. *Law, Legislation and Liberty, Vol. II* (London: Routledge, 1976).

Healas, P. 'Reforming the Self: Enterprise and the Characters of Thatcherism', pp. 72–92, in R. Keat and N. Abercrombie (eds), *Enterprise Culture* (London: Routledge, 1991).

Hegel, G.W.F. [1807] *Phenomenology of Spirit*, trans. A.V. Miller (Oxford: Clarendon Press, 1979).

Hegel, G.W.F. [1821] *Philosophy of Right*, trans. T.M. Knox (Oxford: Oxford University Press, 1949).

Herdt, J.A. 'Alasdair MacIntyre's "Rationality of Traditions" and Tradition-Transcendental Standards of Justification', *The Journal of Religion*, Vol. 78, no. 4 (1998) 524–546.

Himmelfarb, G. *The De-Moralization of Society* (London: IEA, Health and Welfare Unit, 1995).

Holmwood, J. 'Welfare and Citizenship', in Richard Bellamy (ed.), *Theories and Concepts of Politics* (Manchester: Manchester University Press, 1993).

Holmwood, J. and J. Siltanen, 'Work and Welfare in a Changing Europe', *International Journal of Sociology*, Vol. 24, no. 2 (1995) 43–66.

Hudson, W.D. *Modern Moral Philosophy*, first published 1970, second ed. (Houndmills: Macmillan, 1983).

Hume, D. [1739–1740] *A Treatise of Human Nature*, E.C. Mossner (ed.), (London: Penguin, 1969).

Illich, I. *Tools for Conviviality* (Glasgow: William Collins and Sons, 1973).

Jones, T. *Remaking the Labour Party* (London: Routledge, 1996).

Kant, I. [1785] *Groundwork of the Metaphysics of Morals*, trans. H.J. Paton, third edition (London: Hutchinson, 1956).

Katz, M.B. *The Undeserving Poor* (New York: Pantheon Books, 1999).

Keat, R. 'Starship Britain or Universal Enterprise', pp. 1–17, in R. Keat and N. Abercrombie (eds), *Enterprise Culture* (London: Routledge, 1991).

Keat, R. *Cultural Goods and the Limits of the Market* (Houndmills: Palgrave, 2000).

Knight, K. *Aristotelian Philosophy. Ethics and Politics from Aristotle to MacIntyre* (Cambridge: Polity Press, 2007).

Kohlberg, L. *Essays on Moral Development* (New York: Harper and Row, 1984).

Kuna, M. 'MacIntyre on Tradition, Rationality, and Relativism', *Res Publica*, Vol. 11, no. 3 (2005) 251–273.

Kymlicka, W. *Liberalism, Community, and Culture* (Oxford: Clarendon Press, 1989).

Kymlicka, W. *Contemporary Political Philosophy. An Introduction* (Oxford: Oxford University Press, 2002).

Laclau, E. 'Metaphor and Social Antagonisms', pp. 249–257, in G. Nelson and L. Grossberg (eds), *Marxism and the Interpretation of Culture* (University of Illinois: Macmillan, 1988).

Laclau, E. and C. Mouffe, *Hegemony and Socialist Strategy* (London: Verso, 1985).

Lane, R.E. *The Market Experience* (Cambridge: Cambridge University Press, 1991).

Leonard, P. *Postmodern Welfare: Reconstructing an Emancipatory Project* (London: Sage, 1997).

Locke, J. [1683] *Two Treaties of Government*, M. Goldie (ed.) (London: Orion, 1993).

Lyotard, J.-F. *The Post-Modern Condition* (Manchester: Manchester University Press, 1984).

MacIntyre, A. *After Virtue. A Study in Moral Theory*, first published 1981, second ed. (London: Duckworth 1985).

MacIntyre, A. *Whose Justice? Which Rationality?* (London: Duckworth, 1988).

MacIntyre, A. 'I'm Not a Communitarian, But...', *The Responsive Community*, Vol. 1. no. 1 (1991) 91–2.

MacIntyre, A. 'The Spectre of Communitarianism', *Radical Philosophy* (March/April, 1995) 34–5.

MacIntyre, A. *Dependent Rational Animals* (London: Duckworth, 1999).

Macmurray, J. *Conditions of Freedom* (London: Faber & Faber, 1949).

Marshall, T.H. [1949] 'Citizenship and Social Class', pp. 67–127, *Sociology at the Crossroads, and other essays* (London: Heinemann, 1963).

Marx, K. [1843] 'On the Jewish Question', pp. 46–69, in D. McLellan (ed.), *Karl Marx. Selected Writings* (Oxford: Oxford University Press, 2000).

Marx, K. [1844] *Economic and Philosophic Manuscripts of 1844*, D.J. Struick (ed.), trans. M. Milligan (London: Lawrence & Wishart Ltd., 1973).

Marx, K. [1852] 'Letter to Joseph Weydemcyer in New York', p. 58, Vol. 39, in *The Collected Works of Marx and Engels* (London: Lawrence & Wishart Ltd., 1975).

Marx, K. [1859] 'Preface to *A Critique of Political Economy*', pp. 424–427, in D. McLellan (ed.), *Karl Marx. Selected Writings* (Oxford: Oxford University Press, 2000).

Marx, K. [1875] *Critique of the Gotha Programme*, pp. 340–360, in D. Fernbach (ed.), *Karl Marx. The International and After. Political Writings: Volume III* (London: Penguin, 1992).

Marx, K. and F. Engels [1846] *The German Ideology*, pp. 175–208, in D. McLellan (ed.), *Karl Marx. Selected Writings* (Oxford: Oxford University Press, 2000).

Marx, K. and F. Engels [1848] *The Communist Manifesto*, pp. 245–272, in D. McLellan (ed.), *Karl Marx. Selected Writings* (Oxford: Oxford University Press, 2000).

Mead, L.M. 'The Logic of Workfare: The Underclass and Work Policy', in W.J. Wilson (ed.), *The Ghetto Underclass* (New York: Sage, 1993).

Mead, L.M. 'Citizenship and social policy: T.H. Marshall and poverty', pp. 197–230, in E.F. Paul, F. Miller, and J. Paul (eds), *The Welfare State* (Cambridge: Cambridge University Press, 1997).

Miliband, R. [1969] *The State in Capitalist Society* (London: Quartet Books, 1982).

Mill, J.S. [1859] *On Liberty*, G. Himmelfarb (ed.) (London: Penguin, 1989).

Mill, J.S. [1861] *Utilitarianism*, in J. Gray (ed.), *On Liberty and other essays* (Oxford: Oxford University Press, 1991).

Mill, J.S. [1869] *The Subjection of Women*, in J. Gray (ed.), *On Liberty and other essays* (Oxford: Oxford University Press, 1991).

Miller, D. *Market, State, and Community* (Oxford: Clarendon Press, 1989).

Miller, D. 'Virtues, Practices and Justice', pp. 245–264, in J. Horton and S. Mendus (eds), *After MacIntyre* (Cambridge: Polity Press, 1994).

Miller, D. *Principles of Social Justice* (London: Harvard University Press, 1999).

Milner, H. *Social Democracy and Rational Choice* (London: Routledge, 1994).

Mishra, R. *Society and Social Policy*, second ed. (London: Macmillan, 1981).

Mishra, R. *Globalization and the Welfare State* (Cheltenham: Edward Elgar, 1999).

Moore, G.E. *Principia Ethica* (Cambridge: Cambridge University Press, 1903).

Moore, J.W. 'Isolation and Stigmatization: The Development of an Under Class', *Social Problems*, Vol. 33, no. 1 (1985) 1–13.

Mouffe, C. 'Democratic Citizenship and the Political Community', pp. 225–239, in Mouffe (ed.), *Dimensions of Radical Democracy* (London: Verso, 1992a).

Mouffe, C. 'Democratic Politics Today', pp. 1–16, in Mouffe (ed.), *Dimensions of Radical Democracy* (London: Verso, 1992b).

Mouffe, C. 'Deconstruction, Pragmatism and the Politics of Democracy', pp. 1–12, in S. Critchley (ed.), *Deconstruction and Pragmatism* (London: Routledge, 1996).

Mulhall, S. and A. Swift, *Liberals and Communitarians* (Oxford: Blackwell, 1992).

Murray, C. *The Emerging British Underclass* (London: IEA, 1986).

Nietzsche, F. [1886] *Beyond Good and Evil. A Prelude to a Philosophy of the Future*, trans. R.J. Hollingdale (London: Penguin, 1990).

Nietzsche, F. [1888] *The Antichrist*, reprinted in *The Portable Nietzsche* (London: Penguin, 1954).

Nisbet, R. *The Sociological Tradition* (London: Heinemann, 1967).

Nisbet, R. *Conservatism: Dream and Reality* (Milton Keynes: Open University Press, 1986).

Nozick, R. *Anarchy, State and Utopia* (Oxford: Basil Blackwell, 1974).

Nussbaum, M. 'Shame, Separateness, and Political Unity: Aristotle's criticism of Plato', pp. 395–435, in A.O. Rorty (ed.), *Essays on Aristotle's Ethics* (London: University of California Press, 1980).

Nussbaum, M. *The Fragility of Goodness. Luck and ethics is Greek tragedy and philosophy* (Cambridge: Cambridge University Press, 1986).

Nussbaum, M. 'Aristotelian Social Democracy', pp. 203–251, in R.B. Douglas, G.M. Mara, and H.S. Richardson (eds), *Liberalism and the Good* (London: Routledge, 1990).

Nussbaum, M. 'Non-Relative Values: An Aristotelian Approach', pp. 242–269, in M. Nussbaum and A. Sen (eds), *The Quality of Life* (Oxford: Clarendon Press, 1993).

Nussbaum, M. 'Emotions and Women's Capabilities', pp. 332–359, in M. Nussbaum and J. Glover (eds), *Women, Culture, and Development* (Oxford: Clarendon Press, 1995a).

Nussbaum, M. 'Human Capabilities, Female Human Beings', pp. 61–104, in M. Nussbaum and J. Glover (eds), *Women, Culture, and Development* (Oxford: Clarendon Press, 1995b).

Nussbaum, M. 'Compassion: The basic social emotion', *Social Philosophy and Policy*, Vol. 13, no. 1 (1996) 27–58.

Nussbaum, M. *Women and Human Development. The Capabilities Approach* (Cambridge: Cambridge University Press, 2000a).

Nussbaum, M. *Sex and Social Justice* (Oxford: Oxford University Press, 2000b).

Oakeshott, M. *Rationalism in Politics and other essays* (London: Methuen, 1962).

O'Brien, M. and S. Penna, *Theorising Welfare* (London: Sage, 1998).

Okin, S.M. 'Reason and Feeling in Thinking about Justice', *Ethics*, Vol. 99, no. 2 (1989) 229–249.

O'Neill, O. 'Kantian Ethics', pp. 175–185, in P. Singer (ed.), *A Companion to Ethics* (Oxford: Blackwell, 1991).

O'Neill, O. 'Justice, Capabilities, and Vulnerabilities', pp. 140–153, in M. Nussbaum and J. Glover (eds), *Women, Culture, and Development* (Oxford: Clarendon Press, 1995).

Parkin, F. *Class Inequality and Political Order* (London: MacGibbon & Kee, 1971).

Pateman, C. *The Sexual Contract* (Oxford: Polity Press, 1988).

Pateman, C. *The Disorder of Women* (Cambridge: Polity Press, 1989).

Perkin, H. *The Rise of Professional Society. England Since 1880* (London: Routledge, 1989).

Perkin, H. 'The Third Revolution', pp. 35–48, in Kelly (ed.), *Stakeholder Capitalism* (Houndsmill: Macmillan, 1997).

Pettit, P. 'Consequentialism', pp. 230–240, in P. Singer (ed.), *A Companion to Ethics* (Oxford: Blackwell, 1991).

Pierson, C. *Beyond the Welfare State? The New Political Economy of the Welfare State*, second ed. (Oxford: Polity Press, 1998).

Plamenatz, J. *Man and Society. Vols. I & II* (London: Longmans, 1963).

Plant, R. 'The moral basis of welfare provision', pp. 52–96, in H. Plant, P. Lesser, P. Taylor-Gooby (eds), *Political Philosophy and Social Welfare* (London: Routledge & Kegan Paul, 1980).

Plant, R., 'Democratic Socialism and Equality', pp. 135–55, in D. Lipsey and D. Leonard (eds.), *The Socialist Agenda: Crosland's Legacy* (London: Jonathon Cape, 1981).

Plant, R. *Modern Political Thought* (Oxford: Blackwell, 1991).

Plant, R. 'Social Democracy', in D. Marquand and A. Seldon (eds), *The Ideas that Shaped Post-War Britain* (London: Hammersmith, 1996).

Plant, R. 'Social and Economic Rights Revisited', *King's College Law Journal*, Vol. 14, no. 1 (2003) 1–20.

Plato, *The Republic* [Rep], trans. D. Lee (London: Penguin, 2003).

Polanyi, K. *The Great Transformation* (Boston: Beacon Press, 1944).

Popper, K.R. [1966] *The Open Society and its Enemies, Vols. I & II*, first published 1944, revised edition (London: Routledge & Kegan Paul, 1974).

Porter, J. 'Openness and Constraint: Moral Reflection as Tradition-Guided Inquiry in Alasdair MacIntyre's Recent Works', *The Journal of Religion*, Vol. 73, no. 4 (1993) 514–536.

Przeworski, A. *Capitalism and Social Democracy* (Cambridge: Cambridge University Press, 1985).

Quinton, A. *Utilitarian Ethics* (London: Macmillan, 1973).

Rawls, J. *A Theory of Justice* (Oxford: Oxford University Press, 1971).

Rawls, J. [1987] 'The Idea of an Overlapping Consensus', pp. 421–448, in S. Freeman (ed.), *John Rawls. Collected Papers* (London: Harvard University Press, 2001).

Rawls, J. *Political Liberalism* (Chichester: Columbia University Press, 1993).

Rawls, J. [1997] 'The Idea of Public Reason Revisited', pp. 573–615, in S. Freeman (ed.), *John Rawls. Collected Papers* (London: Harvard University Press, 2001).

Raz, J. *The Morality of Freedom* (Oxford: Clarendon Press, 1986).

Ritschel, D. 'Macmillan', in V. George and R. Page (eds), *Modern Thinkers on Welfare* (London: Harvester Wheatsheaf, 1995).

Rothstein, B. *Just Institutions Matter* (Cambridge: Cambridge University Press, 1998).

Rousseau, J.J. [1762] *The Social Contract*, pp. 181–352, in *Jean Jacques Rousseau, The Social Contract and Discourses*, trans. G.D.H. Cole (London: Everyman, 2004).

Ryan, A. 'Mill and the Naturalistic Fallacy,' *Mind*, Vol. 75 (1966) 422–425.

Ryan, A. *Property and Political Theory* (Oxford: Basil Blackwell, 1984).

Sandel, M. *Liberalism and the Limits of Justice* (Cambridge: Cambridge University Press, 1982).

Sandel, M. [1984a] 'The Procedural Republic and the Unencumbered Self', pp. 12–28, in S. Avineri and A. de-Shalit (eds), *Communitarianism and Individualism* (Oxford: Oxford University Press, 1992).

Sandel, M. 'Morality and the Liberal Ideal', *The New Republic*, 7 May (1984b) 15–17.

Sandel, M. [1989] 'Moral Argument and Liberal Toleration: Abortion and Homosexuality', pp. 71–87, in A. Etzioni (ed.), *New Communitarian Thinking* (London: University Press of Virginia, 1995).

Sartre, J.P. [1947] 'The Humanism of Existentialism', trans. B. Frechtman, in W. Baskin (ed.), *Jean-Paul Sartre. Essays in Existentialism* (New York: Citadel Press, 1993).

Scanlon, T.M. 'Fear of Relativism', pp. 219–245, in R. Hursthouse, G. Lawrence, and W. Quinn (eds), *Virtues and Reasons* (Oxford: Clarendon Press, 1995).

Scarre, G. *Utilitarianism* (London: Routledge, 1996).

Schaap, A. 'Agonism in Divided Societies', *Philosophy and Social Criticism*, Vol. 32, no. 2 (2006) 255–277.

Schram, S.C. *Words of Welfare* (Minneapolis: University of Minnesota Press, 1995).

Scott, C.C. *The Question of Ethics. Nietzsche, Foucault, Heidegger* (Indianapolis: Indiana University Press, 1990).

Selznick, P. *The Moral Commonwealth* (Oxford: University of California Press, 1992).

Selznick, P. 'Civilizing Civil Society', pp. 171–184, in A. von Harskamp and A.W. Musschenga (eds), *The Many Faces of Individualism* (Leuven: Peeters, 2001).

Sen, A. 'Rights and Agency', *Philosophy and Public Affairs*, Vol. 11, no. 1. (1982) 3–39.

Sen, A. and Williams, B. 'Introduction: Utilitarianism and Beyond', pp. 1–20, in A. Sen and B. Williams (eds), *Utilitarianism and Beyond* (Cambridge: Cambridge University Press, 1982).

Singer, P. *Practical Ethics* (Cambridge: Cambridge University Press, 1993).

Slote, M. *From Morality to Virtue* (Oxford: Oxford University Press, 1992).

Sorensen, E. [1988] 'The Comparable Worth Debate', pp. 293–299, in J.P. Sterba (ed.), *Morality in Practice* (Belmont: Wadsworth, 1999).

Spicker, P. *Principles of Social Welfare. An Introduction to thinking about the Welfare State* (London: Routledge, 1988).

Stears, M. 'The Vocation of Politics. Principles, Empirical Inquiry and the Politics of Opportunity', *European Journal of Political Theory*, Vol. 4, no. 4 (2005) 325–350.

Swaine, L. *The Liberal Conscience* (Chichester: Columbia University Press, 2006).

Taylor, C. [1979] 'What's Wrong With Negative Liberty', in D. Miller (ed.), *Liberty* (Oxford: Oxford University Press, 1991).

Taylor, C., 'The Nature and Scope of Distributive Justice', pp. 289–317, *Philosophical Papers 2* (Cambridge: Cambridge University Press, 1985).

Taylor, C. *Sources of the Self. The Making of the Modern Identity* (Cambridge: Cambridge University Press, 1989a).

Taylor, C. [1989b] 'Cross Purposes: The Liberal-Communitarian Debate', pp. 181–203, *Philosophical Arguments* (London: Harvard University Press, 1995).

Taylor, C. [1992] 'The Politics of Recognition', in A. Gutmann (ed.), *Multiculturalism. Examining the Politics of Recognition* (New Jersey: Princeton, 1994).

Taylor, C. [1992–93] 'Liberal Politics and the Public Sphere', pp. 184–217, in A. Etzioni (ed.), *New Communitarian Thinking* (London: University Press of Virginia, 1995).

Taylor, C. 'Justice after Virtue', pp. 16–43, in J. Horton and S. Mendus (eds), *After MacIntyre* (Cambridge: Polity Press, 1994).

Tawney, R.H. [1921] *The Acquisitive Society* (London: Fontana, 1966).

Tawney, R.H. *Equality*, first published 1931, third revised edition (London: George Allen & Unwin Ltd., 1938).

Taylor-Gooby, P. 'Postmodernism and Social Policy: A Great Leap Backwards?' *Journal of Social Policy*, Vol. 23, no. 3 (1994) 385–404.

Temple, W. *Personal Religion and the Life of Fellowship* (London: Longmans, Green & Co. Ltd., 1926).

Titmuss, R.M. *Essays on 'the Welfare State'* (London: George Allen & Unwin, 1958).

Titmuss, R.M. [1965] 'Social Welfare and the Art of Giving', pp. 113–127, in B. Abel-Smith and R. Titmuss (eds), *The Philosophy of Welfare. Selected Writings of Richard M. Titmuss* (London: George Allen & Unwin, 1987).

Titmuss, R.M. [1970a] *The Gift Relationship. From human blood to social policy* (London: LSE, 1997).

Titmuss, R.M. [1970b] 'Welfare "Rights", Law and Discretion', in B. Abel-Smith and R. Titmuss (eds), *The Philosophy of Welfare. Selected Writings of Richard M. Titmuss*, London: George Allen & Unwin, 1987.

United Nations [1948] *The Universal Declaration of Human Rights*, in I. Brownlie (ed.), *Basic Documents on Human Rights* (Oxford: Clarendon Press, 1993).

Van den Brink, B. 'A Liberal Account of Self-Limiting Individualism', pp. 91–110, in A. von Harskamp and A.W. Musschenga (eds), *The Many Faces of Individualism* (Leuven: Peeters, 2001).

Van Kersbergen, K. *Social Capitalism. A Study of Christian Democracy and the Welfare State* (London: Routledge, 1995).

Van Parijs, P. 'Competing Justifications of Basic Income', pp. 3–46, in P. van Parijs (ed) *Arguing for Basic Income* (London: Verso, 1992).

Van Parijs, P. *Real Freedom For All* (Oxford: Clarendon Press, 1995).

Walzer, M. *Spheres of Justice. A Defense of Pluralism and Equality* (Oxford: Blackwell, 1983).

Weber, M. [1904–1905] *The Protestant Ethic and the Spirit of Capitalism*, trans. T Parsons (London: George Allen & Unwin, 1930).

Whelan, R. *The Corrosion of Charity* (London: IEA, 1996).

White, S.T. *The Recent Work of Jurgen Habermas* (Cambridge: Cambridge University Press, 1988).

Whitemore, F. 'British Socialism and Democracy in Retrospect', in D. McLellan and S. Sayers (eds), *Socialism and Democracy* (London: Macmillan, 1991).

Wiggins, D. 'Neo-Aristotelian Reflections on Justice', *Mind*, Vol. 113, no. 451 (2004) 477–512.

Wilensky, H. *The Welfare State and Equality: structural and ideological roots of public expenditure* (Berkley: University of California Press, 1975).

Wollstonecraft, M. [1792] *A Vindication of the Rights of Women* (London: Norton, 1988).

Young, I.M. [1993] 'Together in Difference: Transforming the Logic of Group Political Conflict', pp. 155–178, in W. Kymlicka (ed.), *The Rights of Minority Cultures* (Oxford: Oxford University Press, 1995).

Index